I WILL LIFT
EYES
TO THE HILLS!

A personal experience of macular degeneration and miracles.

Dr Liz Lenton

Published in 2016
By Channel View Publishing Plymouth, Channel View, Andurn Estate, Down Thomas, Plymouth, PL9 0AT

www.fishportboats.co.uk

All enquiries to Channel View Publishing Plymouth.

ISBN 978-0-9554023-9-5 (Standard version)

 978-0-9554023-8-8   (large print version)

Profits from the sale of this book will be donated to:

Royal National Institute of Blind People (See page 5)
Registered Charity Number 226227 (England and Wales) and SC039316 (Scotland)
105 Judd Street, London WC1H 9NE *www.rnib.org.uk*

London Eye Hospital Trust
Registered charity number 1147023
http://www.londoneyehospitaltrust.org/
29a Wimpole Street, London, W1G 8GP, UK.

I have chosen the above charities to benefit from the sale of this book. The RNIB not only offers comprehensive advice and help for people with all forms of vision loss (see 'Useful contacts' at the end of this book), but also has a 'Seetheneed' appeal which aims to have sight loss advisors available in all NHS hospitals. When you have read my story you will see why this particularly appealed to me.

The London Eye Hospital Trust is associated with the London Eye Hospital where I was privileged to have treatment. It aims to eradicate the eye disease trachoma which so often causes blindness amongst the poorest nations in the world. Supporting it seemed an appropriate way to help the far less privileged.

Liz Lenton

(For more information on these charities see the last page of this book)

DEDICATIONS

This book is dedicated to Katrina who has encouraged me throughout my whole experience with Macular Degeneration, and convinced me that I should write this book.

Also to Stewart who has been my human rock and reflected God's love for me.

I also wish to thank my editor Clare Blake for her skill, patience and encouragement,

and my good friend Heather for her expert feedback and suggestions.

Some names have been changed and locations disguised to protect identities.

FOREWORD

This book tells a literally eye-opening story. It is the story of a remarkable person who has faced the challenges of life with faith and fortitude, and not least the challenge of macular degeneration. For those who know little about this condition here is an insight into the anxieties and realities of those who have to live with it. For sufferers and carers of AMD here is someone who has travelled that journey and can write about it with courage, honesty and even humour. For all of us, here is a book filled with hope.

I have known Liz and Stewart for over sixteen years. They have a breadth of sympathy and an understanding of humanity which is drawn from a rich and varied experience of life. From their house they look over Plymouth Sound and can lift up their eyes to the Cornish hills beyond. They can also lift up their eyes to a God who in his love for the world bears our sins and carries our sorrows, who changes lives in a way that can even be described as miraculous. My hope is that those who read this book will be able to lift up their eyes to see the world in a way which is filled with new hope and possibility.

Nick McKinnel

Bishop of Plymouth

INTRODUCTION

'Sometimes, life hands you a chance. It hands you something amazing, you almost think it's a dream, but no matter how much you pinch yourself, you don't wake up. It's moments like those that make life really worth living, because no matter how hard times get, there are always those miracle moments that lift you back on your feet.'
Unknown

1. OVERVIEW.

You may have opened this book because you are curious about its title. It could be that you recognise it as the opening words of Psalm 121, but then are perhaps wondering how I can possibly make any connection between the words 'Macular Degeneration' and 'Miracles' in the subtitle. However, I hope you will continue reading as the answer to this question will be revealed as I tell my story and relate my experience with Age Related Macular Degeneration (AMD)[1].

This is, of necessity, a very personal account, so you will learn much about me and my life events. Some of my experience will be similar to any of the tens of millions of people worldwide who suffer from dry AMD, but my reaction to this condition and some of the coping strategies I have used will naturally be personal to me, an ordinary 78 year old British woman. I say 'ordinary' in the sense of the things that are common to our human condition, but, of course, nobody is truly 'ordinary'. I believe that we are created as unique individuals, and life's experiences with our varied reactions to them certainly ensure that one can never find that much referred to, but non-existent person, 'the average'.

Because of this my story will be entirely different from that of anybody else. I have included details of important events in my life because I hope that knowing more about me in this way will not only give you

---

[1] See Appendix 2 for an explanation of this condition

better insight into why I have reacted and coped in the way that I have regarding AMD and other experiences, but also make the book a more interesting one for you to read. My desire is that reading my story might bring encouragement or better understanding to fellow sufferers and those close to them.

I should first mention that I have a medical background. I qualified as a doctor many years ago when, as we used to say in the RAF, 'Pontius was a pilot'. It was in the RAF (not WRAF) that I was first employed as a doctor as a General Duties Medical Officer from 1966 to 1974. I was very much a 'Jack of all trades and master of none' type of medical practitioner with a wide variety of medical appointments in my thirty-five years of medical practice. My medical background has perhaps served to help me find my way round medical terminology more easily and better understand certain implications of treatment in my experience with dry AMD, but in no sense am I writing this book from a medical perspective; indeed, I am not qualified to do that. It is purely a personal account of my own experience. With the passage of years I increasingly feel that I know less and less about more and more. The huge strides taken in all branches of medical science in recent years have left me breathlessly gasping in wonder, unable even to attempt to keep up.

My first reason for writing this book is simply to inform as many people as possible about AMD because there is surprising ignorance about this common condition. It has often been said about rats: 'There will be one not far from you, even though you may not realise it!' and the same could be said of AMD. Not that we, the sufferers, are rats, but the condition is certainly as unwanted as any untamed rat, and much more widespread than most people think.

AMD is the main cause of severe visual impairment in the UK and pioneering ophthalmologist Mr Bobby Qureshi from the London Eye Hospital stated that in the year 2015 alone there were in the region of some 600,000 people suffering from end stage AMD, and many millions more with an early or intermediate form of the disease or other macular diseases like diabetic retinopathy. The good news is that, aside from a fluke accident like tripping over something you have not seen and breaking your neck, AMD is not a killer. The 'Age' bit will be eventually, but not the 'Disease' bit! Although AMD can take your life! I trust, however, that you will find in my story a restoring of hope and a step towards regaining what you have lost.

If you are afflicted with Macular Degeneration, or related to someone with the condition, you probably already know that it would take a miracle to cure it. If you are a sufferer yourself you will have embarked on a growing acquaintance with a most irksome travelling companion on life's path, and no doubt have been avidly searching for any possible means to ditch him. A silent and largely unnoticed presence at first, he eventually starts to make his demands felt like a hungry cat that can no longer be ignored! Also like a cat, he has many different ways of letting you know he is around, perhaps starting with everyday tasks like reading, writing or sewing that gradually become more and more difficult, especially in poor lighting. At first I used my failing sight as a good excuse to duck out of difficult crossword clues, but frustratingly, even when I knew the right answer, writing the letters in the squares proved to be an impossible task. And it wasn't just crosswords. In modern life there are all sorts of little squares you need to fill in, ranging from official forms where you must place your signature strictly inside the box to signing for a parcel delivered to your door. Tick boxes are literally everywhere.

In dry AMD there can be a long period before you experience any symptoms, but once they start they are hard to ignore as it is your central area of vision that is affected. One common problem for sufferers is gradually noticing that you can only read bits of text. The blind spots in your vision cause words or individual letters to go missing, rather like what happens when the ink starts to run out in your printer! I remember travelling as a car passenger and seeing the top word 'Plymouth' on a road sign, but becoming aware as I moved my position that there was another word 'Pavilions' beneath it. However, I could now no longer see the word 'Plymouth'! It was a bit like playing hide and seek. If I moved to look from another angle, the missing word would reappear, but then the word I had originally seen would vanish in its turn - I could never see them both at the same time.

With AMD you may see 'drunken lines' that lean towards each other for support when you know they are really parallel, or lines that should be straight like those on a fence or lamp post will get distorted so they appear curved or kinked. You may also find colours less vibrant or have difficulty telling them apart. More embarrassingly, you may not be able to recognize the faces of people coming towards you. Stewart, my husband, was aware of this, and did his best to whisper a name to me as people approached, but this was not foolproof. Neither of us is very good at putting names to faces and I am also rather deaf, so Stewart's hissed reminders of 'You know – the woman whose daughter ran off with the milkman', or 'The man with bad breath' were risky as though I would know exactly who he meant, there was always a chance of causing offence if they happened to have better hearing than me!

Fortunately, in AMD the peripheral vision remains, so there is some good news - at least total and complete blindness will not overtake you. If you have black areas in your central vision they will not grow to the extent that they take over your whole visual field like a black curtain.

Typically, as an AMD sufferer you will have been exploring every disappointing avenue that might lead to a permanent cure, or at least an effective treatment. If, like me, you have the dry type of AMD, you will have been told that not only is there no cure, but also no treatment. Yet, quite reasonably, you somehow continue to hold on to the hope that one day you will find something that will help. Perhaps you are reading this book now as part of that habitual quest.

On the other hand, you could be someone who has only just had the bottom knocked out of your world by an eye consultant telling you that you have this condition in the dry form for which there is no treatment. It's hard not to be anxious when you start to read up about dry AMD and discover that although it usually progresses only slowly, sooner or later it could cost you most, if not all, of your sight, and then you

11

remember the consultant's words, "Oh, and by the way, just be aware that a case of dry AMD can sometimes also develop into the wet form, for which, although there is some treatment if caught early, you must return promptly as wet AMD is more aggressive in its speed of progression and sight threatening effects."

There's no doubt it's a depressing outlook but this leads me on to the second and more important reason for telling my story - to offer some hope which has been in short supply to sufferers of dry AMD. It is amazing and uplifting to find that since I started to write this book I have become aware of some reasons that give new hope to AMD sufferers. The first has been a further development in the treatment that I personally received which has opened up the possibility of such treatment for AMD sufferers who were formerly considered unsuitable because of previous cataract surgery. The other is a recent development, widely reported in the media, concerning initial treatment trials introducing retinal cells grown from stem cells into the patient's retina in the hope that normal light-sensitive cells will be produced that will take over the function of those damaged by AMD. Both of these are referred to later in this book. It seems that where once hope was almost non-existent for AMD sufferers, at last there is a much brighter outlook on the horizon.

I believe that 'Hope' is an essential ingredient in all medical treatment. Indeed, it is hard to imagine life itself without it! I felt as if all hope had been removed when my vision declined so badly I could no longer do many things I had previously taken for granted like driving. As a result, I had to dramatically change my lifestyle and was struggling to cope, yet it seemed that there was no understanding or concern about this by any professionals. I was not offered help of any kind, or even followed up in clinic. This was the lowest point in my AMD experience. What a change it made when, quite by chance, a glimmer of hope reappeared!

Thinking about what a difference this made to my whole outlook, I have recently reflected once more on my first day as a civilian GP. I sat at my desk before any of the patients arrived and bowed my head in prayer, conscious of the enormous task I had taken on, and not at all certain that I would be adequate for it. I knew that I needed help outside myself, and I was thinking of guidelines that I could employ. I wrote on a piece of paper these words - the Love, the Hope, and the Healing. The order seemed important. I understood that as I lovingly reached out to people by listening to them and getting alongside to help them with their burden, they would feel hope, and this would set the stage for what measure of healing was possible.

Over the years that followed, however bad the diagnosis and poor the prognosis I had to impart to patients, I have always tried, whenever it was honestly possible, not to remove all their hope. I wanted to leave them with something, however small, to grasp on to, even if it was just the simple statement that I would pray for them.

The fact that I have included the word 'miracle' in this book's title could make you think that you are just being tantalised. You may believe that I have experienced a wonderful 'one-off' or an exceedingly rare event that could never happen to you. Or you might be irritated by the use of the word 'miracle' itself with its implication of divine involvement. Well, the miracle in my case might not pass the scrutiny of Lourdes but nonetheless, what has happened to my eyes over the past few months has been nothing short of miraculous, and divine action and intervention there certainly has been for those with willing eyes to see it

Dr Williams School, Dolgellau
With Cader Idris in the background

13

2. SIGNIFICANCE OF THE TITLE'

'I will lift up my eyes to the hills' is the opening statement of Psalm 121. It continues:

'...from whence cometh my help.

My help comes from the Lord who made heaven and Earth.' [2]

I can quote this Psalm in its entirety without looking it up because it was my School Psalm at the girls' boarding school I attended from around the age of thirteen to sixteen years. Dr Williams' School (or DWS as we called it) was situated at Dolgellau in North Wales in the southern part of the Snowdonia National Park beside Cader Idris - the 893m (2,930ft) high seat of the legendary giant 'Idris' – 'cader' being the Welsh word for chair. Cader Idris is the second highest mountain in Wales, surpassed only by Snowdon itself, and selected numbers of pupils who were fit enough were supervised in ascending its slopes each year. I was first at the top in my year which will surprise all who know me as I have never been the most athletic of people! Of course, the achievement was very much a team effort with different leaders at each stage, and all of us supporting each other. It's not difficult to see why Psalm 121 was chosen as the School Psalm for DWS with Cader Idris so close, but it was not just my schooldays that inspired me to choose it as my title.

A choir friend who has been a great supporter through my eyesight problems and constantly encouraged me to write this book about my experiences messaged me out of the blue: "I have a thought for your title! - 'I will lift up my eyes to the hills'." I had been considering a different title, but as I thought about her suggestion, I could see how appropriate it would be. There is an obvious connection with 'eyes', because what happened to mine is the 'raison d'être' for this book and these lines are even more fitting in view of the outcome of my story which, as you will have guessed, is that I can now look with seeing and appreciative eyes towards the hills again.

---

[2] Psalm 121, v 1-2, Spirit Filled Life Bible

Hills have been a big part of my life experience because I have been privileged to live near beautiful mountainous scenery during some formative times in my life, not only at school in North Wales, but also my student pre-clinical three years which I spent in beautiful St Andrews in Scotland - a part of the British Isles known for its mountainous scenery. St Andrews also enjoys a worldwide reputation as the home of golf, and, more recently, as the place where our second in line to the throne, Prince William, met his bride to be, fellow student Catherine Middleton as she then was. It was also the University attended by Mr Bobby Qureshi who designed the ingenious system of lenses that would result in his pioneering eye surgery to help dry Macular Degeneration which I was fortunate enough to have successfully done in April and June of 2015.

'Lifting up' and 'Looking up to the hills' carries an implication of trust and dependency, even pleading towards a divine being for an answer. Again, I want to use the analogy of a cat because I have had a long association with these fascinating animals, and have become very familiar with their mannerisms. I even bred pedigree cats when I was in General Practice as I found cat breeding was an excellent home based hobby for a GP spending hours on call in the days before cell phones. A cat, when it expects something from you, has a way of looking up at you with wide-eyed expectancy and trust that is almost impossible to refuse. Looking heavenward with expectancy and as much trust as I can muster has featured throughout my life to various degrees, sometimes almost unconsciously before I was fully aware that I was actually looking to God.

Certainly in the last few years as my eyesight has rapidly deteriorated I have been looking towards my Maker more than ever, so my old school psalm is particularly apt for my book title. I also like the idea of looking to the hills, rather than to any man-made building, church, temple or shrine, however beautiful and peaceful they might be as if Almighty God could be confined.

I do not wish to alienate readers of a different, uncertain or even no faith by making reference to 'my Maker' and God. It is not an attempt to proselytise, but it would be less than sincere of me to write about myself without revealing something of the importance of my own faith. Some people trust other things, such as their own determination, but if I ask myself what has best helped me to cope with my failing vision, aside from the support given to me by my husband Stewart, any inner strength has come from trusting in God.

PART ONE

MY 'BACKSTORY'

'We know from our clinical experience in the practice of medicine that in diagnosis, prognosis, and treatment, the individual and his background of heredity are just as important, if not more so, as the disease itself.'
Paul Dudley White [3]

'Don't be pushed by your problems be led by your dreams.'
Ralph Waldo Emerson[4]

---

[3] 1886 – 1973. An American physician and cardiologist, one of the leading cardiologists of his day, and a prominent advocate of preventive With Mum & Dad & family car before the war medicine. Joint describer of the Wolff Parkinson White syndrome.
4 1803 – 1882. An American essayist, lecturer, and poet

3. MY EARLY YEARS

'For my part I refuse to be the servant of the past, the slave of yesterday, or the puppet of Fate.'
Reverend E F Dinsmore

My connection with cats dates back even before I was born, when Russell, my brother, or half brother to correctly describe him, was dispatched with a securely tied cardboard box with 'breathing holes' punched in it containing the family 'moggie'- the only cat carrier our family ever used. He had instructions to take the cat to the PDSA (People's Dispensary for Sick Animals) clinic and ask if they would kindly put the animal to sleep as a new baby was expected and his mother could not take the risk of 'Smutty' jumping into the baby's cot, lying on the baby and suffocating the new arrival!

To get to the clinic Russell had to walk several miles along the streets of suburban East London and it gave him a chance to ponder his dilemma. Unlike most 14 year old boys, he was eagerly looking forward to the new baby so part of him wanted to comply with his mother's wishes, but he was also very fond of the cat and thought it was unfair that a so far innocent animal should be headed for the chop. In the end Russell just couldn't do it, so Smutty was freed just before his appointed place of execution to go and take his chances elsewhere. However, my brother's disobedience was soon found out for Smutty arrived home even before Russell! Now it was my father's turn to carry out the distasteful task that his stepson had failed to complete, but Dad also had no stomach for putting down such a loving and loyal pet, so he gave Smutty away to a woman who admired him in the animal clinic's waiting room. This time it took Smutty a little longer to arrive home, but he was back on the doorstep within twelve hours! After that, even my mother felt he had earned his reprieve, and, far from the fate befalling me that my mother had feared, Smutty and I became the best of friends.

When I did arrive I was by all accounts four weeks overdue by the calculations available at the time. "A tendency that has continued," Stewart likes to remind me when we are getting ready to go out. My mother had a difficult home labour and it was a long and anxious wait

18

for the father-to-be who was being calmed and cared for in the house next door. There was a fence about 4ft high between the two gardens but when news came that I had finally arrived, my father leapt over it and rushed upstairs to see his wife and meet his firstborn. Sadly, I was to be their only child as the doctors later informed my parents that my mother would not be able to have any more.

I am told that when my father first took me in his arms he pronounced that I would be either a film star or a doctor! Becoming a doctor was probably only slightly less absurd than becoming a film star, but it was at least something towards which my father might be able to give some pointers. He certainly did his best to guide me through the challenges, especially academic ones that I faced in my school years. For my part, I greatly looked up to him and wished to emulate him for he himself had achieved success in spite of the odds being heavily stacked against him.

My father came from a very poor family where education was neither expected nor encouraged, but he had ambition to do well in life, and so he put himself through evening classes after his day job as a draughtsman at Fords of Dagenham. First he gained London Matriculation so he could gain entry to a degree course, and then he graduated with a BSc from West Ham Technical College. His family gave him absolutely no support in his struggle to gain an education, and did not even bother to make sure food was left for him at the end of his long day. However, his elder sister did try to help at least once. My father would often tell the story of the night he returned home hungry and tired, long after everyone else had gone to bed, arriving just in time to see a mouse finishing off the piece of cheese his sister had intended for him!

My mother had left school early, and so it was to my father that I looked for advice and inspiration. He was my hero - I even took his photo into examinations because I hoped that some of his intelligence and ability might rub off on me. However, in my early years Smutty the cat was my dearest confidant and loving friend. He came into bed with me most nights, and I would put my arm around him and tell him all my troubles. Sometimes I would make his soft fur wet with my tears, but Smutty was a huge comfort and I would quickly fall asleep, soothed by his contented purring.

Generally, if I did feel upset or unfairly treated it was something to do with being disciplined by my mother, or getting on the wrong side of Rita my half sister who was ten years older than me. Rita frequently told everyone, especially me, that she hated me. I just accepted this as a fact, and it did not occur to me in those young days to think that there might have been a reason for it. That was just Rita! She was a much older sister and I had never experienced, nor did I expect, closeness from her, so her expressions of hate did not unduly upset me. Having a much younger sister trying on her high heels and messing up her treasured belongings understandably made her angry. I knew that I was doing wrong but thought I could get away with it! However, I bitterly resented it when I thought she had treated me unfairly .It was only as I got older and began to understand the family history that I started to work out for myself why Rita might have resented me.

Doris, our mother, had been pregnant (with Russell) when she was just 16 years old, the victim of a bigamous and possibly 'shotgun' marriage to a merchant seaman who was often away at sea. I doubt if Rita remembered her father because when her mother discovered that he already had a wife in at least 'one other port' (Malta), she 'upped sticks' and went to live with an aunt near London, taking baby Rita and 5 year old Russell with her. Doris and her mother decided it would be easier to avoid difficult questions and possible scandal if Doris and the children never returned to Swansea so my Grandmother bought a tobacconist and confectioner's shop for Doris in Essex, and it was there that she met my father who was a customer.

It was only years later on my 60th birthday in a very rare display of her inner feelings that Rita opened up and told me the story from her point of view. An attractive, small built doll of a child with enormous dark appealing eyes, Rita had always been the 'apple of everyone's eye' and was around six years old when my father, Ted Stuart, married Doris. Rita was doted on by the whole Stuart family, and Ted's two maiden sisters, Auntie Annie (who had left the cheese out for Dad) and Auntie Ivy, both loved to take Rita out and make a fuss of her. But I was particularly surprised and quite moved to hear Rita say that every day she would skip happily home from school, saying over and over to herself, "I've got a Daddy and he loves me". I never knew that she had any feelings at all for my father. These must have been very painfully suppressed by her in the rejection she later felt as everything changed when I was born. As Rita put it: "...when the 'rightful heir to the Stuart line' came along (ie: me), the 'little doll' was dropped and totally discarded." No wonder that Rita wasted no time in locking me in the dark cupboard under the stairs whenever our mother went out of the house and left Rita in charge. Rita always did her best to inflict the maximum discomfort with my confinement, telling me that "The Whimpies will come and get you!" I had no idea what Whimpies were, but she didn't manage to scare me. All I can remember is my feeling of annoyance at my imprisonment in a dark uncomfortable place when I could have been out doing other things. In fact, the only thing that ever did 'get me' in that dark confined space was a hot iron that my mother hastily deposited there as she rushed off to work after doing some ironing. It made painful contact with my body in several places before I managed to get away from it. I think Rita was called to account that day as I can remember my mother sitting me on the kitchen table and crossly applying salve to all my burns. However, these episodes obviously played on Rita's conscience years after I had almost forgotten them, because she made a public confession about the Whimpies in an impromptu speech she made on my sixtieth birthday. This was at a period when we lived near each other for the first time, and had become good friends.

Although regrettably my childhood relationship with Rita was difficult, there was always a special bond between me and my 'big brother', Russell. I do not really remember him until after the war, but everyone kept his memory alive during it by talking to me about him and showing me photographs. Presumably, like most young boys, Russell might have preferred a baby brother, but he had never given that impression. He was apparently a very willing babysitter and often took me out in my pram, but then the war came along so I did not really see him again until I was at least eight years old.

When war was declared, my father, who had been a Territorial Army officer, became a regular and was often away from home on military service. Initially he was with the Royal Engineers, but later transferred to the Royal Electrical & Mechanical Engineers (REME) when it was formed in 1942. In the early war years we accompanied him to various locations around the country, and I particularly remember Philleigh, a small village near the 'King Harry Ferry' in Cornwall. Philleigh would later be connected with the D-Day invasion preparations when thousands of American troops passed through on their way to the beaches of Normandy and even General Eisenhower himself visited, but my father was stationed there much earlier so I imagine he was probably involved in the construction of anti-invasion defences. Although I was under four years old when we lived there, I would often walk from our lodgings to the army camp barrier and ask the guard for 'my daddy'. On one occasion the camp put on a little show in a field for the families, and I particularly loved the marching and drill displays. From when I was very little I had always loved marching, and still have vivid memories of Dad and me marching in procession round the dining table whenever there was military music on the radio!

Russell also left home to join the RAF as soon as they would take him, and trained as an Air Gunner, but unfortunately sustained injuries in an air crash at the end of his training which meant he was invalided out of the RAF. Russell hated seeing others leaving to serve their country when he was not in uniform, and probably also felt the implied, if not outspoken, reproach of people who had no knowledge of his RAF service and assumed that he was dodging doing his bit.

One day, on impulse, Russell decided to go home from his work in a railway depot via the recruiting offices to see if he could re-enlist. The RN recruiters showed him the door when they found out he had been medically discharged from the RAF, but the Army recruiters next door were not so fussy. With the minimum of formalities, he signed up for military service with the Welsh Guards just because he had been born in Swansea! He was still only 19 years old and our Welsh mother was furious. "You did not need to do that, Russell," she yelled. "You had every right to stay at home and now you will be right in the front line! Everyone knows that the Guards take the brunt of everything!" Little did she know how prophetic her words would turn out.

With both Russell and Dad gone, I was left with only Smutty to comfort me and save me from the 'Whimpies', a 'hating' half-sister, and the frequent short temper of my distraught working mother who had a lot on her plate. Not only was she worried about her menfolk away in the war, but Rita was a withdrawn and somewhat difficult teenager

'Little doll'
Rita
Aged 5

Russell
Welsh
Guardsman

Smutty

Dad with
The
Rightful
Heir to
The 'Stuart
Line'

With Mum &
Dad &
pre-war
family car

Our pond that
had been filled
in before
my birth.
Dad Mowing

whose fussiness over food caused real problems with wartime rations. Rita also refused to leave her bed and come to the shelter with us when the air raid warnings sounded which meant that Mum was even more anxious than she need have been.

My earliest real memory of Russell came around the end of the war when he turned up at our house with two other soldiers and gave me a pair of gold dangly earrings that he had brought from Italy, but the rather adult style made me suspect that they had originally been intended as a present for my mother. There seemed to be a rather strained atmosphere at that meeting, and I was puzzled that Russell did not stay with us but departed soon after with the two other men. It would be a long time before I learned the full story of Russell's visit that day.

4. PLEASE GOD, SEND ME A BANANA!
'Yes, we have no bananas.'
Comedy song - popular in the war

As a child in wartime I enjoyed exploring the streets of our town with other children of my age. We looked for bomb-damaged houses and shrapnel, and I liked to pick the flowers in the abandoned gardens. It seemed such a pity to leave them with nobody to appreciate them.

We lived near Gants Hill Underground station which had not yet been officially opened. However, all the tunnels were already finished and we loved exploring them. It was obviously used as an air raid shelter because we found sections housing rows of bunk beds, but there were also mysterious tunnels barred by manned barriers where all we could see beyond were lights. We understood that it was a secret place to do with the war, and that the electronics firm Plessey had something to do with it.

There was a First Aid station near the top of our road at the entrance to Dr Barnardo's Village Homes. On one occasion my mother rushed me there with my hand wrapped in a tea towel after I had cut it badly trying to climb through the garage window. It turned out that they were only allowed to treat casualties of war, but she persuaded them to give her a field dressing to apply, and someone lent her the bus fare for the two buses we had to catch to get to King George V Hospital along the Southend Road. This was where, much later, I would first be employed as a doctor as a pre-registration house surgeon.

Much is made today of recycling, but it is not a new notion. In the war we had special bins called 'pig bins' for our kitchen waste, and dustbins for dust and ashes from the coal fire if they had not already been used for other useful purposes, like anti-slip scatterings on the snow. I remember getting the rather dirty job of sieving all the contents of the house grates to separate cinders from ash. The cinders from the coal fires were often used again with a little fresh coal or peat while Smutty got the smaller cinders in his dirt box which was just a shoebox lined with newspaper. No plastic then! There were also hessian sacks into which we deposited waste paper and metal cans for 'salvage'. I knew the latter were for the munitions factories as my Auntie Ivy worked in one - war work that was forced on her. Decorative iron railings fixed on walls in front of houses disappeared overnight, cut off and sent away for the war effort.

We youngsters often followed the columns of marching soldiers - British 'Tommies' - for miles along the Southend Road which led to the coast. I remember one turning to me as he marched and saying emphatically "Go home, little girl!" At other times we followed 'Yanks' as they walked along the pavements, chanting: "Got any gum, Chum?"

Later in the war Rita worked as a typist at the American Red Cross in London, and she occasionally brought American servicemen home. I was sometimes allowed to sleep under the dining table instead of retreating to the dank spider-haunted air raid shelter in the garden, and on one occasion one of Rita's visiting GIs passed a whole box of 24 Milky Way bars under the table to me. "All for you, honey," he said. What luxury! It must have been something like two to three month's worth of our sweet ration! At last, having an older sister was beginning to make sense!

We played games in the street, even in the middle of the road, as there were virtually no cars around in those wartime days. Our bread and milk were delivered on floats drawn by sturdy and fairly docile cart horses. However, my best friend Jean's unruly large Red Setter puppy got out one day and chased poor old Peggy, the milk float horse, all the way down the street with the milk float clattering behind her, scattering precious bottles of milk everywhere before she was eventually caught by two men!

We had to do what we could to eke out our rations. Before Russell left for the Army he dug up the back lawn so that it could be planted with potatoes in what was supposed to be our 'Dig for Victory' effort, but it did not seem to be a popular move, and I don't ever remember any potatoes growing there. I guess that my mother did not feel like adding gardening to all the other demands on her time!

A puppy we purchased in Romford market used to play there, mostly yapping at everyone. He was thought to be a Manchester terrier. I am not sure whether it was his much yapping or unruly behaviour which earned him this classification, but when my mother returned one day to find the washing hanging from the line in shreds because the mongrel had been swinging on it, she said he would have to go back to Manchester or anywhere else that would have him!

I loved going to Romford market, the start of my long love of all markets. There was always a great variety of things on sale, and it was fun watching the stallholders with their sales patter. Some balanced all the plates and saucers from a tea-set across both outstretched arms as they told the gathering crowds, on a descending scale, just how much they were not going to ask for the purchase of the whole lot, sometimes at the end throwing in a teapot and jug for good measure! There were always bargains, especially if you were like my mother and embarrassingly good at bartering.

I always went to the clothing shops that lined Green Street Market where the friendly Jewish lady owners and assistants soon got to know me, and took great interest in my progress towards becoming a doctor. I think it gave them vicarious pleasure to think they were contributing to my future career when they reduced the price to rock-bottom for me.

My first 'two wheeler' bike was purchased in Romford Market. My mother brought it home in a taxi and it was a huge surprise as I hadn't asked for one, and hadn't even learned to ride a bike yet. However, I soon managed to do so by sitting on it while holding on to the wall of the corner house, and then propelling the bike alongside it. Eventually, I built up enough confidence to push away from the wall and was soon speeding off along the pavement.

Something else that came from Romford Market was a clutch of 'day old' chicks which my mother purchased because she thought that we could rear them in the back garden and they would provide us with fresh eggs. We were lucky if we got one egg per week on our food ration, and usually we had to make do with powered egg. If the chickens did not lay, they could always be used for the 'pot'. Roast chicken would have made a welcome change from our meagre and boring supplies of corned-beef, spam or gristly sausage. It was a very cold day when we brought the chicks home and we had to go straight out again, so my mother put the chicks in a tray in the bottom of our electric oven, set at the lowest possible temperature, to keep them cosy. When we left, the oven door was open, but when we returned it was closed, and the poor chicks did not even make it to Christmas dinner.

Another precautionary measure carried out in anticipation of my birth, along with the planned demise of the family cat, involved the back garden pond, my father's proud creation, which had to be drained and filled in. At the end of the war when Dad was on demob leave during

27

a spell of hot weather, he dug out the pond again, replenished the concrete surface, and filled it with water from the garden hose so we could use it as a splash pool. Jean and I had great fun playing in the water in our bathing costumes, squealing whenever Dad sprayed us with the garden hose, much to our delight.

15th Ilford
Brownies
outing to
Whipsnade
Zoo

As well as playing in the street and in our reclaimed pond, I enjoyed a variety of activities like attending 'Brownie' meetings, later on moving up to 'Girl Guides'. As Guides we were taken away each year to spend a week under canvas at a Guide Camp in country places like Dorset and Devon. For many of us this was as close as we would get to the annual summer holiday

Winning tent
entry to fancy
dress competition
as 'Three crazy
Campers' at
Guide Camp in
Kingsbridge,
Devon

which is so much a part of family life these days. The Brownie and Guide meetings were held in the Methodist Church Hall round the corner from where we lived, and I was also sent there every Sunday afternoon to Sunday School, clutching a couple of pennies for the collection in my hand.

I was not from a churchgoing family, but somehow I managed to collect a variety of experiences at different places of worship! The Methodist Church Sunday School and 'Church Parade' with the Guides were my first conscious experiences of any church service, although a baptism certificate and my Mother's account of the event bore witness to the fact that I had been christened when I was about one month old at St Andrew's Anglican Church near where my parents used to live.

When I was about 7 or 8 years old, I decided to visit this church for myself and went to it at a time when I hoped there would be a service. Sure enough a church service was about to start so I took a vacant seat in one of the pews. It was not a bit like the Methodist church, so the service was well under way before I suddenly realised it was a Communion service. I knew from my father who had been confirmed, (my mother had not) that you had to be confirmed before you could take communion! Panic!

I made an excuse of not feeling very well to a lady sitting next to me and left the church. However, I was surprised when I looked back after a few minutes to see that she was following me, presumably making sure that I arrived home safely, although she had not been there when I started out. How did she know where I lived? After reaching home, I rushed back to the street corner where she had left me, expecting to see her retracing the long road in the other direction but she had vanished and I saw no trace of her. I thought that she might have been an angel!

I was later to have other experiences of churches where I was puzzled about what was happening, including a Roman Catholic chapel at the convent school I attended just after the war at Ghent in Belgium. I would watch the other pupils and copy what they did when the bell rang, following their lead to stand, kneel, or turn our chairs round to sit on them. There were other occasions too when the priest would put a container looking something like a huge magnifying glass in front of the girls' faces so they could kiss it. When I saw this odd behaviour, I gave my friend a puzzled look. She whispered back "Holy Relic!"

More understandable to me was another type of service that sometimes took place at the Baptist church I attended as a student in St Andrews. Occasionally the floor at the front near the pulpit would be lifted to reveal a large pool full of water. One or two adults took turns to explain to the congregation why they 'believed' and wanted to follow Jesus Christ, and would then separately enter this pool with the minister and perhaps a helper. The minister would say the words of baptism, deftly tip them backwards under the water, and then bring them upright again to be received by helpers with huge towels who would discreetly take them away to get changed. I was very moved by these services and could understand the logic of adult baptism. Eventually, I too would take this step.

When aged about six, a friend and I were once wandering around the neighbourhood looking for bomb damaged houses, when we came across a service taking place in a wooden building that bore a sign saying 'Gospel Hall'. Driven by curiosity as it had always previously been deserted, we quickly accepted the invitation of the open door. A preacher in long white, monk-like robes was apparently about to speak of his work as a missionary abroad so my friend and I took the only two seats together right beneath the pulpit. Before he delivered his message he spent time kneeling in prayer which was quite audible to me but totally incomprehensible. I thought he must be speaking the language of the place where he was serving as a missionary but I have since heard people 'speaking in tongues' and I think that this is what was happening. When he began to preach, he looked straight at us and said that there was no finer thing for a young person to do than to make up their mind to follow Jesus wherever he called.

A similar thing happened to me at my Welsh boarding school when we were at the customary Sunday church service in Dolgellau. A missionary doctor was home on furlough and he specifically asked for any young person present to consider becoming a doctor, adding that the mission field had great need of them. Looking back over my life, I wonder if events in it might have been influenced by the prayers of these people and perhaps of Christians I never knew at events like my christening.

At school in Dolgellau a small group of us sometimes went to a service at the oldest parish church in neighbouring Llanelltyd. After the service I once asked the elderly priest to pray for my brother and sister who were then both estranged from the family as I knew he would take my request seriously. He would never know it, but his prayers were answered years later. They were both reunited with the family and Rita was confirmed at well over 70, while Russell, after many years of debating the existence of God and Christ, also eventually appeared to come to faith after my mother died.

From infancy I was encouraged by my mother to say my prayers before going to bed. This was mainly a list of petitions such as "God bless Daddy, and God bless Russell, and keep them safe and bring them both home soon." Then I always added "PS, Please God, send me a banana!" I had never seen or tasted a fresh banana, although the father of my friend Jean once brought home some dried ones. Bananas were one of the many imported food items we could not get because of the war.

In due course, I am glad to say my prayers were all answered favourably. I have often suspected that God has a sense of humour and in the case of the 'PS' I experienced a personal example of God doing 'exceeding abundantly above all that we ask or think'. Before banana rationing ended in England, my mother and I joined my father when he took a job in the Gold Coast in British West Africa, now known as Ghana, where there were more bananas than I could ever have imagined!

5. POST-WAR ADVENTURES
'God is the same everywhere.'
War and Peace, Leo Tolstoy

Belgium

During the war my father's troops were billeted for a time in a girls' convent school in Ghent, Belgium. When the Mother Superior heard about me, she made Dad promise to send me to school there after the war. To prepare for this, we (Mum, Dad, 18 year old Rita and 8 year old Liz) made a preliminary visit to Belgium as soon as passenger ferry boat services recommenced post-war. We took the boat train from London and crossed as foot passengers to Ostend. I was told during the crossing that I was the first child they had taken cross-Channel since the war. It was interesting then to read in a national paper after our return that a boy had just become the first child to cross the Channel by ferry since the war!

Mum, Rita and me in Belgium preparing for me to go to school in Ghent – looks as if we were caught in the midst of a family disagreement.

We visited people Dad knew in the Belgian towns of Ertvelde, Eeklo, Zelzate and Lokeren, and took in the tourist sites in the major cities. I could not get over it when I saw the 'Menneken Pis' statue in Brussels. It caused us great amusement.

How could anyone get away with making a statue like that? Never mind dressing it up in different uniforms!

Arne, an old drinking buddy of my father, had three daughters. Alicia and Anna were already at the convent school, while Astrid, the youngest daughter, was due to start with me at the beginning of the next term. Until then I attended Astrid's local school where I was received with much friendliness and curiosity. I could not believe it when one little girl brought me a coloured marzipan confection, beautifully made in the shape of a crinoline dressed lady. I had never before seen a sweet too beautiful to eat!

It did not strike me then why a British Army officer's daughter was being treated as having VIP status, but Belgium was still celebrating the end of the war and their liberation from German occupation. The festive season was also approaching, and there was a continuous party atmosphere with much singing and dancing in the streets. These were lined with colourful stalls selling all manner of things. We were struck by the availability of food and drink in contrast to Britain where many things were not available or still rationed.

There was a Flemish expression spoken everywhere with great hilarity, "Niets in de winkel. Alles in de kalder!" (Nothing in the shop. Everything in the cellar!) However, the darker side of the Continental post-war period was also brought home to us by the markings on houses that had been occupied by enemy collaborators. Pictures could also be seen of public hangings and other grisly fates inflicted on those who were seen as traitors by the Belgian people.

After returning to a very austere but happy first post-war British Christmas, we were soon back in Belgium with Arne and his family. On my ninth birthday in January my parents set out from the house very early with Arne, promising a quick return. I waited eagerly for them to come back, while Astrid's mother made me a biscuit cake. It was probably too rich for a child used to British wartime fare, or perhaps my stomach was affected by my upset feelings at being deserted by my parents on my birthday, especially as they still weren't back by my bedtime, but I was terribly sick, throwing up into an unfamiliar low basin that my father had told me was used for washing feet. I could not understand why this caused Alicia and Anna such amusement! I never completely solved the mystery of my parent's absence, but from hints dropped, I gathered that Arne had got too drunk to drive home.

The convent school was a strange adventure. We had to curtsy whenever we encountered the Mother Superior anywhere in the school, and although we attended Saturday morning classes we had Wednesday afternoons free. On Wednesdays and Sundays after church, the whole school went for walks in crocodile fashion beside the canal in Ghent. Another unfamiliar custom to me was that on Wednesday and Saturday lunchtimes we each had a small glass of beer, although I hated the taste (still do) and so tried hard to get out of this. After lunch the nuns and girls joined hands dancing and singing in a huge circle while one nun rhythmically clanged the school bell.

We had a navy blue winter uniform with a strange hat rather like those I later saw worn by air hostesses, while in summer the uniform colour changed to brown with a checked dress and a huge brown hat with a brim. My Belgian school days finished when my demobbed father got tired of his old job as a patent agent in London and applied for a vacancy advertised by the Crown Agents in the Gold Coast.

Back home, Britain indulged in some much needed post-war jollification. Romance was in the air, and the newspapers were full of the engagement of Princess Elizabeth to her handsome Prince Phillip of Greece. There were no TVs then, but just before Mum and I left for Africa we were thrilled to be able to see a film of the wedding in the local cinema. This, incidentally, was the cinema we had been in some two years before when the film was stopped and the manager came onto the stage to inform us all that 'Victory in Europe' had been declared. The bonfires that were lit on that occasion in our street to celebrate left a nasty crater on the road surface. Later, the whole street had a party in an adjacent car park.

Our VE street party with me in tartan skirt and Jean adjusting her hat

Russell was also out of the Army and was struggling to get a job. However, Dad managed to get him one in the firm of patent agents he was leaving. It was there that Russell met his future wife, but the job itself was not a good fit and did not last long, although fortunately the marriage did. In contrast, Russell's wife Doris worked in that firm from leaving school until her eventual retirement, apart from her absence for war service in the WAAF.

Dad left for the Gold Coast, leaving Mum to make arrangements for the house. They had decided not to sell it but keep part of it for themselves, and let the rest to help pay the rates. There was no shortage of tenants in those war-damaged years, and Mum chose an elderly couple she sometimes met at the shops who were about to lose their own accommodation.

My sister Rita did not want to accompany us to Africa, and ran away from home to be with a man who was 'old enough to be her father'. Although my father and brother went after them, they failed to persuade Rita to return. Russell was now 25 years old, and had just

34

started the job at Dad's former patent office, so he stayed behind as caretaker and rent collector, living in the part of the house we were keeping on for our return. Accommodation was still in short supply after the war so it was easier and less expensive for Russell to live there, and it suited my parents to have someone to look after their interests.

Africa

It was quite a shock to my mother and me to see my father from the small windows of our converted Halton Bomber after we landed at Accra Airport. He was quite yellow! In those days it was usual to take bright yellow Mepacrine tablets as a precaution against malaria, but the drawback was that they turned the skin a similar shade. Fortunately for me, I had been prescribed the more palatable Paludrine tablets which were just coming into use, so I did not suffer the same fate. However, I think that once more I gave my guardian angel extra work because somehow I managed to avoid taking most of the tablets.

In Africa I did not attend school, although my father tried his best, without much cooperation from me, to home-tutor me following a correspondence course from an organisation called the Parents' National Education Union (PNEU). I was far more enthusiastic about attending the classes my father had started for the electricians in his department - they seemed much more fun.

While we were out there, India and Pakistan became independent so for the New Year's Eve Fancy Dress party at our local social club, 'The Railway Club', I was dressed as 'New India' in a costume devised for me by a couple of local Indian shop traders, although I was disappointed that this was not a sari, but a tunic over trousers, Punjabi style. I carried a huge heavy, orange, white and green flag and my efforts at waving this nearly brought down 'New India' more efficiently than any political opposition might have done.

We lived in Sekondi in one of a group of bungalows for European railway employees, although my father ran the electrical department in the district of Sekondi and Takoradi. My mother was very popular at the 'Railway Club' because she was something of an entertainer on the piano, and even after we had all retired for the night, there would often be a phone call demanding our presence as the members fancied a bit of a sing-song. Dad would sometimes 'clown around' a bit, but he could play the violin and had a good singing voice. My mother had a trained voice so they often sang popular duets together. Their favourite choice was 'The Desert Song' operetta (Sigmund Romberg & Oscar Hammerstein)

A favourite photo taken with my box Brownie camera – a gift for my arrival in the Gold Coast
It shows an island off the coastal area which included Bushua Beach, Cape Coats castle and Elmina castle (made infamous by the slave trade), and Dixcove Fort
One of these would often be our destination for a Sunday outing

and they sang the title duet beautifully. At other times my father would wrap a tea-towel around his head and give a lively performance of 'The Riff Song' with actions but when my mother sang 'One Alone' it was with great feeling. Only as I now recall this am I struck by what the words would have meant to her.

> *'One alone, to be my own.*
> *I alone to know his caresses…*
> *This would be a magic world to me*
> *If he were mine alone.'*

36

Even just hearing this music again in my head I find my emotions being tugged. The song 'Goodnight, Sweetheart' always indicated an end to their act.

These were some of the good times in my childhood memories, and, even though my parents sometimes had rows, there also seemed to be love. However, problems arose from my father drinking to excess and frequently being the worse for it. Although he was fuddled rather than violent, I hated seeing him like this. There were also constant money worries which my mother never seemed to be able to get to the bottom of. Even though white women were not expected

Dr Williams School, Dolgellau from rear – sketch by my father

to work in that heat my mother got rid of all the houseboys except young Moses who did not want much pay and whom she liked and trusted. Most people employed cooks, but after finding a filthy rat-infested kitchen, she had dismissed the cook and did all the cooking herself. She also took in dressmaking in an attempt to make ends meet. Mum could turn her hand to anything, and back in England she always decorated the house herself, doing everything that needed doing inside, including papering walls and ceilings. As well as dress making, I also learnt these skills from her which were useful when I first had my own property.

Mum mended her own shoes from old tyres, and I even saw her dig up the backyard of our house in England to find a drain that was blocked. She discovered that a tree root was solidly impacted inside, and after breaking the problematic section of the drain to get the root

37

out, she connected a spare part and re-filled the hole with earth, finishing up with a layer of concrete – thus saving a lot of money. She was prepared to do all this hard work to ensure my school fees got paid.

Both my parents had charismatic personalities in different ways. My mother seemed volatile and dominating, and this could be intimidating to me as a child. She was the stricter disciplinarian of the two, and was liberal in her use of slapped bottoms - when she could catch me! I used to run because it really hurt! Dad was my pal. He never smacked me, and had two different 'pet' names for me, 'Barney' and 'Chippie'. I did not know their origin, but they made me feel treasured.

In England he always referred to me as 'his partner' when he did jobs like digging the garden or re-concreting our garden pond. I doubt if I was of any real use but it made me feel important.

I liked to tag along whatever he was doing. He was a bit of an artist, and for a while I accompanied him to the club when it was closed as he was painting a large mural behind the bar. It was a nautical scene of his own composition, and remember clouds with mouths blowing old style sailing ships along. I seem to have inherited some of his artistic inclination as I also do a little painting myself, but I only seem to succeed with painting cats!

Partners!

If the workers in the electrical department were on strike and there was an interruption to the power supply, Dad would be called out to deal with it, and he would take me with him as he visited the big transformer units. I felt proud to be included as I knew that he was relying on me to summon help should anything go wrong. I watched from a distance as he pulled enormous fuses to see if they were faulty. He hated doing it, and I could tell that he had to gather his courage before each one.

In Africa I accompanied my parents to everything as there were no real facilities for children and there were only one other girl and one boy from Europe living in the area, but I hardly remember seeing them or their parents at the club in the evenings. We were frequently invited out to dinner, and I quickly learned appropriate behaviour and how to work my way through the table settings correctly. I also enjoyed ballroom dancing and soon learned to follow different partners, some of whom had very individual styles, which proved useful years later while serving in the RAF. In many ways I seemed to take a shortcut to growing up which was just as well looking further ahead.

We children often roamed around in places where the grownups might not have wanted us to. We liked exploring deep into the bush, risking snakes and other poisonous creepy crawlies, although the greatest risk I was ever aware of came from within our own home when I faced a snake in our latrine. The creature reared up from the box full of sawdust that we needed as we had no water flush like English toilets. Snakes often strike out defensively when they detect nearby vibrations so it was fortunate for me that when I screamed it just slithered quickly away. The tall pans from the latrine were

emptied at dead of night by a 'Latrine Man' who carried them on his head to the 'honey wagon' parked in the road outside our compound. Sadly for him, our 'Buddy (bloody) Black Dog' as he called him (the dog was white and no friend of his) loved to chase him, and the poor man usually slopped most of the contents over himself!

Mum, Me & Friend at Elmina Castle

However, I cannot say that I had no education in Africa. Even though I missed out on a lot of school work, I did acquire something of an older head on young shoulders and this would serve me well in the not too distant future. Perhaps, as I now know, one of the worst risks I ran during my time in Africa was from the strong sunlight because its dangers were far less recognised then, and sunscreens for the skin were rarely used. I also hated wearing sun glasses and never did. Sometimes I wonder if this might have contributed to my current problems with macular degeneration.

6. BASIC EDUCATION

'You alone, O God, are inexhaustible, and ever offering me something new to know, something new to love... And so on for eternity I shall ever be a little child beginning to be taught the lessons of Thy infinite divine nature.'
Cardinal Newman (1801-90)

My schooling started early with evacuation from London to a boarding school at only four years old, but that did not mean getting a head start. Sadly, there was a great lack of continuity about my formal education. Today one often hears about the national curriculum, but if anything similar existed in those days I managed to avoid it!

The boarding school I attended at such an early age was near Oxford and was definitely not a place I would recommend. The older children were set the task of washing us. This included   slapping, and I heard one older girl tell another to make sure to hit us with wet hands as it would hurt more. The adults were not much better. I remember the headmaster once said that every child would get the strap every night until a boy who kept swearing owned up. This was no idle threat, though fortunately, not that physically painful. In my dormitory we were each strapped once over the blankets at leg level, even if you had already fallen asleep.

My father came to visit and found me looking so miserable that he made an instant decision to remove me. He had invited me to take tea and sandwiches with him in the 'posh lounge' used for visiting parents but I protested "I should not be in here!" and when he offered me a sandwich, I worried about accepting it. "I am not supposed to eat these. They are dainty. Ours are made with thick bread and only a scrape of marge and jam." He changed me into my best woollen suit and said he would take me out for a walk, but instead we hitch-hiked all the way home, leaving all my belongings behind. It was only when we arrived home to face the wrath of my mother that I suddenly realised my suit had been put on back to front! Apparently we never

40

did get my trunk and clothing back, nor any refund on the fees my parents had already paid for the next term.

I then started at the primary section of the local authority school in Gant's Hill, Greater London, just down the road from the house I was born in and where we still lived. I was taken by my sister, much to her disgust, to an introductory day for younger siblings. It was a day of fun, though nothing like my schooldays there eventually turned out to be. On this one occasion there were many lovely toys that I never recollected seeing again and lots of climbing, but it did the trick and school at that age was not an unpleasant experience.

I think it must have been a reasonably good school too as several lessons have stayed in my mind. At first the male staff members were off on military service but I shall never forget Mr Petherbridge's lessons when he returned after the war. He enjoyed drama and I remember the great fun we had making cardboard Roman helmets and shields to use as props in the plays he wrote to illustrate our lessons.

As it was wartime I guess the school also got used to comings and goings amongst the pupils. At one stage I certainly remember going to a primary school in Swansea while staying with my maternal grandmother and my youngest aunt. They tried teaching me Welsh, but unless 'Put your hands on your head' ever becomes a useful expression, I do not think what I learned will get me very far.

Sadly, I've come to the conclusion that I don't have much of a gift for languages. During the year at school in Belgium I was supposed to learn French, but all I managed to pick up was some Flemish which nobody in the school should have been speaking. However, the Flemish helped a little when I later took up German in my Welsh boarding school (DWS) because there are some similarities between the two languages. Yet I'd obviously got them a bit confused when I took Stewart back to Belgium just after we got married to visit the family whose children I had been at school with. The family selected a wine from the cellar that originated from the year I'd spent with them, and after a couple of glasses of this I summoned enough courage to

41

launch into Flemish. My friends, politely (I think), remarked that I had obviously been learning German!

When I was at DWS the rather elderly French Mam'selle often chastised me for speaking French with a dreadful Belgian accent. Yet she regretted underestimating my ability to comprehend her Parisienne accent when she made a few rapid exchanges with the other French teacher on the French conversation table, and it quickly became obvious that I had understood every word. She was saying that she did not believe that a young colleague was absent that particular term because she had broken her leg, considering the obvious swelling in this poor unmarried woman's abdomen the previous term!

When I accompanied my parents to West Africa between 1947 and 1949 my education had little to do with any school curriculum or even the PNEU syllabus that my father was supposed to be following with me. We used to say in the Forces that although children moved from school to school when they accompanied their parents and so sometimes lacked continuity in their learning, they got a valuable education in a different sense by experiencing different parts of the world.

On my return from Africa, the headmaster at the Gants Hill school said that, whereas I would have passed the 11+ exam for grammar school 'with flying colours' before I left with my parents, I would need a lot of coaching to get me ready to enter grammar school now. My father quickly found an answer to the problem by sending me to a

Photo I took into exams

private PNEU school located five miles away in Buckhurst Hill. However, my mother seemed less keen on this solution although it was only much later that I discovered the real reasons for her unease. After being at the PNEU school for eighteen months and doing a little cramming in Latin which I had not previously learnt, I easily passed the public school's Common Entrance examination allowing me to go to boarding school when my Father who had rejoined the Army was posted to Wales. It was around the time I started at the PNEU school that I began to run into difficulties with the 'hero worship' I had for my father, although this did not stop me taking his photo into exams.

Although I had asked Jesus into my life at a Varsity and Public Schools camp, I still adopted a 'belt and braces' approach to exams at the PNEU school. When I was taking the Welsh School O-Level Certificate at DWS, I not only took Dad's photograph, but also bent pins which were supposed to bring good luck if you found them on the way to the exams (easily arranged by friends), 'Good Luck' cards and anything else I thought could possibly get me through them. I even resorted to doing a fair bit of work for them! One advantage of a boarding school was that this essential was harder to neglect. More logical than bent pins and the like was my habit of reading over a list of facts, dates or formulae just before entering the examination room, and then before even looking at the exam paper writing everything down on the blotting paper before I forgot. I did, eventually, become quite good at getting a feeling about what questions might be asked in time to actually do some appropriate revision. I was then beginning to rely less on my earthly father's inspiration and more on my Heavenly Father's guidance and began researching past exam papers.

While I was at DWS we had an extra few days of holiday to include the Queen's Coronation on Tuesday 2nd June 1953. Not many people had a TV at that time but one of the fathers brought a set into school for all the girls who weren't lucky enough to return home like me. Dad had been fortunate enough to obtain two tickets for the stands erected at Horse Guards in Whitehall. Mum and Dad agreed that I should accompany him, while Mum watched on our newly acquired TV set. We had to get there by 5am to beat the crowds and make sure of our places, but although it was a pretty miserable wait in the damp weather, spirits were high.

There was a hold-up in the procession just as Princess Margaret's carriage was driving past us and the Horse Guard outriders moved from the rear to either side of the carriage to protect the Sovereign's sister. Unfortunately, the horse of the Guardsman nearest us got rather frisky and he had great difficulty controlling it, a task probably made even harder by the fact that it was all happening under the interested gaze of the Princess. Eventually the poor fellow was unseated, and another military person had to come forward and help him up as he was hampered by his ceremonial uniform. I felt sorry for that poor man. My father said that he would probably be disciplined over it. The parade was very colourful but what impressed me most was the wonderful Queen of Tonga dressed in her beautiful national dress who chose to ride in an open carriage in spite of the rain, dispensing huge smiles and cheerfulness to the crowds as she passed.

I left DWS after a time in the lower sixth form. I was a school prefect at an early age, and due to become Head Girl the following year when I would also take my A-levels. The previous year I had been very fortunate as the Essex Education Authority took the unusual step of paying for me to continue at boarding school rather than moving me just before O-levels when my father's financial problems meant he could no longer continue to pay my fees. At that time the basic information - Pass or Fail - was all we could be told at O-level. Only under exceptional circumstances would we be given an idea of the actual results. My chemistry teacher had said that I would never make a doctor so I was heading for 'Oxbridge' and had already embarked

My Father in the Pakistan Army

on 'Arts' subjects for A-level taking English, History and French along with starting German. However, when my father visited the headmistress he discovered that I had done equally well in Science subjects, and so insisted that I change to them as they would be a better preparation to earn my living as I could not be brought up as 'just a young lady!'

After the summer holiday I did not return to DWS as planned, but enrolled

44

in the two year pre-medical course at SW Essex Technical College to do Chemistry, Physics, Botany and Zoology. Unfortunately, the first year was virtually the O-level course, and I already had O-levels in these subjects, so I should actually have been directed to enter the second year. However, it turned out that I needed a less demanding time of study. My mother and I had already had our travel immunisations to join my father in Karachi where he had gone on secondment to the Pakistan Army, but we were destined never to get there. I cannot imagine what would have happened to my career if we had gone, but that was not the reason for us staying behind. My mother who was a heavy smoker (as was my father) found that along with her smoker's cough she was coughing up blood.

She was diagnosed, to her great shame, with pulmonary TB, an illness she had always associated with dire poverty. After a few formalities, she embarked on an eighteen month period of hospitalisation. This started in a London hospital that she found particularly unpleasant, but fortunately my father got a brief period of compassionate leave and managed to get her transferred to a military hospital in a beautiful area of Surrey near a local beauty spot known as 'The Devil's Punchbowl'.

This left me alone at home which caused considerable concern when people found out. My headmistress at DWS kindly invited me back to school, but I was not sure of the practicalities, especially in terms of financial arrangements. Although I had been sorry to leave DWS, I also did not want to return as it would mean leaving a budding relationship behind. Eventually, on my father's instructions, I let our home to the Army letting agents and moved into digs nearer the college where I was treated just like one of the family. The food was good, and in return I listened at mealtimes to their Dad's reminiscences of WW1 and Gallipoli where he had served.

It was a long and difficult journey to visit my mother in hospital, but my boyfriend often accompanied me. He was Greek and held opposing views to my father on the Cyprus conflict then taking place which earned my father's disapproval. Nonetheless, my mother gave us permission to get engaged as she feared she would not make it out of hospital alive, and thought that he would take care of me.

However, the engagement broke up somewhat painfully for me after we went to different universities because he was obsessively jealous. Even I eventually had to admit that it was never going to work. This whole relationship was a difficult one for me and I believe my 'Guardian Angel' worked overtime to ensure I came out of it to a future that turned out to be miles better than the one I had tried so hard to sort out for myself.

Meanwhile, my mother was struggling with various unpleasant reactions to the drugs she had to take as well as complications arising from the difficult and lengthy surgery she'd undergone. The intention was to remove the middle of three lobes in her right lung, but when they opened her chest they found that the lung was not divided into lobes at all. She even woke up during the operation.

It seemed very likely that Mum would die at this stage and she was convinced that it was only her deep desire to see my father again that kept her clinging to life during the operation and the long recovery period afterwards. Yet eventually she was well enough to leave hospital, and her wish to see my father again was granted when his tour of duty in Pakistan ended, but there would be no fairytale ending. They were not destined to live happily ever after.

7. LESS OF MY EARTHLY FATHER

'The Moving Finger writes: and having writ, Moves on: nor all thy Piety nor Wit shall lure it back to cancel half a line, nor all thy Tears wash out a Word of it.'
Rubaiyat of Omar Khayyam

Had I been old enough to be suspicious, there had already been hints about my father's 'feet of clay' such as the number of women friends who visited or sent gifts when I was at school in Belgium. Rather more of a hint came when my father left us at Liverpool docks on our arrival from West Africa on a cold January day after telling us that somebody had picked his pocket of all his money as we left the ship. I remember

46

shivering in scant summer clothing as my mother and I made our way along the Liverpool streets to get to a bank. However, we did not meet up with my father again there or even back at our house in Gants Hill where we had kept the flat. It turned out that my father had moved in with 'The Laughton Woman' as she became known because she lived in a place of that name. It was quite near the PNEU school that I would be attending, and this was why my mother had been so troubled by this solution to my education needs. Although she could have been spared the worry as I did not fall under this woman's influence, or even that of my father as I saw nothing of him.

Meanwhile, my mother and I moved into our house beside the tenants who had been given notice and were grudgingly arranging to vacate the premises. They clearly resented our presence, and we could see how this couple who had at first appeared so nice had actually made life quite unbearable for Russell. He had left home with no rentcollected or rates paid and we had no idea where he had gone. It was some years before we would meet up with either Rita or Russell again.

Mother and I were still reeling from my father's 'bombshell'. I felt a sense of personal loss that my father was with another woman. My mother though was suffering not only grief at being so callously abandoned by her husband but a great sense of betrayal. She had kept from me the painful knowledge that, before we arrived home, her father-in-law had brought this woman to our house to remove his son's (my father's) belongings. This had been interpreted quite liberally, and included furniture that had been my maternal grandmother's.

What was becoming clearer to me was that my father would make promises that he probably intended to keep, but then either did not, or could not. His promises to me were fanciful and more like wishes he had for me - for example, telling me (and everyone else) that on our return home from Africa I would go to a particular very notable girls' public school. It was a dream! He seemed to partly inhabit a Walter Mitty world and, as time went by, it became hard, perhaps even for

47

him, to distinguish between his romanticising and plain facts. His heavy drinking also contributed to his increasingly erratic behaviour.

The attributes of my earthly father that I was painfully discovering caused me some difficulty with the Christian concept of a Father God. I found it hard to trust His promises, His love for me, and that He would never leave me or forsake me. I remember the period after returning from Africa as a particularly hard time. It must have been dreadful for my mother. Even if her sisters had lived nearer, I doubt she would have told them, and she was much too proud to confide in our neighbours about her plight.

She became so distressed by this huge betrayal and the loss of people she held dear that she did not allow me to leave the house even to visit friends. Obviously she was ill, and I can still remember the evening I eventually managed to escape and run to the next-door neighbour to phone for a doctor. All the time I could hear her shouting out from her bedroom for me to return and not to bother anyone. Fortunately, the doctor who attended was quite astute, and he gave strict instructions to my mother that I had to get out among friends of my own age.

Eventually my father and mother reunited, but this was only the first in a number of separations and liaisons. As well as the 'Laughton Woman', there was 'that Mona Woman', the 'Belgian Woman' as well as the 'Lokeren (in Belgium) Woman' and later two more 'Mrs Stuarts', and these are only the ones I can put a name to! My mother, who professed her continuing love for my father throughout, resisted the total collapse of the marriage and never would grant my father a divorce.

As a consequence, it was finally 'Goodnight Sweetheart' when my father tried unsuccessfully to get their marriage annulled in the High Court in London. He claimed that my mother's first marriage was not bigamous as her 'husband's' original wife had been under age, so that marriage was invalid, and my mother was therefore legally married to Rita and Russell's father. The assertion was that she had therefore bigamously married my father! The court case lasted several days and was reported in the national press. Even the university lecturer for whom I babysat received a press cutting from his mother with all the details. I interrupted my university course and spent most of my 21st birthday year away from St Andrews supporting my mother. On the positive side, I was able to meet up with my ex-flatmate Jenn as she was then working in London, and we attended a term of evening classes together at the London Bible College.

All this was very unsettling, and looking back I can see the hand of God finding a way for me through all the difficulties and distractions (some of my own making), supplying miraculous financial provision enabling me not only to finish my schooling, but also to go on to university and eventually fulfill my father's pronouncement at my birth that I would become a doctor.

8. The 'GREEN LADY' and the 'CAT LADY'
'Whatever you are, be a good one.'
Abraham Lincoln

As a child in West Africa, I noticed that white British people appeared to assume that British and Christian were synonymous. Certainly 'C of E' was the most common insertion in the space marked 'Religion' on forms. This was also the case in the RAF where it often accompanied the name and number on identity tags, whether or not the owner felt any allegiance to the Church of England which was represented on most camp sites. While some others put RC or OD (Other Denomination) and a few specified 'Baptist' or 'Methodist', I simply put 'Christian', feeling denomination to be less important. If I became a war casualty I was perfectly happy to be ministered to by any RAF 'padre'.

I guess that most people facing imminent death might like to receive the possible comforts offered by religion whether or not they had really sorted out in their own mind if they were actual believers, or simply trying to 'be a good person, but not a churchgoer' as many would explain themselves on being asked about their faith. Being good is what Christians should aim at, but it is not what makes them a

Christian. Sadly, I for one, am not as good as two people I can think of who were both adamant that they were not believers, but were certainly very good to me, and helped me at two critical periods in my life.

When my mother was first diagnosed with TB I also had to go to the chest clinic to be checked out. The elderly doctor was assisted by a slightly odd-looking woman in a white coat secured around her middle by ties drawn into a firm bow. A navy blue skirt could be seen below the white coat and black stockings covered noticeably swollen legs. She obviously had 'bad feet' judging by the way her shoes were distorted by irregular bulges at the toes. A flat navy-blue brimmed hat with a band and a badge in front was secured firmly to the bun of her no nonsense hair style by two large hat pins. She was of indeterminate age, but obviously no longer a 'spring chicken'. Her hands looked podgy and her face inclined to hairiness - there were definitely signs of a '5 o'clock shadow'.

She reminded me vaguely of 'Nitty Nora' who came to our primary school at intervals to painfully yank a fine-tooth comb through our hair in search of - as her nickname implies - nits. There the similarity ended, for Miss Barrington was as gentle as 'Nitty Nora' had been rough. She was certainly an outstanding example of the truth of the phrase: 'You can't judge a book by its cover'. She herself often poked fun at her own appearance, saying, "You can see I'm no oil painting," but Mum and I knew that her true beauty was not displayed in her looks.

Miss Barrington had a good speaking voice, as gentle and kind as you could wish to hear at any time of personal stress when it would take on an almost crooning quality. Her duties included taking my full medical history which she did as if she were a doting grandmother, keen to hear every little detail of what had been happening to her favourite grandchild since their last meeting. She was employed as Health Visitor to the chest clinic, and this meant she was also a frequent visitor to our home as my mother needed closely following up after her discharge from hospital. We both enjoyed these visits which were unhurried and punctuated with great merriment for Miss Barrington had a good sense of humour and could see the funny side of seemingly very ordinary circumstances.

She frequently entertained us with tales from her nursing days. She had been employed in the war by what we would call today the Sexually Transmitted Diseases Clinic. It was her job to attempt to track down the contacts of American servicemen who had been diagnosed with a venereal disease. She often had only a first name and a vague description to go on, and so she had to be quite ingenious in how she set about her task. Because they wore green uniforms at that time, Miss Barrington and her colleagues became well known amongst the prostitutes of London's 'East End' as the 'Green Ladies'.

She told us once that she was climbing some outside stairs in a block of flats when she was loudly accosted by a woman who demanded to know what she wanted. She discreetly enquired whether there was a 'Gertie' living in the flats. "Yer. She's 'ere. What d'ya want widg 'er?" came the loud reply. "Well, I just need to speak to her about a personal matter."

She was directed to a door upstairs, and when the woman answered, Miss Barrington quietly and gently explained that she might possibly have been named as a contact. "What d'yer mean?" came the ear-splitting response. "Eh Maisie!" she called down over the walkway to the first woman who was still lurking, curious about the outcome of the visit, and continued at the top of her voice: "This Green Lady sez I got VD. I ain't, 'ave I? You tell 'er!"

Not only did Miss Barrington dispense laughter, but she often called bearing a home-made cake, saying that she had made one for herself and one for us as she had enough ingredients and was coming to visit. In her unobtrusive way she supplied what she could see was lacking in our lives at that time - a good dose of laughter and some good home cooking.

She was easy to talk to and my mother felt able to confide in her and share some of her deep unhappiness and worries. Miss Barrington knew all about my father's infidelities and the continuing distress it was causing my mother, and also that money was scarce because my father diverted most of his salary to his preferred lifestyle.

Miss Barrington surprised us by having a passion for ballet, and would spend all day from early morning queuing outside a box office to get tickets for a particular performance. This was in spite of suffering from the most awful gout which was responsible for the pain and swelling in her hands and feet. Unfortunately, this could only be treated by older medication and this had some bad side effects, but in spite of her many physical problems, she always did her best to rise above them and enjoy life. She wanted me to experience her enjoyment of ballet and took me to some wonderful performances with stars like Sir Frederick Ashton and Dame Margot Fonteyn. I still can't hear the music from 'La Fille Mal Gardee' without picturing us watching the famous 'Ashton Clog Dance' together.

Visits from Miss Barrington did not stop with her retirement, and Mum and I also visited her in her home in North London. She told us to call her 'Rose', but the name did not really suit her and we continued to think of her as Miss Barrington. In her retirement she took up water colour painting, and also produced some very detailed and neat embroidery. I have many little cards with her paintings of colourful birds and several attractive handmade tablecloths that were gifts after I married.

She was most encouraging about my hopes to become a doctor, and, knowing how things stood with my father, she incredibly made me an allowance of £5 per month pocket money which continued until my financial status became more settled once I joined the RAF. I was so glad I managed to get from the RAF station near York where I was based with my husband in time to be at her bedside before she died of kidney complications with her gout. Just before she lapsed into unconsciousness she managed to say, "I knew you would come, my little doctor."

Lynda was another person who insisted that she wasn't a Christian but I believe God worked through her. She was also invaluable to me at a significant time in my life. I first met Lynda when I bought a kitten from her. She lived and worked in a cattery so that she could breed and keep her own cats but unfortunately she had to leave when the

cattery owners found she had far more cats than the number originally agreed. This coincided with my taking on my GP practice after the sudden death of my predecessor for whom I did sessions. The doctor's surgery was then based in a large Victorian house which Stewart and I had bought and Lynda came to live in the flat over our garage and help me.

Flat above our garage occupied by Lynda

Lynda was very versatile and multi-talented. Her role was adapted as circumstances in the practice changed, and she worked for me as both my housekeeper and Practice Administrator at different times. She was very good with the patients and would do all in her power to help and speak up for them. If she had not limited herself to a life where she could keep and breed her cats, she could have done a lot better than being my 'Girl Friday'. If Lynda had a blind spot it concerned the desirability of not increasing her cat population further. If someone came to purchase a kitten she would often send them to another breeder for a wider selection. I chose to be deliberately vague about the precise numbers of her growing cat family scattered over her flat and the garden. I knew that it could get out of hand but I did not want to make an issue of it as in her previous employment because she was so valuable to me.

It became known that I was a Christian doctor, and as there were a number of different Christian organisations in the area, Lynda often had to take calls from people needing to speak to someone in a Christian context. She always put them at ease, but explained that as she wasn't herself a believer she would transfer their call to someone who was. She was always happy to man the reception desk to let others attend surgery prayers.

Once when I was going through a particularly stressful time in the practice over a partnership split, she not only did her best to shield me from anything that might stress me further, but would dispense amazingly appropriate words of comfort and encouragement explaining that this was what she thought a Christian believed, while still emphasising that she herself was not a believer! Although she always spoke up for patients, this was something she seemed reluctant to do for herself. Sadly, she paid dearly for this when she allowed a delay to build up in her own cancer treatment. She died not long after we came to live in Plymouth.

9. FAMILY RECONCILIATIONS

'Blessed are the peacemakers, for they will be called children of God.'
Matthew 5 v9

I explained earlier that before we went to Africa, Rita had left home with an older man, and on our return Russell was also nowhere to be found. He had left the family home because he could not get along with the tenants who rented part of the house. He knew he was letting our parents down in leaving because they had entrusted him to look after their interests and he probably did not want to return to face the music.

One day my friend Jean told me with great excitement that she had seen Rita in our doctor's waiting room with a baby in her arms! Our family doctor was just at the top of our road so it was easy for me to keep watch at surgery times,

Rita & Son

and eventually my patience was rewarded as one day I met her and the

Rita & Partner with Mum and Me sitting in front

baby on their way home. She spoke to me politely enough, but there was no great warmth (that didn't enter our relationship until much later!). She resisted returning with me to see Mum then, but did say she would call one day. She was true to her word and, gradually, 'visiting rights' were established both ways, and we were made welcome by her and the baby's father at their flat about three miles away. He was very keen that Rita and, more importantly, his infant son should restore connections with Rita's side of the family.

Contacting Russell was impossible because he had not only moved out of our family house while we were abroad, but also left his job with the patent agent that Dad had found for him before we left for Africa. However, amazingly, Dad almost bumped into him in Oxford Street in London. Russell had been through several jobs, mainly as a salesman, but none had lasted

Rita, Russ & Me

long. Dad bought him a coffee, reunited him with the family, and set him on the path to permanent employment. He had always done his best to be a good father to Russell who clearly appreciated this, although he despised the way Dad had treated our mother. It could not have been easy for Dad when he married Mum who was five years his senior, and inherited two children, the eldest only twelve years his junior. Added to this, there was much interference from Russell's aunts who were used to having their say in Rita and Russell's upbringing. However, Dad did his best and Russell had reason to thank him for at least two jobs and getting him out of several scrapes.

Russ had a very different war from my father and, sadly, it seemed he was never the same man afterwards. I had not really known him before, but even I could feel that things were not quite right. He enjoyed the company of family, but was very ill at ease with strangers. For a long time, whenever he wanted to buy anything he would send me into the shop to get it for him. People being changed by their war experiences was not uncommon at that time, but it was rarely spoken about or causes looked for. Russ spoke more about his war experiences in old age when dementia allowed him to forget the shameful consequences of telling people too much, just as he forgot that he didn't eat white bread, sausages and several other things, tucking into them with relish when they appeared at the care home meals. Obviously, his memory was not always reliable by then. For example, he would talk about his flying in the RAF which had been as an Air Gunner, but when people assumed he had been a pilot this became a sort of false memory.

He did tell Mum things about his war experiences bit by bit over the years and, later on, she told me. He had served in North Africa and Italy and spoke of seeing fighting around Monte Casino, and leading mules laden with ammunition along tiny mountain tracks beside sheer drops. He described seeing his mates next to him have their heads blown off. He also drove a Bren gun carrier, and once told me that he was with a group of his comrades when he saw a low flying enemy aircraft coming straight for them, and dived under the Bren gun carrier for cover. When the noise stopped he emerged to find just a huge crater where his mates had been standing. If there had been the opportunity to see a doctor, he might, even then, have been called 'shell shocked'. These days he would have been diagnosed with PTSD.

He was probably relieved when he was picked up on a train by the Military Police. He had been getting eyesight problems and had a chit in his pocket from the Army MO referring him to a specialist in Naples, but had no leave of absence permit from his CO. When asked if he was AWOL (Absent without Leave) he simply said, "If you want to call it that". This was where my earlier childhood memory of him in our living room with two other soldiers came in. He had been on his way to a British military prison when he gave his escort the slip at the London mainline railway station, and headed towards our home to see his mother. His escort was compassionate because when they picked him up again they allowed him to complete his journey to visit his mother under their supervision.

I believe that when my father heard about Russell he used his influence to get some commutation of his sentence. He certainly ensured that the way Russ's Army service had ended was overlooked when he encouraged him to apply for a job in one of the REME workshops that were under his command when he was Deputy Assistant Director of Mechanical Engineering at HQ Southern Command.

Russell remained in this workshop for many years after my father retired from his Army post and continued there long after my father's death. Russell didn't see my father at all in the sixteen years after my parents' marriage finally broke up, but he came to his bedside just before his death when he was able to tell Dad that he was still in the job that he had found for him. Russell was very proud of his work at the REME workshop and was greatly respected by everyone there. He studied at evening classes to gain qualifications, and later became Workshop Superintendent. The day after he had to retire, I found him with tears in his eyes. "Yesterday I was somebody ... but today I am nobody," he said.

10. A MEDICAL SCHOOL PLACE!

'Gaudeamus Igitur, Juvenes dum sumus.'
'Let us therefore rejoice, While we are young.'
Traditional ancient student song possibly originating in 1287

From what I have written so far, I may have given the impression that I wanted to become a doctor purely because this was my father's ambition for me, but in fact he just planted the seed of this possibility in my mind. At my interviews for Medical School, the question 'Why do you want to become a doctor?' was always asked. I found it just as hard to verbalise then as I do now. I just knew that I really wanted this above everything. I loved to be able to help people, I liked to fathom what made them as they were, and I found the workings of the animal and the human body fascinating.

Although I applied to medical schools elsewhere, it was always assumed that because I lived in London I would attend one of its numerous medical training establishments in spite of their small

57

allocation of places to females. However, my father had left again, money was scarce, and the foolishness of pressing on in my attempt to study medicine seemed to be confirmed when I did not get a place at any of the London medical schools. Then, out of the blue, a telegram came offering me a place at a Scottish University that I had never heard of before, followed by an offer of a grant from Essex County Education Committee that allowed me to accept it.

My grant had been means-tested on my father's income, but when I overheard my mother on the phone evidently pleading with Dad to pay his share, I picked up the extension phone just in time to hear the callous words: "Tell her she should go out and find a job!" Could I believe my ears? It felt like I had received a physical blow in the core of my being, and I felt shaky inside. Was this really my Dad? I couldn't believe it was happening. It felt like the time when

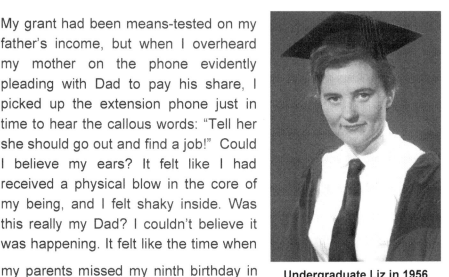

Undergraduate Liz in 1956

my parents missed my ninth birthday in Belgium but a thousand times worse. My contact with Dad had been limited since this latest parental split, and my only means of contacting him was through his bank, presumably to hide his whereabouts from my mother, but with these harsh words the realisation dawned that I too had lost his love, and that his ambition for me to become a doctor had been superseded by his desire to fulfil his own needs. I was not important to him, he was no longer 'my pal', and never again would I hear him call me by his two pet names for me.

Unlike London and many other medical schools, St Andrews, in common with all the Scottish Universities, did not offer exemption from 1st MB ChB[5] which allowed direct entry into 2nd MB so I had to recommence the equivalent of the four A-level subjects I had taken at technical college. This possible drawback was far outweighed by my sense of relief at gaining entry to medicine and the privilege of going to St Andrews which turned out to be a much better university experience than I could ever have imagined.

The colourful traditions and close-knit 'Town & Gown' community at this ancient University, founded around 1413, was unlike anything I had ever experienced, with processions and Pier Walks, and the red coloured gowns of the undergraduates contrasting vividly with its historic grey buildings.

Kate Kennedy Procession at St Andrews University

Me, Mum & Jenn at Student torchlight procession when Baron Robert Boothby of Buchan (1900-86) became Rector of St Andrews University (1958-61)

---

[5] First Bachelor of Medicine & Bachelor of Surgery degree examinations taken at the end of the first year of study

Even though I knew that I could be made to sing a verse of 'The Gaudie' (see below the heading of this chapter) in public as a forfeit for not producing a 'Raisin Receipt' written in perfect Latin for the pound of 'raisins' (grapes or wine) I had given to my senior woman on a certain Monday, it was all infinitely better than commuting daily on the London Underground.

Looking back on this time, the contrast between what my earthly father would not attempt to provide, and the abundance of what a loving heavenly Father did provide, is enormous. I probably would not have lasted the course in London for various reasons, not least of which would have been the long daily commute. God's provision did not stop there either as I was destined to meet people who opened their homes to me, saving my money and providing a place for me to stay when it was not desirable or possible for me to return home. One of these was geography lecturer Professor John Paterson with his wife Evangeline, and I became a babysitter for their three young children. They even took me away to help with the family when he went to give talks on Christian topics in his capacity as an Inter-Varsity Fellowship speaker and I learnt much from them about Christianity.

In the Patersons I saw their faith sacrificially put into action as they kept open house for the students, not only regularly for the Christian Union members on Sunday evenings, but also for any who needed help at any time. This was in spite of the needs of their own growing young family, and poor Evangeline's frequent suffering from total exhaustion. My brother Russell visited me at St Andrews

The Paterson Family

whenever he could, and would often keep John Paterson talking for hours, even once until 5am as he struggled to come to a belief in Christ.

Russ continued the devotion he had displayed for me from my birth, and did his best in every way he could to compensate me for the loss of my father. He would put me on trains to and from school and university, take me to Foyle's bookshop at Charing Cross Road in London to buy me any medical textbooks that I thought might help, and even bought me a microscope. He would take me on holiday with his wife, and had such a generous nature that both she and I had to be careful not to admire anything in a shop window or he would go in and purchase it for us. He was very proud of me and the first to celebrate any of my achievements. Later, when I became a GP he designed handy instruments for me including some that enabled me to communicate better with my deaf patients, and others that amplified the audible heart beat.

I managed to get a little nursing job at the local St Andrews Cottage Hospital for a couple of hours every evening which helped my finances, while in my second year I was also greatly blessed when Jenn, a fellow student, asked me if I would share her uncle's retirement flat with her at no cost. This agreeable arrangement even continued when Jenn left for London to continue her studies to be a 'Lady Almoner' (medical social worker).

Jenn and I took it in turns to cook. We were experimenting a lot with food, and were delighted that the local butchers supplied a great variety of game and offal. However, I sometimes found it a bit difficult as Jenn had an uncanny knack of presenting a beautifully prepared dish of the particular organ that I had been dissecting that day for supper!

After leaving Jenn's flat and going to Dundee for my clinical studies, I went through a phase of examining myself for all the symptoms of every disease we studied and, of course, it was not hard to find that I had experienced most of them at least once, so before I had learned to distinguish the relative significance of symptoms it seemed that I could have been suffering from any number of dire conditions about to strike me down and ruin my life until I concluded that I could not possibly be suffering from them all, so probably had nothing! In fact, ever since I have tended to ignore things about myself that might be a potential medical problem and always think that they will probably go away of their own accord.

Years later this was my attitude to a possible cancerous breast lump when I only took action several months after discovering it when my sister confided that she had just had a cancerous lump removed from her breast. On hearing that I too had this diagnosis she remarked that it was a pity we had not spoken to each other earlier as we could have gone for treatment together.

As it was, she was able to come with me and tell me what to expect as Stewart had left for Plymouth by this stage but I was still in Sussex. I cannot say that I was at all worried about the breast cancer as I seemed to be able to view the whole thing purely from a doctor's perspective, just thinking through what would need to happen next for the patient. I have noticed this tendency in all 'threats' to my health, and often feel I haven't got the time to indulge them so I just distance myself. This frame of mind where I 'rise above it all' and don't allow myself to imagine the worst has seemingly become one of my main coping techniques.

This meant that when I was initially diagnosed with dry AMD I just put it out of my mind and did no additional research on the subject. Perhaps this was one reason why I was so ill prepared when I was later discharged with almost no knowledge of any helpful resources after I had experienced a rapid decline in my visual acuity.

Incidentally, writing about Jenn becoming a 'Lady Almoner' has reminded me of an examination paper I sat in chest diseases. The evening before, I happened to hear a talk on the radio about TB and chest clinics. It updated me on my mother's experience and emphasised the concerns of that time, and I was amazed to find that I could make good use of this information in at least two of the exam questions. When I looked at another question, I could not believe what I was seeing as it asked the differences between a Health Visitor and a Hospital Almoner. Thank you, God! I could so easily compare my 'Green Lady' and my flatmate's work.

Unfortunately, I always got very stressed when sitting examinations, and although I had to take a great many during my university days, my nerves got no better. There always seemed to be so much that could be asked about such a huge subject that one could never feel adequately prepared even when one had worked steadily, and I must admit that this was not always my position. I vowed that after my degree I would never voluntarily sit another exam!

I remember around finals that I prayed; "Lord, if you make me a doctor, I will be a doctor for you." However, I got a bad case of 'cold feet' and was about to make this prayer difficult to answer. I was so convinced I was not doing well in the examinations that when I got to the final item, my oral examination for surgery, I could see no point in giving myself more stress by appearing in person when I believed I had already failed. Leaving a message that I was withdrawing from the exams, I retreated to the safety of the little tenement house in Dundee that I had the good fortune to be buying from my landlady. She had preferred to sell the house to me by instalments in lieu of rent and I raised the finance to do this by letting the spare room to provide extra income. I was sitting drinking a soothing cup of tea, not allowing the seriousness of what I had just done and its consequences to sink in, when I was surprised by a knock on the door. I was even more surprised to find the Dean's secretary with a message saying that the external examiner had agreed to delay his departure until the next train if I would return with her to take the examination. My reluctance must have been evident for she added, "And I have been allowed to tell you that you have done a very good written paper."

Do these many provisions, against so many odds for my medical career, look to you at all like miracles?

MB ChB at Last!

11. RAF MEDICAL CADETSHIP

'First gain the victory and then make the best use of it you can.'
Horatio Nelson

When I got to my penultimate year at university, my mother showed me an advertisement for Army medical cadetships. As it turned out they were not accepting women, but the RAF were. So I applied and was invited to attend a selection procedure at the famous Biggin Hill RAF station of 'Battle of Britain' fame.

I remember not having the vaguest clue about what to expect at this selection procedure. I had to stay there for at least one night, and was accommodated in a room just outside the Womens Royal Air Force (WRAF) block. I had eventually settled down to get some much needed sleep when I was woken up by a great banging of doors and loud women's voices when the WRAF block occupants all returned together from duty. I lay there, quiet as a church mouse, pretending to be asleep, while I tried to figure out if this was somehow part of the selection test to see how I would handle the circumstances. Whether or not it was part of the selection procedure, I ended up becoming the first medical woman cadet, and jolly nearly the last as I believe that until more recently they only ever appointed about six.

The cadetship scheme meant that my university fees would be paid for my remaining two years, and as I was commissioned in the lowly rank of Pilot Officer, I would also receive a salary appropriate to that rank. As someone remarked at my selection panel, I would feel like a millionaire compared with my financial status as a student existing only on a grant, and he did not even know about the individual 'haggis pie' that would sometimes be my only food on days when my grant money was running low.

For my part, I had to serve in the RAF for five years after my pre-registration year which would follow straight after I graduated with a medical degree. At the same time I would be promoted to the rank of Flying Officer with its accompanying salary which was higher than the remuneration normally earned by the NHS (National Health Service)[6] pre-registration doctors, even though for this year I would be seconded to the NHS so I could complete two house jobs at approved hospitals, each lasting six months. On the downside, the RAF did not pay members of the Medical Cadetship Scheme the terminal gratuity normally paid to short service officers at the end of their term of service.

Although I was now paid by the RAF for my remaining two student years, I had virtually nothing to do with it. I did not even wear uniform, although after being accepted into the RAF I had been on a three day introductory course at RAF Freckleton near Lytham St Annes in Lancashire where we were kitted out with some basic wardrobe items like RAF shirts, a raincoat and epaulette 'sliders' with rank braid to fit onto both, plus two very hardwearing white towels which I still have.

We had to buy our own uniforms from one of the firms of military tailors, and staff from Gieves & Hawkes, Moss Bros and Alkit visited RAF Freckleton to measure us for our uniforms. I selected Gieves which was affectionately known as 'thieves' and I could soon see why as I ended up parting with what seemed a huge amount from what at first appeared to be a welcome 'windfall' of an initial clothing

---

[6] State provided healthcare in the UK funded from taxation

allowance. I decided to wait to order a uniform greatcoat which even in the early 1960s was going to set me back £80. In fact, I never did obtain one, and managed to get away with just my RAF raincoat during my whole 8 years service.

The man from Gieves was priceless! He could have been a butler from 'Downton Abbey'. "I think I'll add an extra two inches to the length of your skirt, Madam - for the dignity of the service!" I was not even wearing a fashionable mini-skirt. Mind you, as trousers formed no part of my uniform, I was quite glad of this precaution at certain times in my life as an RAF MO. A supply of printed personal visiting cards - a size larger than for men - also had to be ordered. On arrival at any new posting, three of these had to be deposited on the silver platter placed for that purpose in the Officers Mess reception.

There was only a taxi-load of us on this introductory course. I know because we all missed the last bus back from Blackpool one night. We never met again after we each returned to our respective universities - a pity because the chap from Glasgow was rather nice. Our small select group was introduced to some useful tips about RAF life such as coming to attention and saluting if within sight of the RAF ensign being raised at the start of the day and lowered at the end, and not wearing any outdoor clothing in the public rooms of the Mess. A forgotten hat on your head in the ante-room could cost you a round of drinks, whereas wearing a hat at breakfast in an Army Officer's Mess meant that the officer in question preferred no conversation. Newspapers were allowed at the table only at breakfast, a standard I have been keen to preserve throughout our married life! Curiously, when entering the office of another officer of any rank you would wear your hat in order to salute them smartly because you never saluted with an uncovered head - so the salute was not returned in this case.

We also had to learn the rank structure and insignia and their equivalents in all three British services plus American if only to recognise who to salute, when and how. I always felt self conscious about saluting, and even on my last posting at RAF North Luffenham in Rutland, I was constantly but affectionately teased about this by some officers in the RAF Regiment (experts in RAF drill and ceremonial) who were also based there. "Come on Liz, you teach our chaps first aid, let us teach you how to salute!"

After my two NHS house jobs as House Surgeon at King George V Hospital in Ilford and House Physician at King's Cross Hospital for Infectious Diseases in Dundee, I was promoted to the rank of Flight Lieutenant and went on several introductory courses with the RAF. These were at RAF Feltwell in Norfolk where we learned about the service generally, and the Medical Training Establishment at RAF Halton near Aylesbury where we learned about the Medical Branch and tropical diseases and what forms to fill out and when.

Finally, we went to RAF Farnborough in Hampshire where we did our aeromedical training. As well as learning about human airborne physiology, this involved participating in nerve-wracking experiences like being spun round individually at great speed on a large human centrifuge or being exposed to high altitude conditions in a decompression chamber. The centrifuge gave us the experience of forces several times greater than gravity that the pilots of high performance aircraft would encounter when undertaking certain manoeuvres. Likewise, the decompression chamber simulated what might happen if an aircraft lost pressurisation for some reason, and the crew was exposed to atmospheric conditions at which the human body was not designed to function. This would be more serious if the oxygen supply to their masks also failed, and therefore we had our supply cut off to see how it affected our performance of simple tasks. The child's toy I was given where I had to put various sizes of balls into the right holes for their size presented no problem to me at all. I just put them all through the largest size hole! My recollection was of sorting them out really well!

We did an abbreviated Officer Training course in the OCTU (Officer Cadet Training Unit) at RAF Feltwell. There were about a dozen of us, a motley crew consisting mainly of newly qualified dentists and doctors with little service training, but also two former Ceylon Air Force officers who had been Sandhurst trained, and a few returning ex-servicemen. Officially, we comprised the PQRE course (Professionally Qualified and Re-entrants), but it was nick-named the 'Peculiar and Retread' course for obvious reasons!

We were supposed to march everywhere, but because of the poor example to normal officer cadets they soon forbade us to march anywhere except inside a hangar - and what a sight that was! We had one man who could not get fitted with a uniform and wore something like a 'flasher mac' everywhere, one who could not tell left from right, two who could not get their arms to work in proper sequence with their legs, and two very smartly drilled ex Sandhurst officers who were the only ones who half managed to keep in time with me marching in high heels.

We also had to learn how to hold a Court Martial or hear a Charge. We each had to take turns in either presiding over the proceedings, or being the prisoner, the escort, or the Flight Sergeant who would give out the commands to the accused and escort. Nobody seemed very good at giving the orders, and we ended up on one occasion with the prisoner and escort marching in a divergent path from each other towards the front of the stage on which this was all taking place. Their steps were getting shorter and shorter, but still no order, not even to halt, was forthcoming. Eventually, with a three foot drop ahead of him, the 'prisoner' could not resist the old chestnut: "Well, say something, if only good-bye!" Ironically, as luck would have it, the guy who did not know his left from his right had drawn the role of the Flight Sergeant giving the orders on this occasion.

On another occasion, some of the men were chatting up a group of Princess Mary's Nursing Service Sisters in the Officers Mess. An orienteering exercise was planned next day which meant getting to a map reference where we would set up camp for the night. Our chaps thought it would be fun if these nursing officers could join us for a drink and a bite to eat at the camp, but they were overheard by one of the directing staff who told them that all the directing staff from the CO down must also be invited.

68

What a charade that brought about! I don't know if much orienteering was done, but I was dropped off at the campsite later after staying for an appointment with 'Gieves' the Military Outfitters. I had been well briefed by the corporal cook from the Officers Mess, and I had with me a good supply of frozen lobster tails, the CO's favourite starter, and enough fillet steaks and all the accompaniments to serve everyone. I also had to cook them. I was a woman, wasn't I? Somehow the Mess silver and formal tablecloths also arrived with the all important wines and bar equipment. With all the preparation putting up the marquee and adjoining bar tent, and digging the latrines etc, the two-man sleeping tents were only hastily erected just as the CO's car was expected. As if specially rigged to do so, they each collapsed on cue just after he had passed. If he knew, he did not look back, and apart from the damage caused to the paintwork of the CO's car because it had been parked too close to the fire, all the guests left without any mishaps.

We were too tired to do anything about the tents and settled down in the marquee for the night with me in the separate bar tent. I was not very comfortable as it had no proper groundsheet. The other unforeseen difficulty was the short dark walk to the latrine. It was necessary to visit in twos with somebody to hold the torch, but nobody was volunteering to escort me, not even the dental officer I was dating at the time, for fear of being ribbed by the others. We had more comedy potential than the average episode of 'Dad's Army'!

My being a woman was evidently seen as a bit of a problem if an early morning conversation I heard coming from the other side of the door to my room in the Mess at RAF Freckleton was anything to go by. "What shall I do about the officer in this room?...Well, it's a woman!" "Just make a lot of noise when you take the tea, knock loud, and wait for an answer before you go in." At RAF Farnborough, they chickened out and booked me into a small B&B near the station's main gate where I shared bathroom facilities with their normal clients - all male travelling salesmen, because they could not take responsibility for me in the Officers Mess where there were no women's quarters!

At my posting to RAF Linton-on-Ouse in Yorkshire where the Fleet Air Arm did their flying training, I was similarly booked into a delightful B&B that served enormous breakfasts. The reason I was given was that it was '...because of all the Midshipmen in the Officers Mess'. I am not quite sure whether it was I or the Midshipmen who were considered the likely corrupting influence!

12. FIRST POSTING - MALTA
'Tmiem tajjeb isewwi kollox.'
'All is well that ends well.'
Maltese Proverb (possibly after Shakespeare)

My first posting was to RAF Luqa in Malta. At the end of our basic RAF training we were asked to write down our preferences for posting, presumably so they could make some attempt to match us with the posts available. I wrote 'Overseas - as far away as possible'. However, others were posted further away so perhaps I should have been more specific. Everyone told me that there must have been a mistake with my posting as there were no WRAF in Malta - but I

RAF MO

was RAF, and, as I would discover, that made quite a distinction, even if for practical purposes I wore WRAF-style uniform!

A blast of hot air greeted us as the door of the RAF Britannia aircraft was opened at RAF Luqa. It was May, and already the green vegetation and colourful spring flowers were giving way to the more usual dry and sandy brown colour that was normally the visitor's first impression on coming in to land on the island. It was a joint RAF and civilian airport and this defined some of my future duties. I was joining a team including a Wing Commander as Senior Medical Officer assisted by a British CMP (Civilian Medical Practitioner) employed by

70

MOD (Ministry of Defence) and I was to be the UMO (Unit Medical Officer).

The differences were mainly those of seniority and ultimate responsibility as we all did the same job. Our prime task was to look after the safety of the aircrew and aircraft and form part of the backup to the fire and rescue services if there were any aircraft incidents or accidents. We also acted as Port Medical Officers ready to give advice or supervise anything to do with medical hazards or communicable diseases.

Malta was a key staging post for RAF flights between the UK and the Far and Middle East. Casualty evacuation also played an important part and we had a small 'Casevac' ward in the Medical Centre where casualties or patients being medically evacuated back to the UK and staging through Malta could be looked after by dedicated 'Casevac' nurses who would also accompany them on the flights if required. We had up to two PMRAFNS nursing sisters who took it in turns to carry out these duties, but lent us a hand when they were not busy with their Casevac work. The station Medical Centre also housed a dental surgery with one dental officer and a hygienist.

There was another active airfield, RAF (formerly RNAS) Hal Far, for which we held medical responsibility, plus other non-flying units such as the signals unit at RAF Siggiewi and radar units at RAF Madliena on the east coast and RAF Dingli on the 720ft high western Dingli cliffs. The RAF Air HQ was a separate unit at Florianna outside the capital Valletta, but they had their own small medical unit staffed by an RAF doctor for whom we provided cover when needed. Most of the RAF personnel worked at RAF Luqa and were either accommodated there in Barracks or Messes if they were single or unaccompanied, while married personnel with families rented either RAF Married Quarters or Civilian Hirings all over the island. (There was also a Transit Mess for crews passing through.)

As serving officers we obviously had a role in the event of hostilities and the Medical Centre (in common with many UK flying stations, particularly those associated with the 'V Bombers') had a fully equipped decontamination unit in case of a nuclear incident. I found this decontamination centre that was usually lying idle particularly useful as it was a convenient place to take patients to examine their eyes in complete darkness or make use of the silence and lack of distraction for medical hypnosis. We also had our own dispensary, a small operating theatre and a ward where we could supervise patients if required, rather than sending them to the Royal Naval Hospital Bighi, situated near Grand Harbour opposite Valletta. There was an Army Maternity Unit at Mtarfa near the old capital Mdina known as the 'Silent City', whose services we always used because RAF doctors were not allowed to undertake home deliveries as we had to be always available in case of an aircraft accident, so ante-natal care was all we could provide for our maternity patients. Our Station Medical Centre, or 'Sick Quarters' as it was still called out of habit, was staffed by a fairly large team of Medical Branch Airmen including a few local members of RAF(Malta) under a Flight Sergeant. We also had our own ambulances and dedicated drivers. Most of our morning work, like any other doctor, involved holding surgeries for staff and families with a medical problem - 'Sick Parade' we used to call it. I think the name derived from any military person who could not attend a normal parade, the alternative being to pack a 'small kit' and form an orderly queue to be seen by the MO.

Later in the day there would be immunisation and other clinics, followed by 'home visits' although, as we had our own transport, we usually sent a driver to bring patients to see us. Our facilities in the centre were much better than trying to examine a patient on the far side of a low double bed in poor lighting with dogs or children joining in. It was a 'win-win' as it meant we could make a thorough examination and save ourselves time while also remaining available on the airfield. The rest of the time would be taken up with routine medical examinations of all RAF personnel. All aircrew had to have a full

Stewart in flying kit 'bone dome'and oxygen mask which had to be checked by the MO

medical examination at least annually, and the MO would also inspect their flying kit, especially their flying helmets ('bone domes' as they were called) and oxygen masks. Outside working hours one of us would be on call for the whole of the island.

I thought Malta was charming and I loved the historical connections. I was allocated a driver, SAC (Senior Aircraftsman) Bonici who also taught me to drive as I had had no previous opportunity to learn. He used the time spent in driving practice to introduce me to the island, including many parts not normally frequented by tourists. SAC Bonici was a longtime Maltese service member of RAF(Malta) and a part-time rogue, but a loveable one. There was not much about Malta in all its echelons, legal or otherwise, that he did not know of. He became a good and long standing friend.

Bonici had quite a few medals, and one day he needed to wear them with his best uniform as he was about to be presented with a special commendation. He could not find his medals so he asked his wife to help. "The Virgin Mary has them," she said, "So you cannot have them now." "What do you mean? What does the Virgin Mary want with my medals? Stop messing about, woman. Go and get them!" "No, I can't do that because you might get ill again," she replied. "What do you mean? How can having my medals make me ill? You're not making sense, woman!" "Well," she said, "You know when you were very ill with peritonitis and it was touch and go whether you would make it - I took your medals to the Virgin Mary at the church and put them with her statue in the glass case, asking her to make you well." "Well, go and borrow them back for a day," he said, "Surely she won't mind that." But apparently his wife thought she would, so Bonici had to confess what had happened to his boss, the MT Officer. Fortunately, his CO had exactly the same medals so he was able to lend them to his embarrassed driver.

Talking of transport, there was then an excellent system in operation with the Maltese buses (the only public transport remaining after the small railway 1883-1931 was closed). All bus routes radiated from a hub outside the entrance gate of the capital Valletta, but on such a small island it was no real hardship if you had to go to Valletta on one bus before catching another bus to your destination. Each vehicle was always well maintained and gleamed with pride of ownership in spite of its age and often almost vintage appearance. Although the external livery was coloured according to their route, the interiors around the front window were often personalised by their owner drivers making each journey a novel experience. The buses had different colours for each route and this made travelling a simple matter. You might need to take the green bus from your starting point but change to the mauve bus at Valletta to reach your destination, and if you arrived with little time to spare you could easily spot your bus as it was about to depart and jump onto it. How much easier that would be for sufferers of AMD!

Unfortunately, everything changed after Malta became a republic in 1974 as the Dom Mintoff Government decreed that from 1975 all buses should be the same colour (green), and routes distinguished by their destination sign. People said it was Dom Mintoff himself who brought about the change because he believed that having the coloured bus system could give the wrong impression that Malta's population was illiterate!

13. COURTSHIP and MARRIAGE

'Faith is putting one's foot down in the mist and finding it on a rock.'
Anon

There was no WRAF in Malta, and, apart from the occasional presence of a Casevac nurse, I was the only woman in the Officers Mess. I had left my dental officer 'date' from training with disappointingly, no greater commitment from him than a promise to write and visit as soon as possible. Time passed and apart from the occasional letter nothing seemed to be happening. Meanwhile, I was getting quite a lot of attention of the wrong kind.

My mother thought the breakdown of my parents' marriage would put me off marrying. It was not that I'd decided not to marry, but experience had certainly made me much more cautious in giving my trust. I knew I wanted my future husband to be a Christian so that we

74

could share important values, and he had to be kind. I was twenty-nine years old and couldn't help wishing to marry and have children before I became an 'elderly prim' ('medical speak' for a more mature woman expecting a first baby).

I remember praying about this one evening, my Bible soaked with tears, and within a short space of time two things happened. I met one of the eligible bachelors on the station who until then had been away on detachments with his squadron. Everybody kept telling me not to settle for my dental officer before meeting Stewart because I would be sure to like him more, but what did these men know? Stewart asked me out a few times, and to my surprise, I did feel very comfortable with him and also discovered that we shared many interests. However, soon afterwards, as if to stop this new relationship in its tracks, my dental officer 'date' finally arrived in Malta to see me.

Meal times in the Mess became farcical because Stewart seemed determined not to leave me on my own with my visitor, and so I ended up with Stewart sitting on one side and the dentist on the other! I felt it all seemed rather unfair to the poor fellow who had come such a long way to see me, and so I suggested that he and I visit the North end of the Island and stay there for a while. We went ahead with this plan, even though Stewart took me to one side to say he did not want me to do it. I felt rather irritated at this because I thought that he had no right to be telling me what to do, but this was the first real indication from him that he had feelings for me.

In Malta the furthest distance from anywhere can only be 19 miles, but because it was such a small island visiting the North always seemed like going to Scotland from London. I must have seemed pre-occupied, and so the dentist never told me he had actually come to Malta to ask me to marry him. I only learned that later. After an hour or so on the beach, the dentist suddenly said, "You want to be back with that Stewart chap, don't you?" and drove me back.

I did not expect to see Stewart alone in the Mess almost as if waiting for me, because he would normally have been out sailing. The relationship that then developed between us was my most wonderful and most miraculous answer to prayer, giving me so much more than I could ever have imagined, and making a far wiser choice than I would ever have made for myself.

Sadly, my poor dentist friend then found himself in a most miserable situation. Naturally, he wanted to take the first plane out of Malta and head back home, but unfortunately this proved impossible as for days on end no seat was available on either RAF or civilian aircraft as it was right at the peak of the holiday season.

Dependable Bonici came to the rescue and seemed to know exactly what the unhappy man needed. By day, he drove him in my car to places few Brits would know about, and then took him to spend his evenings in secluded bars where he could pour out his sorrows to his new-found friend over several beers, before finally delivering him safely back to his bed at a time when he would be unlikely to meet anyone.

Eventually, Bonici believed that the time had come for him personally to take action to put an end to this distressing situation. I had seen this before when he presented me for my driving test for the third time. Because the customary 'sweetener' had not been handed over to the test site officials with the paperwork, I found on my first test that the four oil drums within which the learner driver had to park the car were placed impossibly close, while the next time I had not even turned the key in the ignition to drive over to this parking test when I was told I had failed! Bonici asked me if I would leave it to him, and I soon found myself in the office of the chief of police who asked if I would mind going for a test drive with two of his officers. I did not mind, so I had a proper driving test which I then passed.

Now Bonici was once again asking if I minded leaving it to him. All he would tell me was that someone owed him a favour, but I trusted him completely so I asked no more. The result for my unhappy friend was that he was flown safely away from the island on a civilian flight that left the very next day.

76

This left Stewart and me free to consider our future, and, although he fortunately did not feel that he needed to ask my father's permission before we announced our engagement, there was one permission that as serving officers we both had to obtain. We sat down together and wrote our formal official letters to the Station Commander, 'Sir, I have the honour to request permission to marry (Name, Rank and Number). I have the honour to be, Sir, your obedient servant...'

We decided to deliver these letters in person to the Station Commander at his residence after our evening meal. He invited us in and was clearly mystified to see us there together. When he read the contents of our letters he expressed even more shock: "I always pride myself on knowing exactly what is happening in my station, but I had no idea that you were even seeing each other!" He gave us a congratulatory drink and then took us up to the old flight control tower because the Red Arrows RAF aerobatic team was due to arrive at the station. They arrived with all their lights on during a stunning crimson sunset, swooping low over the end of the runway at about

100 feet in a diamond nine formation, trailing red, white and blue smoke while, at the same time, two Lightning fighter jets started a formation take-off in the opposite direction with their twin afterburners streaming lilac behind them. We had just witnessed one of the most spectacular aviation sights and it permanently etched itself in our memories as an unforgettable part of our engagement.

Flight Lieutenant engaged to Flight Lieutenant! 4th September 1966 RAF Luqa, Malta

This was announced in the Daily Telegraph in September, and to our surprise, we also featured on Malta Television and in the RAF News. Thinking of this later, I felt like threatening to write a follow up story to this happy event when I was finding it difficult to get posted home to join my husband after our marriage! Although it was somewhat of a whirlwind romance there was no point in waiting any longer because we would not be able to spend any more time together as Stewart already knew he had been selected to join a course at the Central Flying School at RAF Little Rissington in the UK to become a flying instructor.

Stewart finished his tour in Malta and returned home in November, and I followed in December just four days before our wedding day. My mother had moved into my little tenement house in Dundee on my posting to Malta to look after it and another two letting properties I had also acquired nearby. She did an amazing job of arranging our wedding with me out of the country. The only problem she mentioned to me was my choice of music to walk in to. The Director of Music said that its real name was 'Behold, the conquering hero comes!'

Before Stewart left Malta, his parents had called to meet my mother in Dundee when his father was on a business trip in the area, but unfortunately the two mothers did not 'hit it off'. My mother felt that Stewart's mother was rather disapproving, and so she was keen to establish that Stewart was lucky to be marrying me! However, it turned out that what Stewart's mother really took exception to was that I came from a broken home because, as she put it once later, it might be a tendency that I would repeat. I eventually met Stewart's parents myself when I stayed with them on my way back from Malta to Dundee before the wedding. I soon realised that I was not exactly what Stewart's mother had hoped for in her first daughter-in-law. She left us in no doubt that furthermore we were most inconsiderate in holding our wedding in Scotland at that time of year because it meant that none of her friends or family would be able to attend - Scotland being almost in the Arctic in her mind!

Despite that, my future in-laws did come to Scotland for the wedding, and I met them again the day before at the Scores Hotel in St Andrews where they stayed along with Stewart, his married sister, and his brother who was his best man, and his very welcoming Aunty Peggy who was his godmother. This was also where we held our wedding reception, and I enjoyed being able to return some of the hospitality and affection shown to me by my St Andrews friends.

78

Unfortunately, my sister Rita declined our invitation. Although my relationship with her had become closer, my 'proper wedding' reminded her that I was still the younger sister who had everything she did not. It took until the late 1980s when both she and her then husband and Stewart and I lived in Sussex for us to become real friends, but she recently surprised me by saying, "Love you," as we parted after one of our fleeting visits back to Sussex from Plymouth.

Stewart and I were married in St Andrews University Chapel. Russ gave me away, and the little Paterson daughter was my bridesmaid. Stewart became my human rock and constant dependable support.

Medical women, like lawyers and dentists, were in the RAF not the WRAF, so that, as stipulated by their professional bodies, they could have equal pay with the men. However, this was only the basic pay and did not apply to various allowances, the largest of which was marriage allowance, which rather unfairly, men were paid, but for which women were not eligible.

In my time in the RAF female medical officers were quite rare. I remember going to see one very senior woman MO to discuss the duties of being a Medical Officer to the WRAF team at the Nijmegen marches in Holland when I ended up being allocated this duty one year. She was at the RAF Hospital Cosford, and my husband flew

Nijmegen Marches (4 days) - 5am surgery and part of WRAF team

79

me to meet her in a Jet Provost training aircraft after he had qualified as a flying instructor and I was the Unit Medical Officer at RAF Linton-on-Ouse, a flying training station near York.

One of the delights for me was being able to do all sorts of flying such as aerobatics, formation flying, low altitude flying and night flying with Stewart as I was supposed to get as much air experience as possible in my role as MO, although, as my Station Commander pointed out, the idea was actually to experience flying with as many different pilots as possible. In addition to the usual station doctor's duties, my role on that flying training station was to teach aviation physiology, First Aid and personal equipment flight safety hazards to the student pilots.

Showing Medical Centre where I was SMO to the inspecting Commandant of the WRAF in 1972

Another meeting with a senior woman MO occurred in Bahrain, but this was less happy. We had been married for only just over three years when Stewart was sent on an unaccompanied posting to RAF Salalah on the southern coast of Oman. We both managed to get time off at Christmas to meet up in Bahrain, but I found that I was expected to be 'appropriately accommodated' in the WRAF Officers Quarters and Stewart in the main Officers Mess! We were met on arrival at the WRAF Officer Quarters by a forbidding medical woman who was totally unsympathetic to our situation. She announced sternly to Stewart that he need not think his presence was going to be tolerated there. In Stewart's mind she thought wrong, but we were saved from 'the dragon's fire' by a married couple who had previously been stationed with us at Linton-on-Ouse who invited us both to stay in their married quarters.

My only other encounter with a woman MO was when I took over from a female SMO at an RAF station where, as a woman, she and her

80

navigator husband were accommodated in a Nissen hut because she was not entitled to occupy the SMO's ex-officio quarter in her own right. One of my first duties on that station was to condemn that Nissen hut accommodation, but fortunately Stewart managed to get special permission to occupy the SMO's quarter on my behalf. However, I am not sure that even this would satisfy the various equal rights legislations of today.

Being in the RAF rather than the WRAF meant that I could be, and mostly was, the only service woman on the station so that as the only woman officer at RAF Linton-on-Ouse when HRH Princess Margaret was the Reviewing Officer at one of the numerous passing out parades, I was designated to accompany her before and after lunch in the Officers Mess. This included taking her to the special 'cloakroom' prepared for visiting royalty, and thereafter I became known as Flight Loo-tenant!

Flight Lieutenant in those days was recognised as a male rank only. The equivalent WRAF rank was Flight Officer. This caused confusion at RAF Lyneham where I had to stay the night on the way to my first posting in Malta. I went to book in and the receptionist looked at me in horror. "Oh, I did not know he was married!" she said. "I have booked him to share with an Army Major!" I had to explain that I was not his wife but was actually the Flight Lieutenant. I sometimes regretted that I did not see what the Major was like before I was hastily booked into a single room!

Similar confusion occurred when Stewart and I got engaged (September 1966) because our engagement announcement appeared to indicate that two males, both Flight Lieutenants, were getting engaged. Today that would not raise too many eyebrows, but in those days it would have been enough to be dismissed from the service even if civilian law had allowed it.

As an RAF Officer it meant that when I met and married my RAF pilot at the end of his tour in Malta, I had to return to Malta without him to serve out my tour that had only just commenced. Unlike WRAF officers, we could not leave the service on marriage should we wish to, and to add insult to injury, as a woman I would not be eligible for the 'Married Unaccompanied Allowance' paid in recognition of having to keep two separate homes going, which my male counterparts would be paid if they went on an overseas posting without their wives. I was in exactly the same situation but in reverse. I had to put in a special request to be posted back to the UK to be with my husband, a posting which took several months to arrange.

However, I am not complaining because apart from the difficulty in managing to be posted together while I was committed to serve my five contracted years, I very much enjoyed my time in the RAF. In fact, I stayed on a further three years in annual bites as long as I could see that the postings would work out, taking me up to eight years which was the maximum that I could do on a short service commission. I liked the variety of my work in the RAF. Although as medical officers we were subject to military discipline and the 'chain of command', as clinicians nobody could interfere with our professional judgement simply on grounds of rank, and our duties as a doctor always took precedence over other possible service roles.

In addition to my other medical training, I also had civilian training in hypnotherapy for medicine and dentistry, and had some fascinating experiences using hypnotherapy as a medical tool. It was particularly good for improving confidence and concentration and not only for dental anxiety but also dental anaesthesia.

Once I was asked to help a student pilot who had difficulty passing a certain phase in his training. Students were required to fly with their instructor just before a test flight so that the test for a particular level was always the second flight. This student always appeared to be tired and performed uncharacteristically poorly on the second assessment flight. With his instructor's help to explain what he should be doing better and how he could improve, I managed to use positive suggestion to build up his confidence and combat the fatigue that overcame him on the second flight, giving him poor results. He then managed to come off his 'review' status, normally the stage preceding the dreaded 'Chop' which signalled removal from flying training.

Unfortunately, my success did create comment from senior ranks who clearly knew nothing of medical hypnosis, and thought I might have students flying around the sky under the influence of the sort of stage-show hypnosis prevalent on popular TV shows at the time where people ended up doing comical things.

When I left the RAF we bought a lovely old cottage in Rutland, then the smallest UK county, although soon to be swallowed up by Leicestershire. I worked in Family Planning clinics in Peterborough, Leicestershire and Rutland, and did some consultant venereology clinics (as they were then called) in Peterborough and Kings Lynn as a locum. This was a time when GPs were holding out for extra payment for doing family planning, and therefore it was decreed that hospital clinics should be prepared to give this advice. It seemed strange to be fitting family planning devices in my VD sessions, and doing quite a lot of venereology in my family planning clinics where they were glad to make use of my experience in this field.

Squadron Leader (W) about to be dined out of the service in January 1974 At RAF North Luffenham in Rutland

I am wearing the type of formal mess dress in vogue at the time.
It is the female equivalent of the male officers' Mess Kit worn by my husband. 'Not bad' you might think but consider this was worn when non-serving ladies would be wearing their most formal long evening gowns. I was even ordered by one station commander to never wear it again on his station.
It has since been replaced

Even before I finally left the RAF, Stewart had applied to rejoin his old squadron back in Malta, but had been assured by MOD that this definitely would not happen, so we went ahead and bought our 'Floral

Cottage'. We should have known that the opposite would come to pass because Stewart was duly posted back to Malta for his last tour of duty, meaning the cottage had to be sold which I arranged before joining him. My mother and aunt came periodically from Bristol to stay there until it was sold, and my mother inherited our cat.

It was sixteen years since I had last seen or had any means of communication with my father. I had no idea where he was, although he had written to my mother-in-law after our wedding complaining that he had not been invited, and that he had seen in a newspaper report that Russell had given me away. We had some free time before leaving for Malta, and I wanted Stewart to meet him, and so with Sherlock Holmes tenacity we followed a vague trail all over the southern counties, eventually ending up in Chelmsford, Essex where he was living with a pleasant Jamaican woman called Jayne.

We had a few meetings with them, both at their home and ours, before we left for Malta. My regret was that neither Stewart nor I felt we had connected with the real man. We had great difficulty in getting behind his veneer of boasting and romanticising, and it was often difficult to distinguish between the two. We were not to know it then, but this was the last possible chance for Stewart to meet my father.

For me, it was something of a relief that there had been a reconciliation of sorts with Dad, particularly knowing Stewart's mother's attitude to broken homes. I was glad that Stewart had the chance to make up his own mind about my father, although obviously he could never have approved of his actions and lifestyle. However, Stewart showed Dad respect and made him welcome in our home.

It was good to have nothing about me that Stewart did not know, not that I ever really believed it would make any difference to how he felt about me. Stewart was so different from my father, being totally transparent and virtually incapable of telling a lie. He had already become a unifying force in our family with his dependable and loving attitude embracing every family member. My mother adored him and could not have wished for a more considerate and loving son-in-law who made her a monthly allowance and was always solicitous of her welfare.

My brother respected him greatly and Rita always enjoyed his company, even trusting him enough to come cross-Channel sailing in our boat with Stewart at the helm. She was a nervous flyer, but was later happy to go on a commercial flight when she knew that Stewart would be the Captain. Perhaps her confidence was partly inspired by James Bond because Rita always remarked on how much Stewart (in those days) resembled Sean Connery!

14. MALTA REVISITED

'In Malta, the Wars of Religion reached their climax. If both sides believed that they saw Paradise in the bright sky above them, they had a close and very intimate knowledge of Hell.'
The Great Siege, Ernle Bradford

Malta the second time was fun! For the first time in my marriage I had no professional duties, in spite of an impressive document with a big red seal (much more impressive than my degree) from the outgoing British Governor General before Malta became a republic in 1974 which granted me permission to practice medicine there. This now hangs with my other professional certificates over the cat litter trays, whereas our Queen's Commissions enjoy a suitably elevated status hanging in our loo - a place favoured for this purpose by many of our RAF friends.

However, the Dom Mintoff regime was not giving work permits to foreign civilians unless they had skills unavailable in Malta, and even then the policy was to train a Maltese national to take over from them. My Family Planning qualification might have counted because this Roman Catholic country had not previously promoted this, but to train another doctor in Family Planning would not take long. So I was condemned to three years of Mediterranean sea, sun and social life! The latter included several important functions prior to the withdrawal of all British Forces from the island in 1979, including an impressive ceremony of 'Beating the Retreat' by the Royal Marines in front of the

Royal Yacht 'Britannia' at the historic Fort St Angelo, then the RN Headquarters.

During our stay in Malta we also joined congregations in various churches at different times. These included the station church at RAF Luqa and the Anglican chapel at the St Andrew's Royal Marine barracks near where we lived. We were also in the choir of the Anglican Cathedral in Valletta for a time. However, quite a stir was being caused at the small Royal Naval Anglican church at Mtarfa which had now become the main British Forces hospital for the island and was no longer in the control of the Army but was a Royal Navy establishment. The RN chaplain there had become strongly influenced by the charismatic movement then sweeping through many churches of different denominations.

This influence brought an increase in love and care for each other among the members of the little church's congregation which grew steadily as people became aware of the great happiness and joy of attending services, both on Sundays and outside the usual times of worship. They also believed in healing and miracles for which they prayed at regular times, inviting any with problems for special ministry and prayer. The members were friendly and welcoming to all who were curious enough to visit so it was not surprising that the church became popular with many retired 'ex-pats' on the island as they found an extended family there that made up for missing their own.

We met quite a few interesting people in that little Naval church including the wives of two prominent authors who lived on the island which led to our also meeting their husbands who were a bit more resistant to the charms of RN Mtarfa's place of worship. One of these was Australian author Hugh Atkinson who would visit us for the evening, bringing a bottle of milk which he used to add to our whisky as a token gesture to the medical advice to drink milk rather than alcohol because of his incipient stomach ulcer. We often thought that a bottle of whisky would have been more use to replace the one that would inevitably disappear during the course of his visit.

The other author was Ernle Bradford who was a prolific historical writer, mostly about events in that part of the world as in his books 'The Great Siege: Malta 1565', and 'Ulysses Found'. Both men were fascinating to talk to in their different ways. One woman I met at the Mtarfa church was Moira, the wife of President Dom Mintoff. It was public knowledge that their marriage was not one 'made in heaven' but when people appealed to Moira to use her influence with her husband to help with a problem, she would herself often help in whatever way she could, usually by very practical personal efforts that even extended to doing menial voluntary tasks like washing up for a Roman Catholic charitable organisation.

Once when listening to the local radio I happened to hear an advertisement for a future interview with the newly incoming Minister to the Church of Scotland on the Island, and I could not believe it when following the word 'Reverend' I heard the name of one of my fellow St Andrews students who I sometimes met at John and Evangeline's home! I had to phone to make sure that it was the same man, and this was followed shortly afterwards by a visit from him in full leather motorbike gear and helmet. Stewart was flying at the time and therefore not in when Colin entered our home and greeted me with a big hug.

I happened to see the shocked expression of my Maltese 'maid' out of the corner of my eye. Whether it was true or not, her reaction reminded me of the tale we had often heard, that if a Maltese couple had not produced a child after being married for a year or so, the priest would call and his presence would be advertised by an open umbrella being placed in the window. It was hoped that his visit would remedy the situation!

Once more in Malta I was in a sunny climate, often with reflections from the sea, but still I rarely wore sunglasses. We had our own boat 'Meriel Seaforth' (a 29ft Maurice Griffiths bermudan rig cutter), and at the end of our tour we started to sail it back to the UK. It was an eventful trip and our experiences included riding out storms off the coast of Sicily. Just south of Naples we decided to return to Malta rather than pressing on which turned out to be a very good decision, as later we heard about terrible storms we would otherwise have run into in which several small boats were dismasted.

Even so, on our return through the straits of Messina we were faced with huge whirlpools ahead. Ulysses encountering Scylla and Charybdis in the Odyssey came to mind, but Stewart managed to carefully manoeuvre the boat through them. I knew nothing of the technicalities, but there was some tricky sailing in that area. However, Stewart had qualified as a Yacht Master Offshore Skipper so I was content just to follow his orders.

After escaping Charybdis the whirlpool, and passing Scylla on the Italian mainland side, the following wind grew much stronger and Stewart saw that the instruments were registering a speed greater than our little boat could normally achieve. With both headsails boomed out, we had too much sail up, but Stewart could not leave the helm which was on a knife edge – if he let go, even for a few seconds, he could easily lose control. There was only one option left. Calmly, he told me to move forward and take down the boat's mainsail. There was no hint in his voice that this might be impossible with the strong wind filling the sail, so I just did it! Almost immediately, the boat became much easier to handle, and Scylla's sea monster, if she was still exerting any influence, didn't get us!

During this tour in Malta we made two rather sad trips home to the UK because both our fathers died. Stewart's father was receiving radiotherapy for an unusual cancer in his neck, and Stewart managed to get to see him when he flew to the UK in a Canberra aircraft. He had actually set out the day before, but had to return to Malta just after take-off because of an instrument failure, and so he flew out the next day instead.

While he was home his father had a stroke and Stewart was given permission to stay at home, and I was also flown back to help with the nursing. Had Stewart's original flight gone ahead without delay, he would not have been at home at the time of his father's stroke and subsequent death. Stewart's mother had vowed to keep her husband at home, but one thing she feared was being in the house alone if he died there. He died during the night after my arrival and I was able to save disturbing the doctor to confirm this. Stewart's brother and sister arrived that morning so all three children were with her at this traumatic time, and the least likely to be able to get there was actually the first arrival. How is this for divine providence?

A similar thing happened to me when a message came via the Ministry of Defence that my father had been admitted to Millbank Military Hospital in London and requested my presence. The RAF got me on the first flight out of Malta that day on a civilian flight with British Airways. The RAF also sent cars both to pick me up at my home and meet me at Heathrow Airport. I was driven straight to the hospital where I found Dad's Jamaican 'wife', Jayne, with him. He had been admitted with severe abdominal pain, and they were waiting for the results of investigations before giving strong pain relief. The diagnosis was terminal primary liver cancer.

Russ also came to the hospital and Dad was pleased to see him. He was amazed to hear that Russell was still in the REME workshop job that he had found for him twenty years earlier. He asked after the 'Little Girl' (Rita) but probably thought I was pacifying him when I told him she was just outside. She was indeed, but had been having such an emotional time in her own life that she could not handle going to his bedside. Dad suffered an agonising time before getting any pain relief, and death came soon after.

I shared a room at the hospital with Jayne and it became obvious from talking to her that there had been a marriage ceremony carried out by her father who was a Methodist Minister. My father had obviously decided to ignore the High Court ruling on the case he had instigated when I was a student and I had the unpleasant task of telling Jayne that there had been no divorce from my mother. Although she would not now be able to claim a widow's pension, I ensured that she was able to have my father's car transferred to her ownership and continue living in their house.

At the funeral Russell said that he nearly fell into the grave himself when the coffin was lowered as he noticed that Dad's date of birth on the coffin made him only two years Russell's senior! With his ever present financial problems, my father had not wanted to retire, and in order to get a job as a lecturer at his old technical college he had altered his birth certificate with a few simple strokes of his pen to read 1920 instead of 1910!

15. TEST TUBE BABIES

'Finding a stone wall blocking your path - cut steps in it that others may climb over.'
Anon

While Stewart and I were at RAF Linton-on-Ouse, I returned to my old teaching hospital in Dundee to have an operation to improve my fertility. A Naval Sea Prince communications aircraft flew me to nearby RAF Leuchars, but when I was due to return Stewart surprised me by coming to collect me in a Jet Provost training aircraft as the Sea Prince was unserviceable. He brought all my flying gear, but forgot to bring my flying boots. I raised quite a few eyebrows when some visiting Danish fighter pilots caught sight of me climbing into an ejector seat in my stiletto heels and nylons at RAF Leuchars. What was the RAF coming to? I was even more embarrassed when I arrived back at base and had to climb out of the aircraft in front of students I'd been teaching about the medical aspects of flying, including the hazards of sharp objects in the cockpit and the fire risks of nylon, particularly next to the skin!

Unfortunately the Dundee fertility operation did not work, but in 1968 a newspaper headline caught my eye. A physiologist, Dr Robert Edwards, had achieved fertilisation of a human egg in the laboratory, and in collaboration with Mr Patrick Steptoe, a gynaecologist from Oldham, hoped to be able to develop a technique that would eventually allow women with my problem to become pregnant. I wrote at once to this pioneering partnership and they agreed to accept me for their experimental treatment. They were encouraged that I was medically trained, and hoped I might be the first to conceive because they thought they could rely on me to understand that they might have to terminate the experiment if there were unforeseen problems.

They encountered a great deal of opposition to what they were doing even from medical sources, and had to do their best to hide what was taking place from the ever present press reporters, hungry for news. Accordingly, the consultants were extremely careful not to draw attention to their joint visits to Dr Kershaw's Hospital, Oldham where we were being treated in conditions of great secrecy. Staff members kept a constant lookout for unwanted visitors, and even suspected an Anglican priest who came to visit me after I attended his church one Sunday prior to my admission.

Nothing about the treatment was easy. The timing not only had to agree with Steptoe's and Edward's other commitments, but also my fertility cycle and getting the necessary leave of absence from the RAF for both Stewart and myself, not to mention the availability of the hospital services required. For me, it involved taking tablets at a certain time, and collecting all the urine I passed over a set period for hormone analysis. Imagine carrying these not very discreet containers everywhere!

On one occasion we were away on the Yorkshire coast and an injection had to be given at precisely 3am. I had the choice of taking the treatment to the local casualty department to be injected, or talking Stewart through the procedure. He had never done this before, and unfortunately, as he injected it into my buttock I had forgotten to explain what I meant by 'draw back', meaning to pull back the plunger to ensure that the needle was not in a blood vessel. He pulled the needle right out so I had to have the painful bit (for both of us) repeated!

When my urine hormonal levels and all other indicators were favourable, we had to go to the hospital at the appointed time where I would be anaesthetised prior to harvesting the egg cells using a laparoscope. In the meantime, Stewart had to provide his fresh sample, and this could not arrive late. A very basic patient lavatory was not very conducive to this!

When Stewart was posted to Oman in 1970 the practical difficulties of participation were insurmountable, so we had to call a temporary halt to our involvement with the project until he returned the next year. When we ended up back in Malta we did return to the UK for one more attempt, but we were not destined for success.

Bob Edwards, the scientist, had a much better bedside manner than the gynaecologist, Mr Steptoe, and he would frequently return after they had both seen us at the bedside to make sure that we had understood everything. He was a lovely man and his pioneering work helped many millions of couples. I was very pleased that he eventually gained recognition with a well deserved Nobel Prize and a knighthood.

We sent a congratulatory telegram in 1978 to Robert Edwards and Patrick Steptoe on the successful birth of Louise Brown, the first IVF baby, and I added the question, "Any hope for these geriatrics?" I was then forty-one. Robert Edwards phoned back and said they would be prepared to try. Apparently, there were even some advantages for an older mother in being able to select specific eggs to use, but I had perhaps too much knowledge of the potential problems of an elderly pregnancy. I also thought that it would be unfair if a child had a mother who could easily be mistaken for her grandmother, and as I had recently returned to general practice and people were counting on me, I eventually made the hard decision not to try again.

When I was first embarking on my own experimental IVF treatment, I was approached by a distressed patient who had gone through the trauma of unfairly losing custody of her two children in a hurtful divorce. Since then she had remarried and she and her second husband desperately wanted children, but sadly he turned out to have a low sperm count. At their insistence, I decided to investigate the possibilities of AID (Artificial Insemination by Donor), but I couldn't find anything affordable of practical benefit to them. The couple wanted a child so badly that, after I had read up a lot about it, including all the guidelines and legalities from professional bodies, they eventually managed to convince me that I should attempt this procedure for them. A potential supply of young, healthy, anonymous donors from all three services existed on the base. I got two volunteers who had completed their families and were requesting a vasectomy which was just becoming prevalent at the time. It was a great advantage having the medical records of all concerned. I devised a system of keeping the donor sample at the correct temperature and delivered it to the husband who inseminated his wife with it after they had made love. This way his own sperm might also be potentiated.

Happily, a pregnancy was achieved just before they went on an overseas tour, and a healthy little girl was born while they were abroad. They gave her one of my names, and asked me to become a godmother, so I have been able to keep in touch with the family. Their daughter has been a great delight and blessing to them, and she now has her own lovely children.

16. QUESTS and BEQUESTS
'Organ donation is not a tragedy but it can be a beautiful light in the midst of one.'
Organ Donation Poster

On returning from Malta the second time, Stewart came out of the RAF and started putting himself through the process of getting his civilian Airline Transport Pilot Licence at considerable expense. Fortunately, he took a record minimum of flying hours to do this which meant that our funds were not too drastically depleted even though I had not worked for three years and still had no job. When Stewart secured a job flying out of Gatwick with Dan Air we moved from our RAF married quarters in the Hillingdon area to East Grinstead near the airport.

In the RAF we had not been considered suitable as adoptive parents because of the difficulty of following service families with their frequent postings, but once we were in Hillingdon we made contact with a London adoption agency that had taken the unusual step of featuring children who were proving difficult to place on television. There was a family of four children which they didn't want to split up and the agency was delighted that we had come forward, especially since the Social Services responsible for the children's care was also in Hillingdon.

It seemed that it might be meant to happen. We bought a large Victorian house in East Grinstead with five bedrooms and even a complete train set in situ in one of the rooms. At this stage we were not allowed to meet the children, but we had lots of questions for the young social worker who came to interview us. However, she worried that we did not have enough experience with children and might expect too much of them. She told us that the children would be better off in a family with children already. We asked if they got many families who would be able to take another four youngsters, but although she thought not, we couldn't get her to change her mind. In her view it was better for the children to remain in care! Our efforts to have a family one way or another were proving very upsetting emotionally.

I started looking at the jobs section of the BMJ (British Medical Journal) and saw an advertisement for a post at the National Eye Bank of the Corneo-Plastic Unit of the Queen Victoria Hospital (QVH) at East Grinstead. This famous and prestigious unit grew up around the need for pioneering facial reconstructive and plastic surgery for predominantly wartime servicemen, including Battle of Britain aircrew who had sustained terrible burns and facial trauma (the famous 'Guinea Pig Club'), and to this day QVH remains one of the best respected regional centres for specialist plastic and reconstructive surgery and rehabilitation in the UK. Mr Saj Khan, who who would later operate on my eyes at the London Eye Hospital, had also previously worked at this unit, and this was one of the factors that gave me confidence to go ahead with my own operations.

I applied and was accepted for the post which consisted of a nominal seven sessions, rising later to eight sessions. However, these were not worked at specific times but spread over the whole week at any time of day or night when I would get called out to attend to a dead eye donor. On one occasion I was amused when I was in the Corneo-Plastic Unit office to hear one of the young secretaries answering the phone saying, "Queen Victoria speaking. Can I help you?"

You could say that the Eye Bank was a 'dead end job' because it involved removing eyes from donors after their death. The corneas were used for corneal grafting into patients' eyes with damaged or diseased corneas. Occasionally, other parts of the eye were used like the sclera or conjunctiva, although the stage of being able to transplant whole eyes as in the case of limbs and other organs has still not been reached.

It was my job to ensure that a good supply of fresh corneas was available for the transplant operations booked to take place. This involved liaising with people in different positions in various hospitals situated across a wide area of Southeast England. Sometimes my contact would be a hospital porter, sometimes a mortuary attendant and sometimes a secretary. My predecessor handed me a list of contacts, usually just single names. In those days single names alone were rarely used so it felt a bit 'cloak and dagger' speaking to 'Fred' or 'Jack' and asking them if there had been any suitable deaths. They knew what I wanted - the younger the better - and preferably someone who had died only in the previous few hours. I also needed to know the cause of death.

If they seemed suitable, I would then take the telephone number and details of the next of kin to see if I could obtain consent to use the eyes of their loved ones. This required a lot of tact and diplomacy, but it was surprising how often people found it a comfort, especially in the case of a young death, that something positive could come from it. I took pride in making a cosmetically good job of the procedure and leaving no trace of the surgery so they looked peaceful with their eyes closed when the relatives came to view them.

I used to say that I could have compiled an Egon Ronay guide to mortuaries as I got to know many different ones! It was amazing how they varied. During bad flu epidemics I sometimes even had to kneel on the floor beside rows of corpses laid out in primitive accommodation to surgically remove the eyes.

Once I was called out to a deceased donor in a large mortuary I knew well. It was always important for me to know the cause of death, and my call-out message informed me that this middle-aged woman had a history of bouts of depression and a previously recorded attempt at suicide. Now she had apparently succeeded with an overdose.

As was my custom, I first did an external inspection of the body to try and ascertain whether there was any infectious disease or something that would make the donor eyes unsuitable for use, and I noticed a strange linear red mark in the skin of her neck. Just then the Coroner's Officer happened to walk by, so I enquired if the woman had attempted to hang herself before taking the overdose. This resulted in further enquiries by the police leading to her husband's confession that he had strangled her because she would not stop nagging!

Strangely, I had been given the correct time of death in a message from her husband when he made contact about her eyes, whereas her GP had calculated a different time of death when giving notification to the Coroner of a sudden death. The husband, of course, was able to be precise! By the time the Home Office pathologist arrived to do the suspicious death post-mortem a good set of fingertip bruises had shown up on her neck. The red line I had noticed had been caused by a necklace she had worn. Bruises take time to appear post-mortem, but eventually the crime should have come to light, although if a routine post-mortem had been done right away it could have been overlooked, so, if you are planning to murder your wife, make sure she hasn't donated her eyes first!

After starting the Eye Bank job I also went to a local hospital post-graduate Medical Centre to update myself with medical advances and meet colleagues. As a result I was approached by a Dr Edgar Blair who was a GP in a dispensing and training general practice but also did some hospital sessions in anaesthetics. He was a keen Freemason and wanted to be able to give more time to it, so he invited me to join his practice as a part time GP assistant. I agreed as it fitted in well with my Eye Bank job, and got me back into dealing with live patients again at a stage, unlike my cornea donors, when I could at least attempt to do something for them!

I got on well with Edgar, and usually carried out my sessions for him when he was at the hospital doing anaesthetics.   One day he had already started a session in the practice when I took over to allow him to go to the hospital. I received a phone call from a mother who said that the doctor had just seen her son and diagnosed Rubella (German Measles). She asked whether she could take him with her to the old people's home where she worked. My reply was that Rubella was usually mild but a real   problem for pregnant women. I told her that it would be a good idea to let him play with as many little girls as possible so they would catch the infection before they became pregnant as there were no immunisations for Rubella then. She replied, "But my son is 16!"

Edgar's plan was to partially retire so he could concentrate more on his Freemasonry. He was already in partnership with a neighbouring doctor to mutually provide off-duty cover, but Edgar hoped that I would at first share and then gradually take over his side of the practice. Sadly, my assistantship was short because poor Edgar died suddenly of a heart attack while attending a meeting at a new Lodge.

After his death I went into partnership with the remaining partner who had his surgery in a nearby village, and Stewart and I bought the large Victorian house that also contained the surgery from Edgar's widow. I was surprised to find that I now had my own practice and because my RAF service counted towards my seniority I was recognised by the Family Practitioner Committee as a general practice principal right away. It was a situation I would never have predicted as I had not been thinking that far ahead. Now it was a reality I could hardly believe it and found it more than a little daunting. I knew I would not be able to do it alone. I would have to rely on my Heavenly Father to help and guide me.

**The large Victorian House with the surgery which was
entered by the far side of the left picture**

The new surgery was eventually built on the other side of the house

17. PARTING WORDS

*'Peace I leave with you; my peace I give to you; I do not give it to
you as the world does. Do not let your hearts be distressed or
lacking in courage.'*
John 14.v 27

Just before we moved house, my mother was staying with us in East
Grinstead and we were trying to keep her with us as long as possible,
because we were worried that she was not looking after herself
properly in Bristol, but eventually she insisted on returning to her
house as she said she had things she must attend to. A few days
after her return, she phoned somewhat unexpectedly, and the strange
topic of conversation was that her cat, which had accompanied her on

98

her visit, was pining for one of my two cats. I wondered if she wanted me to take my cat to live with her but I did not think that would be ideal for her, never mind what her cat wanted!

I puzzled about this afterwards, wondering if the cat conversation was actually about her own needs rather than the cat's, although she had denied that there was any other problem. I made a mental note that we should visit her as soon as we could. When after only another two days I again received a phone-call, I had no doubt in my mind that something was wrong. She had even taken the unusual step of calling her doctor to visit because she had felt dizzy when trying to walk the short distance to her bank and had to turn back. The doctor left her a prescription for the dizziness on the living room table but she could hardly walk across the room to pick it up, let alone take it to a chemist.

The timing of her call was fortunate, not only because I happened to be at home, but it was my weekend off and Stewart was also expected home from a flight with no further flights rostered until the Monday, so we were able to rush off to Bristol and fetch her. After packing her, the cat and her bags into the car, she asked us to make a slight detour on the way home to take her to see the house and surgery we were about to buy. However, during the journey she was clearly getting even more ill. We had to stop several times because she was nauseous and eventually she seemed to lapse into a semi-conscious state so we quickly drove straight home. Surprisingly, she perked up as we reached our front door. Looking around her, she saw we were already back in East Grinstead and said disappointedly, "But I thought you were going to show me your new house and surgery!"

We summoned a local doctor who said he thought Mum looked terminally ill, and the consultant he called in confirmed that she had a chest infection and a failing heart. He prescribed some tablets before taking us to one side where she couldn't hear him and telling us that nothing more could be done for her, and that the outcome was uncertain.

Russell and Rita came as soon as they could and were able to see her, although Rita could only pay a brief visit before returning home. However, Russ continued to stay with us, although both he and Stewart had to go to work on the Monday. I spent the day by Mum's bedside on my own, and we had a quiet but pleasant time together.

I think she had suspected even before we left Bristol that she might be dying, and when we were on our own together she said, "I would like to stay with you, but I have a feeling I won't be able to - but, if that is the case, I feel ready." I replied that I did not know if she was dying or not, but she said, "Don't be upset…no matter how clever, no doctor can tell you just when you will die. I have always done my best for you children, and, if I am permitted, I will continue to do what I can for you. I hope that you will all stick together." Then she added rather puzzlingly that there would not be as much as she would have liked for us after she had gone, but there should be enough money for us all to have a small sum, including Stewart.

By this point her breathing was becoming raspy, and she herself noticed the noise and asked if there were people outside shovelling gravel! A bit later she mistakenly thought Russell was in the room, and wanted to try and comfort him as she knew how badly he would take her death so she addressed him, saying, "Now don't be all down in the mouth when I've gone, Russ. Promise me." She appeared to settle down to sleep through the night and we all managed to get a little rest. I returned to her room just before eight in the morning in time to see her take her last breath, while at precisely that moment her cat locked into the little room next to her bedroom let out a strange loud yowl that I had never heard him make before. Russell heard it too and immediately knew Mum had died.

If anybody can be said to have had a good death, it was Mum, in contrast to quite a lot of her life which had often been difficult although she had been much more content in her later years, even before my father's death. Russell, who remained until after her funeral, was impressed by the peacefulness of her dying, and remarked that he wished that he knew how she had managed it because he would like to know how to achieve something similar when his turn came. He also said, "It makes you believe that there is a God." Her funeral was held in the country church near the new house that she had so wanted to see. She was buried there in the lovely attached cemetery, and Russell made a wooden cross for her grave.

It was amazing that I was free to be with Mum all the time she needed me. On the day she died I should have been finding donor eyes for the Eye Bank. She even helped me with this because it was her wish that her body be donated for any medical purpose for which it might be useful. Her eyes were taken by a colleague, and her funeral flowers were made into arrangements and taken to the Eye Ward where the patients who had received her corneas were being nursed post-operatively.

Her three sisters were at her funeral including her oldest sister who had only just returned to Canada from a UK visit to see her family, including Mum. She kept repeating, "It should have been me." She had always thought that, as the eldest, she would be the first of the sisters to die, and was obviously quite shocked to have lost a younger sibling. Unfortunately, I felt I could not allow her to see her sister's body, because, although donating her eyes would not have left any upsetting evidence, there were visible marks where maxillofacial surgeons had taken advantage of her bequest to operate on her face, and I considered this would be too upsetting for her sister to see, especially as she had seen her alive so recently.

The mystery of her 'leaving us all something' was solved when we discovered that she had managed to build up her bank account to amass a considerable balance. She had obviously been living very frugally if the cupboards in her house were anything to go by. The only food items she seemed to have were packets of jelly which she had stockpiled as there must have been about thirty of them!

Her furniture came in handy for Russell and Doris when they moved into our attic flat a few years later. In the meantime, after Mum's house was sold, they put what they wanted into store. Doris had a passion for renewing drawer linings, and one day she called me urgently as she had made a discovery under the paper linings in the chest of drawers that had come from my mother's house. There was a serious amount of money in bank notes that had since gone out of currency. We had to apply to the Bank of England to get them changed.

I then remembered that when my mother eventually got my father's permission to sell the house that they still jointly owned at the time of the court case he had brought against her, she had managed to keep most of the money, a fact about which he was predictably not happy. For the first time I could remember, my mother had done something totally self indulgent. She had taken herself off on a visit to see her sister in Vancouver, and from there crossed the border to the United States where she saw that Greyhound Buses were selling long distance roaming tickets at very low cost in honour of some special anniversary and bought one. She had the time of her life, and post-cards arrived from almost every American city. We were delighted for her, and assumed that after buying her little Bristol property she had blown most of what was left from the sale of the house on this amazing trip. We were obviously wrong!

It did not bother us that she might have used all her remaining capital on that trip because she deserved it and it had given her so much pleasure. Apparently, a senator had engaged her in conversation at one of her stopovers and the next day he personally took her on a conducted tour of the White House. She could not get over the generosity she came across everywhere she went, and especially the fact that one hotel had kept her as their guest for several days until her luggage which had gone astray was reunited with her. "They even left a small box of chocolates every night for me instead of the single chocolate the other guests got," she told us in amazement.

18. A CIVILIAN DOCTOR and COUNTRY LIFE

'Incidentally, it's easy to write prescriptions, but difficult to come to an understanding with people.'
A Country Doctor, Franz Kafka

I had promised God, 'If You make me a doctor, I will be a doctor for You,' and when I had my own practice I was able to do more to keep this promise. I had good relationships with several religious organisations located in that part of West Sussex, as well as being involved in the 'Healing Ministry' of the local parish church.

A new rector came to the village just after me, and together we set up a bible study group and a mid-week Communion and Healing service. We were committed to dealing with the whole person comprising all three of its interdependent parts, body, mind and spirit. We wanted to show that the church's Ministry of Healing could be a partnership between medical science, which God had also provided, and the prayer and pastoral ministry of the church, working alongside each other. This contrasted with some people's view that you could only have one and not the other, or even, as certain sects taught, that medicine and biblical healing were in opposition to each other.

I remember a young Bible College student being brought to my surgery in the back of a car. He was suffering so badly with a severe asthma attack that, had I not been there, he would probably not have made it to the hospital. It was touch and go, and as I crouched in the car beside him administering injections, his friends were praying like mad. He had got it badly wrong when he threw away all his medication after a prayer for healing. Owing to his hospitalisation, he missed hearing the college principal's strong words of warning to all the students following this episode: "Keep taking the tablets until you check with the doctor!" However, he was unlikely to repeat that mistake.

Neighbours expressed concern about one particular woman who looked very poorly and seemed to be wasting away, but we never saw her at the surgery. Ultra-reserved, she quickly dismissed enquiries about her health on the increasingly rare occasions when she ventured outside her door. It was when the neighbours began to notice an unpleasant smell coming from her that they asked if I could help. I was on thin ice because she had not asked for assistance, but I did call on her and she told me that she believed in the power of prayer. When I told her that I did too, she tolerated me but would not let me examine what was obviously the source of her problem as I could see stained rags at her neckline that were evidently covering her breast.

She was a Christian Scientist and believed that if she, or anyone else, looked at the ulcerating growth, it would interfere with her faith for healing. However, she herself was getting sickened by the smell which made her policy of denial difficult. On the grounds that it would make it smell less and feel better if the nurse was permitted to call regularly to cleanse and dress the area, we managed to supervise her gradual demise and offer as much help as we could, although she only permitted it if she did not see it as medical treatment of her cancer.

Every shooting season the strip of overgrown land on the site of a telephone exchange next to our house and surgery became the refuge of an unlikely couple of birds because they were both cock pheasants! One day this land was fenced off like a building plot, but BT denied that they planned to sell it although it was clearly surplus to requirements as there was no longer a need for the telephone exchange to expand with modern technology advances. This reassured us, because we had always hoped eventually to obtain it for a purpose-built surgery. It was ideally situated for our purposes but properties anywhere in our village rarely came on the market and were at a premium because we were on a main railway line with good access to the capital and the airport, so we knew it would attract plenty of interest. We were glad when BT said that they weren't selling as we already had a large mortgage for the combined house and surgery that we had purchased from Edgar's widow, but then, much too soon for us, it was suddenly put up for auction by closed bids.

Fortunately, we were able to get assistance with a special mortgage scheme for doctors, but only for the value as assessed by a District Valuer from outside our immediate area. The closed bids meant that we were committed to purchase for what we bid without knowing what the other bids were, and there would be no second chance to get it right as the land would be awarded to the highest bidder. There were eighty interested parties.

Stewart managed to get an agreement that the value of the land would be deemed to be whatever it took to purchase it, but if we outbid the next person by a large amount, the excess would have to be paid from our own pockets. Rough calculations and much prayer ensued. I asked God to give Stewart the figure to bid as it was no good if we both came up with different ideas. We let it go right to the last moment, taking the sealed bid in person to the Hastings office just five minutes before the midday deadline. A phone call later confirmed that Stewart had got it just right with no excess to pay. Miracles come in many forms!

Our beautiful new surgery building was named Rapha House. 'Rapha' is the name used to describe God as a God who heals. One day when I was at communion I got a distinct picture in my mind of a wooden cross being pressed into wet plaster. I knew immediately what cross I was meant to use for this purpose. I had tried to buy a simple wooden cross in an airport shop in Tel Aviv as I flew home from an exciting trip exploring Biblical places. I was told it was not for sale as it was a sample of wood from the Holy Land - but they could give it to me! After the service I rushed to get it from my bedside drawer and took it straight round to the surgery under construction.

I had no idea at what stage the building was, and it seemed deserted until I reached the main consulting room at its rear. There I found the plasterer with his trowel loaded with the first batch of plaster which he was just about to apply to the walls. I explained that I would like a very discreet imprint of the cross placed somewhere in each room in an unobtrusive position. He was very understanding and asked if I was prepared to leave the positioning to him. This I did. Many a time a patient sitting in the building would suddenly become aware of a cross imprint. It seemed to have a soothing effect and often opened the way to discussions that might otherwise never have taken place.

I noticed one of my patients who was not a known churchgoer at one of our regular Sunday services when I was leading the prayers, and he told me later that when I prayed for any sick in our village, a problem with his arm disappeared. I expressed pleasant surprise, but he did not as he obviously thought that the healing ministry he had heard about worked in this way!

Our village church was unique in that both the Anglican and Roman Catholic (RC) and United Reformed Church (URC) celebrated an annual joint communion service. Anglican and URC participants could receive the bread and wine from clerics of either of these denominations, although the URC frequently did not have a minister and our church had taken over their pastoral care to some extent. However, the RC communicants were exclusively served by a RC priest, one of the monks from a nearby Abbey.

I had a branch surgery in this Abbey where I saw patients from their lay community and also provided medical care for the nuns from the convent. My little consulting room was separated by only a thin partition wall from an office belonging to one of the priests, and I sometimes felt a bit self-conscious when a patient asked me to pray for them during the consultation if he was in his room.

I once drove out of the surgery on a patient visit, but had a strong feeling that I should visit one of our URC families instead - an elderly couple who also had the wife's widowed sister living with them. For once I was not short of time so I did this, and was greeted by: "Oh, doctor! We have just been praying that you would come." The widow had been feeling unwell, but as her symptoms were vague she did not feel she could ask for a visit or go to the surgery. In fact, she needed urgent attention so I got her into hospital where she had an immediate restorative blood transfusion. In time, both she and her brother-in-law died, leaving the wife, her sister, alone. This lady always requested me to fit in a visit to her when I could spare the time - simply to pray.

The practice covered a wide area and I appreciated having a great variety of patients as they ranged through the whole social scale. Whether they were countess, celebrity, lawyer or labourer, I counted it a great privilege to be welcomed into their homes and their confidence. I once had a peer of the realm discussing his mother's management in my little consulting room which, before we moved

The old surgery dispensary

surgery, was more antiquated than Dr Finlay's Casebook. I computerised my side of the practice and was one of the first GPs in the country to do so, although my GP partner did not wish to participate. As a country practice it had its own dispensary, and it is amazing to think that when I took over we still had a system where patients collected their dispensed medicines from a small two-way cupboard, a bit like a serving hatch, built into the outside wall of the house. It had a bolted door on the inside, and what seemed to be a stained glass door on the outside which disguised it slightly to the uninitiated, but it was an open secret in the village. Surprisingly, I never heard of any medicines going missing, and only once or twice was I aware that something had been picked up by the wrong patient but it was always replaced before any harm was done.

Another old-fashioned aspect of the original surgery was the sound masking for patient confidentiality. This took the form of a floor standing radio that had seen better days, crackling away in the waiting room. However, any patient who dared to switch off the source of the irritating noise would get a severe reprimand from one of the receptionists: "Do you think it's on for your benefit?" She was no Dr Finlay's friendly Janet.

Once I had learned how to pluck and dress them, one unusual bonus I enjoyed in my life as a country GP was finding braces of pheasants hanging in our outbuildings after shoots on the neighbouring country estates. These were joined at Christmas by generous presents of good wine and spirits in spite of the fact that I did no private medicine as some patients would have liked. Other than the fees paid for insurance medicals and BMA recommended charges for form filling outside our NHS contracted work, I felt uncomfortable mixing medicine with money, and I could not see why anyone should want to pay me extra for what I did. Stewart always tells me that I am under-confident in my abilities, but while that may be true, I did not feel I could do any more for patients who paid as I was already committed to do my best for everyone.

Life outside the practice had its lighter moments. I became quite experienced in cooking for large numbers as I took on the task of producing Harvest Suppers for the church, and also did all the cooking when the church held socials for the village.

Catering at a Harvest Supper and an Edwardian Music Hall entertainment

As Gladys Pugh in Hi-De-Hi

There was a very successful Edwardian Music Hall Evening, while at another social the choir did a very funny take-off (written by Jon Fielder[7]) of 'Hi-de-Hi' which was a successful TV comedy series at the time. I also did some cooking for the masses after the Great Storm of 1987.

---

[7] 1955-2015 Teacher and composer. His 'Ragamuffin Man' was performed at the Theatre Royal, Drury Lane in March 2005 in aid of the Loomba Trust Foundation to support the education of 500 children orphaned by the tsunami disaster in Nagapattinum in South India

Storm Damage to our Victorian House as a falling chimney destroyed a visiting Doctor's car and a toilet roll wrapped itself round the aerial

As the storm moved across SE England Rapha House Surgery withstood it well even though we were in its main path, it caused chaos. Hardly a tree was left standing in our formerly tree lined road as the spiralling winds blew trees from both sides across it so that no cars could get through. These were no saplings, but hefty trees with huge trunks that had to be cut up before vehicles could pass again.

The tall Scots pines along the boundary between our Victorian house and Rapha House suffered badly. One uprooted our water main as it fell, while another took out the electricity cable. Our telephone supply also got disconnected, but as we were a doctors' practice BT did a wonderful job in quickly restoring our phone lines, although this was an ongoing process as no sooner was the line repaired than it went dead again because of all the clearance work going on.

Looking from Rapha House.
Arrow shows obsolete drug collection cupboard in the Victorian House

The water main was also attended to fairly quickly, but we had to wait a long time for the electricity. In fact, the village was cut off by road for

Roof damage over Russell's Flat

several days after the storm, and it was ten days before all the electricity was reconnected. Since we had a gas-fired AGA Lynda and I kept soup 'on the go' for everyone, giving special attention to the occupants of a large house opposite who were all single elderly people in bedsits. Our own house did have

109

some damage as a chimney stack had toppled. Fortunately, it did not fall towards the flat where Russell and Doris now lived, but it did land on the car of a visiting doctor who was staying in our house for the night before returning to Wales. His car was a write-off and, as if in a set for a comedy film, the toilet roll from one of the bathrooms had come down and wrapped itself round his car aerial forming a mocking flag in the wind.

Stewart had risked life and limb to go outside at the start of the storm to remove his car to the safety of the garage as he had returned late from a flight and left it in front of the house. He had not realised how foolhardy he was being as it had been hard to judge the full ferocity of the storm from inside the house, but it was fortunate he did so as his car was now the only serviceable one of three as I had also left mine outside in case of call-outs. A crude but functional solar pool heating device had been set up by my predecessor between two out-buildings near the swimming pool. It was sheets of corrugated iron with pumped water flowing across the sun heated corrugations to a collection

chamber on the other side and back to the pool. Now all the corrugated sheets had been lifted and rolled up, resembling a giant opened sardine can unceremoniously dumped over the hedge into the road. Amazingly, Lynda who lived in a flat above our garage slept through it all!

Swimming pools crude solar heating device stripped from the top of the out-buildings into the road

Although the village was cut off we had very few patients as the storm damage kept them otherwise occupied! One minor casualty was a very tired tree surgeon who was stripping branches from the trees which had severed our electricity lines and accidentally cut through the branch which he was sitting on. After a reviving cup of tea, he insisted on getting back to work in spite of his rib injury. Luckily, the felled branches had cushioned his fall.

A conscientious dermatologist who lived in the village reported for duty at the surgery as she could not get to the hospital where she normally worked. We knew there was a possible childbirth that we might have to deal with as the midwife was not available, and debated which one of us would be the better temporary obstetrician, but, fortunately, the baby had the good sense not to put us to the test!

Another person who ended up doing things that went far beyond his job description was our Rector. He went from door to door checking that residents were all right, and could be seen perched in precarious positions carrying out emergency repairs at many a house in the village. My brother was far more impressed by this practical act of service than any of the sermons he'd heard.

Rapha House Surgery when the village was cut off by snow one year after the great 1987 storm

One day I received a call from a young nun who always reminded me of Maria in the 'Sound of Music' as she cheerily breezed through the convent greeting the other nuns. She asked if she could come to see me on a private matter. I asked if she could give me some idea what it was about so that I could judge the length of appointment. Her reply was: "Think of the worst thing that could happen to me."

I had to remind myself that she was a nun when my mind automatically shot to what other young women meant when they said

111

Opening of Rapha House Surgery with the two oldest patients Lady Mary Grayburn (100) & George Walker (94)

something like this. But I had been right first time. We managed to get her taken on by an organisation in another area that found foster homes for single pregnant women where they could go and stay before and after having their babies until mother and baby managed to find somewhere of their own. This nun had come from a large family that she missed a lot, and she doted on her new baby. She clearly had an alternative calling to raise a family rather than pursue her life in the order.

During my time as a GP I also trained as a Christian Counsellor at CWR[8] in Waverley Abbey House near Farnham. I had the privilege of being taught by their late founder Rev Selwyn Hughes, one of the pioneering forces for Christian counselling in this country. My lasting memory of Selwyn is his teaching about marriage with tears spilling over as the loss of his own beloved Enid was still fresh, but he would not relinquish this duty as he thought the whole subject of marriage was so important. I also did a year's biblical studies course there so feel that I owe this organisation a great deal.

John Wimber, a well known name in the Christian healing ministry, came a few times to Brighton to hold Christian training seminars on healing. He was a gentle, if large, modest American. ("Yes, there are some!" I joked with my American relatives). John believed in standing back and waiting to see what God would do, and it was exciting to hear numerous people claim to be healed.

---

[8]Crusade for World Revival

We were all encouraged to pray for healing for any around us who requested it, and a woman that I had been praying for rushed up to John Wimber, thanking God for healing her deafness. I realise that I am in no position to vouch for the long-term outcomes, but seeing people apparently healed, and reading John Wimber's books which described many other healings made me conclude that not all of them could be just wishful thinking. Sadly, having a healing ministry does not mean you live forever, and John Wimber died all too soon for those who loved and admired him. I believe we need to keep an open mind where miracles are concerned as God moves in mysterious ways and it is not for us to make assumptions.

This was the case with the surgery. My time as a GP came gradually to an end through a series of circumstances that Stewart and I could not have predicted, and, even if space allowed me to tell you the sequence of events in detail, I still would not be able to explain why it happened or why Rapha House Surgery is now a private house.

To give a sense of timescale in the story of my eyes, it was around this time that I was first referred to an ophthalmologist because of an optician's findings who suspected early dry AMD. However, I thought no more of it at the time as I didn't notice anything wrong with my eyesight.

Once Rapha House Surgery was up and running, we took advantage of an unexpected offer from a developer to buy the Victorian house we lived in where the old surgery had been. However, we kept part of the land and started building a new house for ourselves, taking out a bridging loan to buy a short-term house to live in until it was ready. It seemed ideal as the builder constructing our house also wanted to buy our temporary home to develop once we moved into the new one.

Unfortunately, he went bankrupt, taking large sums of money we had paid him upfront against advice because we wanted to help him with his cash-flow problems. He also had not paid his workers and used the excuse that we had not paid him! His men retaliated with sabotage and put concrete in the plumbing. On one occasion after landing from a flight, Stewart unusually decided to look at the new building before going home. He got there to find a stopcock had been deliberately opened so that water was cascading down the stairs.

We prayed, our friends prayed, even complete strangers prayed about our situation. Money was haemorrhaging from our finances, and we had nowhere to turn for more. We employed the best of the workers directly on a weekly basis to finish the house for us, hoping that it would not spin out for too long, but even after we moved into the new house and sold the temporary house, we were financially very much worse off.

I was in the process of completing the handover of the practice to another doctor who had been working with me when Stewart's airline, the much loved 'Dan Air', was taken over by British Airways. Ironically, he had elected to stay flying the Boeing 727 which he enjoyed, rather than being transferred to their newer Boeing 737 fleet. Had he done so, it would have meant that he was kept on by BA. As it was, he was made redundant, and later had to pay for his own very expensive conversion with BA to fly the Boeing 737 before he could get another job.

As a result, I increased the number of my clinical assistant sessions to include two Day Hospitals, Medicine for the Elderly, Psychiatry for the Elderly, Oncology (briefly), and several Dermatology sessions. At the time I was driving between seven different hospitals in Sussex and Surrey, but then I broke my leg and was forced to cut back.

This happened when I was on my way to church for the midnight service on Christmas Eve in 1993. I was probably tired after an exhausting day cooking for a houseful of Christmas guests as I wandered off the garden path which was in the shadow caused by a boat we were renovating, and somehow managed to fall down a small terraced wall. This was not as some might suspect because I had been sampling too much of the cooking brandy as I am virtually teetotal!

I felt a sickening snap in my lower leg as I landed and immediately knew something was broken. I stumbled and fell towards the

114

pavement (sidewalk) where I lay while I waited for the ambulance, resisting all kind offers from passing fellow churchgoers to move me, or worse, my foot which was now at an odd angle owing to a dislocated ankle. When the ambulance crew came and moved my leg to put it in an inflatable boot splint the relief was sheer bliss as I was beginning to get cramp in my calf and I knew that it would not be kind to the damaged part.

I had seen many patients in Orthopaedic wards in plaster and traction, but now had valuable personal experience of what had previously been only theoretical knowledge concerning difficulties with essential bodily functions related to this position and the pain killers prescribed. It was not a pleasant experience! I also had several operations and was stuck in hospital over both Christmas and New Year. Russell asked me: "How come God could let this happen to you when you do so much for him?" However, he seemed happy with my answer, "I don't think He would suspend the laws of gravity just for me!"

I did myself wonder why the good Lord had seen fit to wait until this stage when I had virtually given up general practice to allow me this experience, but if it had to happen just then, I could not have made better preparation to be absent from home over the festive season if I had been given prior notice! I had prepared everything that could be done in advance for all the meals for the expected houseful of festive season guests. In fact, I had never been so organised, even down to selecting and labelling all the containers in which to serve everything included in each meal. All Stewart and Rita had to do was follow my detailed written timetable of the cooking plan.

The only note of regret I felt was that I had no appetite even to try the small portion of wild boar they kindly brought into the hospital for me, in spite of the fact that the hospital fare was very meagre and on Boxing Day we were only offered an egg roll for our main meal. Generally, I never lose my appetite, but I don't fancy breaking my leg again just to keep my weight down!

As I recuperated at home we had a chance to rethink our circumstances, and, as we were no longer confined to living within the expensive practice area, we decided to sell our purpose-built house and move further afield to improve our finances. Stewart, who by now had another flying job based at Gatwick, did much of the house hunting alone as I was still in plaster and on crutches.

One day he went to an estate agent in an area he liked, and they asked what he really wanted. The answer surprised them. "A three bedroomed bungalow with at least two reception rooms and an indoor swimming pool," he said with my broken leg in mind. They almost fell around laughing, explaining that they had never encountered anything of that description in the area. Yet remarkably, the next day they phoned to say someone had just come into the office with exactly what Stewart had described. We loved that bungalow and it was even better than the house we had designed for ourselves. Rather like what I got when all those years ago I prayed for a husband!

As a result of the early 1990s recession or being swallowed up by larger concerns, airlines went broke or were taken over, and pilots lost their jobs, including Stewart who was unemployed for three consecutive winters. Then after a few years flying the Boeing 737, a peach of a job came his way as Stewart was offered a direct command flying the 400 seat Lockheed TriStar (L10-11) for Caledonian Airways, an unusual opportunity for Stewart to fly a wide-bodied aircraft for the first time.

I had also rationalised my jobs, and was now working totally in dermatology. Giving up completely had crossed my mind, but a shortage of dermatologists meant that instead I took on more contracts. But Stewart was now approaching 60 years old and, although not at retirement age, France was not allowing Captains of over 60 years to overfly or land in France. Rather than becoming a First Officer again, he took the option to leave.

We planned to retire to Australia where we had already selected the place we wanted to live and almost bought the house, but Stewart did not want to hang up his goggles just yet so took a job flying out of Plymouth for a further 18 months on the turbo-prop De Havilland Dash-8, another type of aircraft he had not flown before and enjoyed

116

flying. Once I'd had my operation for breast cancer in Sussex, I joined Stewart in Plymouth and continued my radiotherapy treatment their at Derriford Hospital.

We had bought a superb waterside view, but the house needed major renovation to be worthy of it, so we 'camped' in the house for eighteen months while the builders worked around us. The ubiquitous builder's dust posed challenges to Stewart who struggled to emerge for work smartly dressed with brightly polished shoes, while I longed for some peace and quiet to rest after driving myself to my daily radiotherapy treatment. I had no professional contacts in the area, and soon decided to leave it that way. Now, at last, it was time to retire!

19. IN RETIREMENT
'Do not fear going forward slowly. Fear only to stand still.'
Chinese Proverb

Plymouth is pleasantly situated on the Devon coast just at its border with Cornwall and so it is an ideal starting place to explore both these lovely English counties. It was when we were investigating the part of Cornwall that we can see just across the water from our house that we found ourselves outside the National Coastwatch Institution (NCI) at Rame Head. We had never heard of the NCI, but were immediately interested because in our fairly advanced plans to emigrate to New South Wales Stewart planned to join a similar volunteer organisation we had found in Port Stevens as it could use skills from both his aeronautical career and his hobby of off-shore sailing. It was not long before he became a Watch Keeper at this NCI Station.

Meanwhile, I had started accepting people for counselling, mostly referred by CWR, the organisation I had trained with. Until I came they had no other trained counsellors in our area, but were often approached by people living there who wanted this type of counselling. Again, I could not bring myself to charge for this as I saw it as a Christian service, but I did suggest one or two charities that would be grateful for appropriate donations.

117

We also discovered that a branch of 'Community Family Trust', a nationwide organisation, was to be set up in Plymouth. This organisation's 'raison d'etre' was to teach relationship skills for couples in an attempt to stem the rising tide of family breakdown. We had good reason to be grateful for our own marriage, and could see the importance of a strong marriage for family life and nurturing children, while I had personal experience of the problems caused by family breakdown. Stewart and I became founder trustees and trainers of the Plymouth branch.

When the woman who had initiated it gave up because of lack of funding for her salary, we took over running the organisation. It was not religiously orientated, but designed to be accessible by all. We taught general relationship skills and started running regular monthly marriage preparation and mentor training workshops in our house with its pleasant view overlooking Plymouth Sound, serving lunch on the all-day workshops. People were encouraged onto the course, not just when planning to get married, but at all stages in their relationship with cohabiting and marriage 'refresher' couples welcomed as well.

In his duties with the NCI Stewart started to take photographs of fishing boats to assist identification and correct logging of boats that passed the Watch, and was soon asked to do the same thing for other Coastwatch Stations. I accompanied Stewart on his quest to find registered fishing boats of all sizes and over time he built up a photographic record of most of the registered boats in Devon and Cornwall. We both enjoyed discovering many little known places where a certain fishing boat might be found, so it was no hardship to include the Scilly Isles when Falmouth Maritime Museum persuaded him to do this in order to complete the collection and publish this 'unique reference'.

The commercial viability of such books was uncertain so publishers were reluctant to take it on, and this resulted in us setting up our own publishing concern. We worked together on our first two books: *The Fishing Boats and Ports of Cornwall'* and *'The Fishing Boats and*

Ports of Devon' which are not only a photographic collection of the registered fishing boats, but also a description of the places they operated from. I wrote an introduction for each book, explaining how they could be used by the non-fishing boat enthusiast to explore the coastline.

The books were quite popular, especially the Cornish book which we updated and rewrote after selling the initial 1,000 copies. Other books followed including a booklet entitled: *'What is the Meaning of the Letters and Numbers on Fishing Boats?'* written in response to a request made by bookshops who had bought our earlier books. These books have become valuable reference tools, and our website has been useful for the media and others requiring fishing boat photography. When we started to research a similar book about Wales we found we had to stay away from home quite a bit, and therefore decided to hand over the Plymouth Community Family Trust to others. Eventually, I also had to give up counselling because the combined effects of deafness and AMD made it difficult to catch the subtle shades of both facial and verbal expression in my patients' communication which can reveal so much to the counsellor.

We have managed to take some lovely holidays, notably in both South and North America, and South Africa where Simonstown in the Cape Province was another place we seriously considered retiring to. I had wanted to go to India since childhood, but Stewart did not want any experience of 'Delhi Belly'. However, he could not refuse me on my 70th birthday, and we did a grand tour of Rajasthan on a 'Citadel and Palaces' tour which we extended with a few days in Kathmandu. We found ourselves in the company of only three other couples with whom we could not have been better suited if we had been friends who had booked a holiday together.

One special occasion, among so many on the tour, was coincidentally on my birthday when we lunched in the Bhawa Palace in Jodhpur just two months before Liz Hurley had her Indian wedding there. One of the two other special birthdays in our group involved a visit to the 'Rat Temple' where you have to go shoeless, stepping carefully amongst the rats that swarm everywhere. I was so pleased to discover that I had some disposable airline socks with me. Let's just say that I enjoyed my birthday treat more!

In common with many retired couples, we found that taking cruises was a delightful way of travelling with no tiresome packing and unpacking, while the excellent on-board cuisine obviated any need to eat ashore which neatly solved the issue of Stewart's 'Delhi Belly' phobia. Yet it looked like an unfortunate start to one trip when we had to spend three days in a Barcelona hotel waiting for our cruise ship in dry dock to be ready to sail, especially when we learned that several stops on our itinerary including Malta and Alexandria had been cancelled as our Suez Canal passage was pre-booked for a certain date. Not many cruise ships sail non-stop through the Mediterranean, and we were particularly disappointed to miss our nostalgic reminder of Malta. The guided walks and bus tours arranged in Barcelona while we waited seemed a poor exchange, but worse was to come.

We had not yet had time to unpack the body-belt we normally used to carry valuables, and it was a blow to discover on our way back to the ship that our credit cards were missing. The police said they knew exactly which pick-pocket gang was involved. Apparently, they worked in and around the 'Catedral de Barcelona' and the Christmas Market, but the gang was much too clever to ever get caught with stolen items. The police told us that even when they were convinced they had seen one of them take something, it always vanished by the time they managed to search the individual concerned.

We had to cancel all our credit cards, and although the cruise company helpfully said they would allow us to settle our onboard expenses later, it still meant we only had limited spending power ashore. However, what could have been an absolute disaster miraculously became quite the opposite. We got to know so many fellow passengers and crew members who sought us out to offer sympathy and support that we felt surrounded by friendship for the whole cruise, especially two couples from Kent who have remained firm friends ever since. One of them even offered to buy anything we wanted on his credit card, trusting us to repay him on our return to the UK.

Surprisingly, not having any 'plastic' actually turned out to be a positive advantage when Indian traders pressed 'bargains' on us. Our pleas of: "No cash" which they countered with "We accept plastic!" could be truthfully answered to their amazement with the statement, "No plastic either!" All this is just one more example when I believe I have seen a loving Heavenly Father in action, taking something unpleasant and working it out for my good. How could I possibly not see it as another kind of miracle?!

Even then the excitement of this trip was not over as when we approached the beginning of the Red Sea 'anti-pirate' measures were put in place including razor wire around areas of possible boarding access and large swing weights and hoses readied for use against intruders. Although we were in a loose convoy and never far from a protective military escort, several crew members stood guard on deck 24/7, and rather excitingly, we were given an anti-piracy briefing and drill as well as the usual safety drill.

In Oman, Stewart was able to show me Salalah where he had been posted for his unaccompanied tour in the RAF in 1970. In that year there was a political coup, and the old Sultan had asked Stewart for political asylum after he had been deposed by his son. The new Sultan Qaboos sometimes visited and dined in the small RAF Salalah Officers Mess so Stewart had met him several times. When we re-visited Salalah and Muscat on the cruise the other passengers and the crew must have wondered if there were VIPs on board that they did not know about when they saw the government officials in gleaming limousines who had come to meet us. They were members of the Royal Protocol Team and they took us to see all the impressive advances that had been made since 1970. Their hospitality was overwhelming.

In 2012 I had a strange year medically. It started after a lovely transatlantic trip on the Queen Mary 2 so I should have been feeling good, but I felt generally unwell and found a large tender lump under my right arm so I was referred to a breast surgeon. He ordered several investigations including a mammogram that quite coincidentally showed areas of carcinoma in situ, because an earlier different scan followed by a biopsy had indicated lymphoma as the most likely cause of my symptoms.

Every woman over fifty will have her own way of describing to a man the excruciating experience of mammography. I was about to embellish mine! As the suspect areas would be impossible to see during the operation with just the naked eye, my breast was threaded with two steel wires in the imaging department of one hospital, and I then walked with these in place to the operating theatre of a nearby private hospital.

I couldn't help feeling somewhat anxious as I waited for a full report on the excised node which would give a better picture of what type of lymphoma I had. During this time I visited Buckfast Abbey which I always enjoy doing, and whilst there took the opportunity to pray in their lovely prayer chapel which is dominated by an enormous stained glass window depicting Christ with His arms invitingly open. When I finished I realised that I had already overstayed my available time, but did not want to leave before I had found a helpful book in the bookshop. There were masses of books on the shelves and I did not know where to start so I asked God to guide me. Right away, I spotted a small book and pulled it out. It was called *In the Palm of God's Hand* and on opening it I saw the words 'Lymphoma' and 'Derriford Hospital, Plymouth'. The author - Wendy Bray - was local to me and I found her book very helpful, as has been her friendship via Facebook since.

Two operations were necessary, but there was still no certainty that all suspect breast tissue had gone, but I decided against having a double mastectomy to be certain. All this took some time, and meanwhile a better, and yet more puzzling, revised diagnosis had come from the histology of the lymph node.

Apparently, I had toxoplasmosis which is caught from cat faeces, either directly or indirectly from sources such as unwashed vegetables. I was puzzled for two reasons. Firstly, I have had an almost constant association with cats from my birth, and as a child this relationship was far less hygienic so surely I should have caught it then. Secondly, it didn't fit because I continued to feel ill, and toxoplasmosis is usually fairly mild and short-lived in healthy adults. I eventually saw an immunologist, but it was too late for the reference laboratory in Swansea to track down information on the strain and possible source of my infection. I was about to receive some treatment which is usually held in reserve as it can prove more unpleasant than the illness, but then, quite out of the blue, I started to feel better.

My main concern then was for my eyes. Although toxoplasmosis eye complications in adults are usually associated with weakened immune systems, I did not want to risk any further trouble there. Fortunately, my ophthalmologist found only the expected signs of the dry AMD which, apart from a few distortions of lines, was not yet presenting much difficulty. It is now three years since this spate of odd happenings, and, apart from the fact that I shall never now be able to audition for a part in 'Calendar Girls', there have been no further ill effects.

Since I have been on the 'other side of the fence' as a patient, I have continued my medical education with personal experience of some investigations not available to me when I was in practice, receiving interesting but unwanted updates in the fields of nephrology, gastroenterology, gynaecology and cardiology! No wonder they say that when you retire you wonder how you ever had time to work.

20. SELL-BY DATE
'Though grey our heads, our thoughts and aims are green; Like damaged clocks, whose hand and bell dissent; Folly sings six, while Nature points at twelve.'
Edward Young (1683-1765)

In case you thought that ageing is all about 'senior moments' and 'viagra', I have to tell you that there are other 'treats' in store in those twilight years. When was it that I permitted myself to use the adjectives 'old' or 'elderly' in relation to me? As the years pass by, most people will tell you that they feel exactly the same as the year before. It is not as if we are a piece of cheese in a fridge with an 'eat by' date of the 5th June which on the strike of midnight on that date must 'go off'. If we have 'date stamps', we do not know it, and some of us start to 'go off' sooner than the stamp should perhaps pronounce, while others preserve their palatability much longer. I felt as though I was in the latter group until somewhere after the age of 70 years I started to be struck by the disparity between how I saw myself, and the image I conjured up if I heard someone of my chronological age described. I needed to realise that this was how other people probably now saw me!

Almost by definition, AMD tends to make its presence felt just before or after retirement, the time when many people are coming to terms with a different kind of identity crisis, far less recognised than the one most of us will have experienced in adolescence, but perhaps a time in which the sufferer feels even more hopeless as there is little hope of future improvement. The termination of specific employment can give rise to a sense of lack of purpose and self-worth, while redundancy of once valued skills threatens self-esteem and morale. It is said that illness is a great leveller, but surely this can just as truly be said of 'old age'.

One of the sad facts about AMD is that by robbing you of the important ability of adequate eyesight, it imposes limitations that can make you feel helpless to the point of panic as all your independence feels threatened. For one thing, it makes it much more difficult to find some post-retirement activity that will redeem self-esteem, whether taking on a social responsibility to put something back into society, helping others, or even excelling at some recreational activity. The sufferer becomes dependent on others to a greater or lesser extent, and can feel a burden to them, particularly as the duty of care often falls on those they would most wish to protect. Valuable relationships can thus become strained.

Sufferers may also need to swallow their pride and be forced down the difficult route of asking for help from people who have not offered it or even anticipated its need. Sometimes there are also worries because this will clearly inconvenience the person approached. Rather than do this, or when there seems to be no-one they can turn to for help, people with advanced AMD may gradually withdraw from social activity and friendships, becoming housebound and solitary. All this accentuates the loss of self esteem that may already be present from the other factors that I have just outlined in the ageing process and, almost inevitably, depression becomes much harder to avoid.

My mother used to say: "Old Age never comes alone." Only now that I am there am I able to see the truth of this, but personal experience always makes us a better judge of things. I thought I was quite sympathetic to my patients when I was in general practice, but I only truly realised what it was like to be in hospital totally dependent on others when I broke my leg. This was certainly a novel experience for me as I had enjoyed good health throughout my working years; indeed, there was not much opportunity to do otherwise as I had often worked as a single-handed practitioner. I once did nine months on constant call 24/7 with nobody else available to provide any off duty cover so I had sole responsibility. Fortunately, my practice was a country one where the patients knew me and were generally very considerate. Stewart complained that I only got ill on holiday, and other doctor colleagues say that they have also experienced this.

In the introduction I explained that I have not been able to keep up with all the changes in medical practice since my retirement, but you can see in this last chapter that I have made great strides in extending my knowledge after a fashion through my experiences as a patient. Notwithstanding what I have just said about the value of personal experience, I want to go on record as saying, "I do not need, or want, any more updates!" Old age is certainly not for wimps! And by this I do not mean I like the opposite. As Stewart always remarks when I say that I do not like growing old, "The alternative is even less attractive!"

Other women collect diamonds, but I am worth more to Stewart in spare parts with two top of the range hearing aids, a 'state of the art' pacemaker, and now two fantastic, but expensive, implants in my eyes. Just after my last costly eye operation, I made this observation to a friend and he said, "You'll have to make sure that you last a bit longer then!" Well, he was an accountant!

AMD is not the only age-related condition I have experienced. As well as poor vision, I have already mentioned my deafness, which is also age-related (presbycusis), and which, as for many other elderly people, has been a growing problem over the years. Deafness in various forms has been a feature on my mother's side of the family. A cousin had an undiagnosed hearing problem in infancy resulting in a speech defect which, coupled with his strong Welsh accent, made him totally incomprehensible to me. He also had to ask an adult what I was saying, so, as you can imagine, our relationship did not go places!

In spite of the family history, I had not expected to be afflicted by growing hearing difficulties just a few years into my retirement, and I tried to counter the loss by investing in various expensive private hearing aids, none of which seemed to work very well. However, when digital hearing devices became available on the NHS, I was fortunate in being referred to an excellent audiology centre where I was prescribed cutting-edge hearing devices that are both discreet and practical.

However, no hearing aid seems perfect, especially if there is any background noise. It has proved to be something of a social inconvenience and embarrassment, and it can be quite isolating. It made counselling impossible because I was no longer able to catch the very quiet voice that is sometimes all people can summon up when they want to make reference to things they find difficult to disclose. They need immediate understanding and reassurance, and the last thing they want is someone misunderstanding or asking them to repeat part of a long and convoluted story that they might already be struggling to 'get off their chest'.

This, combined with the growing inability to see the fleeting changes in a facial expression that could give a clue to some hidden or suppressed emotion, made me realise that counselling was something I could no longer do, robbing me of one of the main things that had given my post-retirement life a sense of usefulness. I tried other skills to compensate for those I had lost, but I could no longer do any art or sewing. Needle threading, even with the gadgets supplied with sewing machines was beyond my capability, but I found I could still knit in spite of the odd dropped stitch or misdirected needle that created extra stitches. It was good enough for tea cosies!

I spent more time communicating with friends on Facebook, and if odd-looking words sometimes appeared, they didn't worry about it! My iPad has a very useful camera so I often like to take pictures of places I visit to accompany my postings. There were some lovely blue flowers in our garden absolutely alive with bees which I wanted a photo of, but unfortunately, I ended up with several horrible unintended 'selfies' as I had not noticed the small setting change. This is a recurring problem with some electronic devices as, even though you can choose the option of bigger text, some important functions or choices you may also want to select are still very small, making it easy to miss them[9].

One of the age-related problems I am very keen to avoid is that of dementia in its various forms. I watched my dear brother Russell's sad decline into this condition over 16 years. When they retired, Russ and his wife Doris came to live on the top floor of our large Victorian house in West Sussex. We later also brought our elderly disabled Aunt Lillian from Bristol to live in a nursing home near us. Russell's visits to her were usually short even though he had loved his Aunt 'Dill' as he called her from infancy, because he hated seeing her the way she then was though she fortunately did not suffer from dementia.

---

[9] See Related matters; I. My Favourite Things

However, his wife Doris did have dementia related to a slight stroke she had when nearly 80 years old. She was three years older than Russell, and became obese after the stroke, further increasing her disability. He looked after her himself, often refusing the attentions of a neighbour I paid to look after them in their home in Suffolk where they had been living for the ten years following our move from the Victorian house. When this neighbour went on a long visit to Australia, I arranged for Russell and Doris to come on a holiday to a 'Hotel for the Elderly' which was actually a very nice care-home. My anxieties about how I could persuade them to accept long-term residential care were over when Russell suddenly asked if they could permanently live there, even though he still insisted it was his job to look after his wife and not the care home staff.

For Doris, there was a merciful release when her inactivity caused a blood clot to lodge in her lung. We dreaded the effect of her loss on Russ as they had been married for 53 years, and they were inseparable. However, within two weeks after her death Russell did not know that he had ever been married, and could not even recognise her in his wedding photographs. He lived another twelve years without her.

Russ often said to me as he looked around Aunt Lillian's nursing home, "If I get like this, I want you to shoot me." Later, he made it clear that he hoped for euthanasia if things got too bad for him. I told him that I could not do this, but assured him that I would never let him suffer. I thought that at least I would always be able to ensure this and I did my best to look after him and supervise his care in his declining years. Sadly, I could not keep my promise to him that I would not let him suffer. I never thought that the medical and nursing professions would be so concerned about following protocols that they would deny a dying old man adequate pain relief in case his crying out was not due to pain but just another   manifestation of his dementia.

The on-call system and other circumstances also resulted in unacceptable delays once the need for strong analgesia had been agreed. He took five days to die a slow and tormented death without adequate pain relief in spite of being skeletal as he had been unable to take solid food for many months because of swallowing difficulties. I tried, but was powerless to help him. I had no authority. Perhaps I felt then, more than ever, the age-related uselessness of my own medical qualifications. I eventually sensed that Russ was also afraid to die, so I kept telling him to "...just go to sleep." A lullaby my mother used to sing to me came into my head. There was a fair chance that she had sung it for him too:

> 'Go to sleep, my baby,
> Close your pretty eyes.
> Angels up above you
> Look down on you from the sky.'

It is amazing how powerful music can be! It seemed to quieten him and he closed his eyes and died shortly afterwards. Russell always suffered from a lack of self-worth, but his value to me as a brother was beyond price. He should not have died in this way.

21. MUSIC and CHOIR

'If music be the food of love, play on...'
Twelfth Night, William Shakespeare

I have included this section because the subject is important to me, and I am unlikely to be alone in this respect amongst others with AMD or poor vision. In recent years it has been found that music is more than the food of love. It can also be the food of memory, and apparently nourishes both mind and body by promoting relaxation and other states that encourage the proper functioning of all our internal systems. Most people won't be surprised to hear that Scandinavian research on the positive psychological and physical effects of music[10] has found that music can remove stress, but it was also suggested that repeated exposure to certain music could replace medication in

---

[10] Töres Theorell: Psychological Health Effects of Musical Experiences: Theories, Studies and Reflections in Music Health Sciences. (Springer Briefs in Psychology, 2014)

calming excitable patients. The overall conclusion was that it could even benefit metabolism itself.

Some of the research involved singing in choirs. I was amazed to learn their finding that listening to and performing music could enhance coping strategies, and also help individuals to deal with problems by facilitating new ways of thinking. I certainly found that music played a part in keeping Russell stimulated when he had dementia. By playing certain CDs it was even possible to get him to dance with me, something he had never done before.

He had a lovely tenor voice, but his inhibitions meant that it was rarely heard outside the family. Not so once he got dementia when he would entertain many of his fellow residents and their carers with pleasing renditions of 'You Are Love', 'Deep in my Heart, Dear,' and other songs, mostly from Ivor Novello musicals and other West End productions that he and Doris had seen together in the early days of their marriage and for which Doris used to accompany him on the piano while he sang. I cannot say if he was remembering her when he sang, but the music certainly lifted his spirits and also helped him deal with things he found difficult as he would just burst into song. He even went to 'Gather lilacs' in the dentist's chair!

I mentioned earlier that Stewart and I have belonged to church choirs wherever we have lived. In fact, the first thing that drew attention to my need for reading spectacles in middle age was when I had difficulty distinguishing just which line a note of music was on. If I got it wrong, it might not have been particularly noticeable in the large Ditching Choral Society I then belonged to in West Sussex, but it would have made an all-important difference to the effect produced in the small church choir where I also regularly sang.

For sixteen years we have been members of the choir at what is now the Minster Church of St Andrew in Plymouth. It has provided enjoyable social contact for me which has sometimes been in short supply since I have not been able to drive, making it less easy to get out and about, while as my eyesight has worsened, how well I have coped in choir has been a useful weekly barometer of the progress of the condition.

I am grateful to successive Directors of Music for allowing me to continue in spite of the progressive difficulties I experienced with reading my music, and latterly, even in reading the conductor's facial expressions. Fortunately, that doesn't apply to seeing arm movements, for as cats say, "When in doubt, wash," and every chorister knows, 'When in doubt, watch the conductor!'

I must say that our conductors were remarkably tolerant as I tried out new gadgets to help me read the music better, even though some of them had bright lights which probably dazzled both conductor and congregation. I soon found that it was easiest to use just a simple magnifying glass because by the time I was organised with the other gadgets, the choir had moved on in the music. Lighting could be a problem though, and it was often my turn to be dazzled when, on what had been a dull day, unexpected and normally welcome sunlight would suddenly stream in through the windows straight into my eyes.

My useful lorgnette inheritance

To my surprise, what became my favourite magnifiers turned up as part of what I had originally taken to be just an Art-Deco marcasite clip-brooch, part of my late mother-in-law's effects that I had inherited. The 'brooch' had lain forgotten in my jewellery box for years as I am not a great lover of marcasite as it was the only type of jewellery I could afford in my teens. I can't remember how one day I came to discover that the 'brooch' had a spring mechanism whereby the folded back part of the clip opened to form a very handy pair of lorgnettes. From that time on they were in daily use as I always had them clipped to some part of my clothing or on a neck chain, ready to use whenever extra magnification was required. I grew to love them, and this felt particularly good because they not only served a very practical purpose, but it was as if Mum Lenton was doing posthumously what neither of us had managed to do during her lifetime, and that finally something about our relationship felt comfortable after getting off to such a bad start.

It was particularly upsetting therefore to find one day that the brooch was missing from the chain around my neck, yet another casualty to my lack of visual awareness. No matter how hard we searched we could not find it, but to our great delight Stewart found a similar item on an American e-bay site. He did not hesitate to pay the full price to secure it at once without risking losing it at auction.

You might wonder as I did, particularly after my eye operation, why I could not just have been given a stronger lens to correct my reading if I was helped by such a small magnification as that provided by my 'Marcasite magnifiers'. The answer was convincingly demonstrated to me by my hospital optometrist who allowed me to try such a stronger correction whereupon I found that I would have to hold any reading material somewhere around the end of my nose to be able to read it! This would make it impossible for me to both read the music and watch the conductor.

My local optician later thought that the additional sight correction could be provided if I wore contact lenses (which are obviously closer to the eye) in tandem with a pair of low strength off-the-shelf 'Ready-Read' spectacles which would then also free my hands to hold my music more comfortably. I discovered from LEH that there was no bar to using contact lenses in principle, but, to my great disappointment, the contact lens specialist found that my 'Dry Eye'[11] condition was too severe for me to wear them as my eyes did not have enough lubrication.

---

[11] See Related Matters IV: 'A Dry Eye in the House?

When reading you can take your own time, but singing has to be done to a set beat and there is no time for hesitation - one not only has the notes to interpret but also the words that must be sung to them. This means you need the ability to scan and take in a lot at once, an ability which I was clearly losing. I discovered that my best option was to enlarge the music as much as possible, and, ideally, to learn the words by heart - or, at least, have the words written separately in large lettering. This caused some hilarity on one occasion when our organist produced a huge enlargement, the maximum achievable with the office photocopier. Of course, it was far too big to hold like that, but was just right when I cut it up and pasted it onto a sheet of manageable size. It just meant that I turned the pages more quickly than everyone else!

A tenor in the row behind once told me he was glad he was able to read the large printed words over my shoulder. Tenors, in company with basses and altos, provide the all-important harmonies in singing, and actually have a slightly similar problem to mine because they sometimes cannot read the words quickly enough. The trouble is that the words are often written in incredibly small print either above or below the notes so you need to either be young enough to have exceptional eyesight or remember to bring your spectacles! Another problem is that sometimes after the first verse in a hymn, the rest of the words will be printed in stanzas at the bottom of the page or even on a separate one. In such cases, singers may wish they possessed two eyes capable of working independently of each other!

Talking of the need to remember to bring spectacles, Stewart discovered that his were missing just before the start of one formal church occasion when many visitors were expected. The only remedy was his mother's legacy to me as I could probably manage as I had learnt most things by heart. Consequently, this most masculine of men had to use this most feminine pair of decorative lorgnettes. He could have carried it off singing with the other basses on the back row of the choir, but he also had to read the lesson, and so his puzzling choice of feminine-style reading accessory, now gleaming brilliantly from the brightly lit lectern, must have caused something of a distraction from the words of the, albeit beautifully read, second lesson!

Reading music is usually easier for sopranos who generally sing the recognisable and more predictable melody. Yet this means the congregation will be following them, so it is important for the sopranos to make sure they notice those irritating changes recently made to well-loved more familiar words.

Although it is also important for the other parts to get the words right, it is their harmony that is most missed if they stop singing. Stewart often gets appreciative comments from members of the congregation around us when we go to different churches on holiday, because he can provide enriching harmony to the old hymn tunes he has sung since his youth. This ability has often proved a useful conversation starter, even resulting in social contacts that we otherwise might not have had, not to mention countless invitations to join their church choirs.

Choir membership also imparts all the other benefits of belonging to a small group such as getting to know people better and receiving their support and encouragement as well as gaining a sense of belonging. These morale boosting effects were so valuable to me as I struggled with my vision, especially the friendship and support of the talented soprano that I usually sit next to. As well as providing clear words and a strong musical lead for me to follow, she has helped me find my place in the music or even the music itself when I could not distinguish it amongst all the similar sheets in my folder, and has supported me in many other ways, including preventing me resigning from the choir and urging me not to give up my pursuit of finding a solution to my eyesight problems. Her 'day job' as a librarian also meant she was in a good position to offer help in researching anything that might assist my fight against dry AMD. As it turned out, I chanced on something online myself, but I knew she was right behind me in my endeavours, and she now shares my enthusiasm to help and enlighten others with my condition. This book comes to you in no small measure because she has encouraged me to write it.

A non-musical perk is that choir members are certain of a reserved seat for special services like Christmas and Easter when the church is packed to capacity. However, I never envisaged that sitting in the choir stalls near the organ could pose any kind of danger until we joined a certain village church choir. On one Pentecost Sunday, the Sunday fifty days after Easter when christians remember the time when the Holy Spirit came upon the disciples of Jesus in the form of tongues of fire, the rather elderly church organ must have caught the flame of Pentecost because it somewhat alarmingly began to belch acrid smoke, threatening to engulf both it and the poor choristers who had to retreat into the safety of the vestry!

Perhaps the greatest benefit of all is that music transports you to a world apart from other concerns. There is no doubt that making music in its various forms, no matter how elementary one's performance, feels beneficial, especially in a group setting with other instrumentalists or singers. There is already something satisfying in being able to perform a challenging piece of music alone, but when you join with others who augment the sound and enrich its quality with various harmonies, it lifts the satisfaction to a whole different level. It is almost as if you become part of one living organism as you move together delicately or with increased intensity or tempo, thrilling at the quality of the sound produced. It can be quite skin-tingling. Being able to perform with others in this way is one of the qualities that make music so valuable as a means of enhancing self esteem, something people are increasingly recognising as important these days.

Another important aspect of this was revealed in April 2016[12] following research carried out by the Royal College of Music with Tenovus Cancer Care among cancer patients, their carers and those bereaved by cancer which found that singing in a choir for just one hour boosts levels of immune proteins. People in these groups are often affected by stress and depression which can adversely affect their general

---

[12] In ecancermedicalscience. http://ecancer.org/journal/10/631.php

health and immune system just when they need all the help they can get from it, particularly for those personally battling the disease. This study shows that there is a scientific foundation behind anecdotal beliefs that singing in choirs can make people feel better. Preliminary findings demonstrate that it not only improves mood state, but modulates components of the immune system which means that singing in choir rehearsals could help put people in the best possible position to receive treatment and maintain remission.

It will not have escaped the notice of those with AMD and their carers that cancer patients and those close to them are not the only ones subject to stress and frustration, depression and social isolation. If this makes you wish that you could tap into the benefits of group singing but you feel you lack experience, don't despair because the opportunities to do so have never been greater with so many community choirs starting up nowadays. There is a great range of choirs to choose from including ones for popular music, rock and gospel as well as classical or church choirs, just as there are choirs who welcome singers of all ages and experience, even complete beginners.

A neighbour of mine faithfully followed her husband's passion for barbershop singing for years, but although she loved it, she always believed that she could not sing herself. Then one day at a barbershop convention a voice coach told her that, given help and perseverance, everyone can sing. Now she is an ardent member of a local women's barbershop group and has never looked back. So if you want to enjoy singing with others, even if you cannot read music, might I encourage you to have a go? In the UK the Gareth Malone website[13] is useful while the link[14] below gives a list of choirs in the USA with website links.

Music is a truly wonderful thing and it has yet another ability that becomes more and more valuable as time goes on. There is   nothing

---

[13] http://www.garethmalone.com/sing/choirs
[14] http://www.choirs.org.uk/international%20choirs/usa.html

like a piece of music for taking you back in vivid awareness, alerting all your senses to a forgotten place or time when it previously impacted them. No wonder music can stimulate patients with dementia. Are you, like me, more able to remember words when they are set to music? As I struggled with my vision, I discovered that my years as a chorister had enabled me to memorise scripture and comforting words that were now so helpful to me.

A favourite passage of mine from my counselling days for encouraging people who lacked self esteem came from the beautiful words of Psalm 139 which begins, 'O Lord, You have searched me and known me.' [15] Bernadette Farrell, a modern composer (born 1957), has arranged a beautiful setting of this to music that we often sing in the church choir. The fourth verse is my favourite:

> *'For you created me and shaped me,*
> *Gave me life within my mother's womb.*
> *For the wonder of who I am, I praise you:*
> *Safe in your hands, all creation is made new.'*

This song strengthened my assurance that God knew everything about me, my past, my present and my future. It encouraged me to continue trusting Him, however bad my eyesight became. Yet it didn't stop the troubling question at the back of my mind: 'Would these words memorised from sacred songs and hymns be all I had to rely on at some stage?' Eventually, I had to use a magnifying glass even with the huge enlargements, and my thoughts turned reluctantly to giving up singing in the choir, but then, when it seemed I had reached a dead end, I discovered I could have the operation on my eyes.

---

[15] Spirit Filled Life Bible

PART TWO

LOOKING NOW THROUGH DIFFERENT EYES

'Men succeed when they realise that their failures are
the   preparation for their victories.'
Ralph Waldo Emerson[16]

'Hope is wishing something would happen. Faith is believing
something will happen. Courage is making something happen.'
Unknown origin

---

[16] 1803 – 1882 An American essayist, lecturer, and poet

22. SEEING LESS
'Enable with perpetual light the dullness of our blinded sight.'
'Come, Holy Ghost' (Veni, Creator Spiritus), 9th C. hymn

What happened concerning my eyes in the first half of 2015 was certainly miraculous in my opinion! There was a time when the 'London Eye' meant only a big wheel to me. Now it would represent a big change in my life when I was already into my late 70s. To be strictly accurate, the word 'Hospital' needs to be added after the word 'Eye' to give the complete picture. Who would have thought even twenty years ago that I would be able to put a few words into something called 'Google' and it would come up with information at just the right time to lead me into what would turn out to be a life changing experience?

The dry AMD diagnosed in my eyes twenty years earlier started to deteriorate quite quickly over just a few years. In 2011 I was just beginning to notice symptoms, but by 2014 they became much more troublesome, and by Spring 2015 I was no longer considered legally fit to drive. This was a devastating blow as there is little public transport where we live. The nearest bus stop is almost a hilly mile away and I do not cope well with hills, but, in any case, it is a very infrequent service and only allows a short while in Plymouth before the return bus departs.

It was a very difficult time, and for a while I felt there was no help and no hope. I had been discharged by the NHS and felt I had been left adrift without any professional guidance or supervision. I obviously need to explain this further, but first I should tell my story from my earliest awareness of having dry AMD.

I started getting my eyes tested regularly from around the age of 43 when I first suspected that I needed to wear spectacles for reading. This is pretty much a normal rite of passage into middle age! After one of these routine eye tests in the 1990's I was sent to the Worthing Hospital Eye Clinic where I was told that I had some early signs of dry AMD. They explained that this was a form of macular disease where drusen - tiny yellowish fatty deposits - build up in a layer of the retina

139

and interfere with the function of the photoreceptor cells of the macula to cause problems with central vision [17]. They told me that no treatment was available, but the good news was that usually it didn't progress quickly, and that I might not have any symptoms relating to the condition for many years, if at all.

At that time I had no visual symptoms other than the usual middle-aged feeling that my arms were too short to hold my book far enough away to be able to read it! I was fine as long as I was wearing spectacles, and therefore didn't really take the diagnosis particularly seriously. As far as I was concerned, there was no problem with my eyes. I was sure I would not have been able to work as a dermatologist at the hospital, a role I performed alongside my GP work, if that were the case as it relied heavily on good eyesight for diagnosis of the skin conditions and the minor surgery associated with it.

In fact, I gave no further thought to the AMD diagnosis until we first moved to Plymouth when an optician said he would like to refer me to the local Eye Hospital for a further opinion. In 2010 I had another appointment at the Royal Eye Infirmary in Plymouth because another optician found my vision had needed significant further correction after a relatively short interval. Fortunately, fluorescein angiography (which shows up the blood vessels in the eye) showed no 'wet' AMD so I still did not have any treatment, but I was advised to purchase and take some approved dietary supplements recommended by AREDS (Age Related Eye Disease Studies) [18] but not available on the NHS.

I was told I might experience distortions in my vision where straight lines appeared kinked, and I might also notice small blind spots or less distinct areas. I was given a special grid chart (Amsler Chart) [19] to check my eyes from time to time and asked to trace round any areas

---

[17] See Appendix 1 & 2
[18] See Appendix 4 - Vitamins and Dietary Supplements
[19] See Appendix 2

where lines looked distorted as this would help record further changes in my vision. I had started to notice some symptoms, but over time I noticed more. In everyday life it seemed I had learned to adapt by using head movements to compensate for any lack in my general vision, but now I was beginning to experience problems with the printed word including written music.

Much depends on having the right sort of lighting with AMD. Dim lighting is not the only problem, as too much illumination can cause unpleasant glare effects so that bright light coming through windows, which most people can tolerate, may have an unpleasant dazzling effect for the AMD sufferer that makes it difficult to see. Although the eye clinic had not said that they wanted to see me again unless it looked as if wet AMD might be developing, I saw the ophthalmologist again privately in 2012 after my toxoplasmosis diagnosis to make sure my eyes had not been affected. Fortunately, they had not, and dry AMD was still the only diagnosis.

In February 2015 my optician surprised me by telling me that my visual acuity had fallen below the legal level required to drive a car. It was a shock because I felt I only had problems reading or doing fine work and was still seeing the world around me quite well. My only difficulty with driving had appeared to be when I had to read small print on notices, such as drawing up beside a barrier and needing to read instructions on how to operate it. However, this was not generally an issue as I did not usually drive very far from home so there was no need to read signposts!

The optician also spotted an area on my retina that was possibly moving towards wet AMD, so referred me urgently to the local Eye Hospital where I again had fluorescein angiography. Unfortunately, I was not informed of the results, but I knew that if it was wet AMD I would need an injection as soon as possible so when I heard nothing I became concerned that my records or a letter to me had gone astray. I eventually phoned the secretary to see if I had been allocated a follow-up appointment, and was taken aback to be told that I had been discharged from the clinic! I presumed that this was because I had no wet AMD, and there was still no treatment for the dry form.

This time was the low point in my story. I felt abandoned and totally cut off from expert help. Coincidentally, again due to a mix up, I had also lost contact with the Macular Society that I had joined the previous year where I was on the waiting list to have some instruction in 'eccentric reading'[20]. There were other frustrations, one being that I very much regretted that I could no longer get to the gym now I could not drive myself. I had some exercise machines at home, but found it much more enjoyable at the gym/fitness centre which I had previously attended almost every day. It helped me stay fit and kept my weight down, both of which were important for my general health, especially in relation to my blood pressure and the macular degeneration, but also provided me with good social contact which I really valued.

Not being able to drive any more also meant an end to many small but enjoyable activities outside the home where I had only had myself to consider. Now I could no longer take myself out for a stroll along the beach, pop out to the shops, visit the hairdresser or chiropodist, drop in on friends or take in a meeting or service at a different church. All spontaneity and independence seemed to have been removed from my life. Depression lurked not far from my door, and I could not help thinking of the many poor souls similarly afflicted who lacked the support and resources that I was privileged to enjoy. They could be truly cut off, alone, and worst of all, without hope.

Looking back now, I can see that being apparently deprived of all official sources of help actually worked out for my ultimate good. Otherwise, I would have followed the normal route of low vision aids and 'eccentric vision' instruction to help me make the most of my remaining sight, rather than finding, as I shall explain later, something that actually restored visual function. First, however, I needed to taste the hopelessness felt by everyone threatened with severe vision loss

---

[20] see Related Matters - A Sideways Look

from whatever cause, and experience the distress of the major lifestyle changes it forces.

Sometimes I would try to convince myself that everything was normal, but I could never keep it up for long. I couldn't even tell whether someone approaching was addressing me or the person standing next to me because I could not see the speaker's eyes, a small thing I had previously taken for granted. I'd always been good at getting splinters out, threading needles, diagnosing skin blemishes etc, but now I could no longer do these simple tasks. Reminders of limitations crept up on me when I would least expect them.
 I hated hearing:

> My button has come off (a sewing job!)
> Read this. It will give you the answers.
> What is this spot on my lip?
> Can I share your hymn book? (I could then no longer see it!)
> Tell me the number on your credit card.
> Can you write down your address for me?
> Just fill in this form before you see the doctor, dentist, etc.
> Place your signature strictly within the box.
> Careful! There might be bones in this fish.
> Sit here facing the window (dazzle greatest).
> Come round for a quiet chat?
> Have you seen N—? Is she at the meeting?

I could no longer see if the fruit I was selecting had blemishes or exactly what I was putting into my mouth on my fork. More embarrassingly, I could not always distinguish which of the toilet symbols was wearing a little skirt! All were reminders of how my life was changing! I was so thankful that I had already learned a great many things by heart like the order of church services and the location of things on my computer screen because I now needed to rely on this rather than read things afresh each time.

Because I relied greatly on having learnt so many hymns by heart, I now regretted that so many of the traditional words had been   slightly altered. I am sure some changes make it easier for younger people to understand the meaning, but others seem to make no real difference and I couldn't help feeling that they could just as easily have been left as they were. It certainly made it more difficult for 'old timers' like me who are apt to sing what we are used to rather than the newer versions. Oh well, I am sure that God can sort it all out even if we cannot. It reminds me of being at an international church service in Lourdes where we all prayed in our own different languages. It makes you realise that this is what God hears all the time!

23. LIFESTYLE CHANGES - IN TANDEM

'Love is not love. Which alters when it alteration finds,'
William Shakespeare

The effects of AMD not only created changes in my lifestyle, but also meant that Stewart had to make modifications to his. He had to be available to take me to appointments or drive me to places where we could enjoy a level walk so I could get essential exercise. This was often fitted in after he had indulged his own preferred form of exercise with a small white ball which had already involved quite a lot of walking!

He started to think more about shopping than many men do, and would often pop into shops to bring home essential supplies on his way back from doing other things. The alternative was that he would not only have to read labels of cans and packets on supermarket shelves for me, but also increasingly find them as I had lost the ability to glance down a row of shelves and spot the item I needed. An additional hindrance was the infuriating tendency of supermarket staff to rearrange everything at intervals, making it difficult even for customers with good sight to dash in and quickly select what they wanted without having to search through all the aisles which inevitably means ending up with extra items in the shopping basket!

Lighting in supermarkets was also difficult, although, to be honest, this had already been causing problems long before I noticed any AMD symptoms. It seemed to do something strange to my vision and I often felt quite disorientated as soon as I entered through the doors, although I was never quite able to work out what was actually having the effect on my eyes. All I knew was that it made me feel strange -

almost as if I had been transported 'Star-Trek' style to a different world. I felt sure that it was a cunning commercial device to confuse you into a zombie-like state where you wandered around picking up random items from the shelves - I think Stewart believes this is what happens to me, anyway. "When you know what you want, just go straight for it and don't look around all the time. I can shop much quicker than you because I know what I want!" He has probably lived to regret setting himself up as an expert shopper.

Another thing I found most unhelpful was when I went to look for vitamins and supplements designed to help those with poor vision and AMD, as no matter what branch of a well known High Street chemist I was in, they always seemed to be located right at the bottom of the stack of shelves instead of being helpfully displayed in plain view as you would expect. You'd have thought this would also make good sense commercially, but, no matter how many managers or supervisors I spoke to about it, they always remained in the most difficult place to see.

You might find something ironic in a Christian saying that one of the worst places for her is church! Lighting levels can be critical, and very bright can be just as bad as too dim. In our church there are bright chandeliers giving what most find to be good lighting, but there are shadowy areas too, and my eyes never seem to catch up in scanning between the two as one of the effects of AMD is to make such adjustments slower. It seems strange to think that supermarkets and churches have anything whatsoever in common but in this case they do!

A special holiday had to be cancelled in summer 2012, when I had Toxoplasmosis, so as some compensation for this we took a Caribbean cruise in the November. My eyes were already noticeably affected by AMD and Stewart thought that the face of my ladies' wristwatch would eventually prove too small as I had already given up trying to read the little date box. In St Martin he bought me a lovely large-faced ladies' watch with more visible luminous markings. We saw no ladies' watches with bold black figures which we later discovered would actually have been a better choice for my vision needs, and as the AMD progressed I found that there was not really a good enough contrast between the silvery reflective watch face and the gold and pale green luminous markings to easily read them. One of my joys at present is that I can once again read this treasured watch easily, even though I often forget and out of habit keep asking Stewart the time! I wish I could so easily rectify the sense of loss I feel over a special gold brooch that Stewart gave me on our wedding day which I lost because I could not see well enough to fasten the safety clasp securely.

Stewart was very helpful as my vision decreased. He amazed me by thinking ahead to my needs the whole time. He would advise me of obstacles in my path in case I tripped over them, although sometimes he couldn't resist reminding me of a time years earlier when I still had good eyesight but somehow managed to trip over a white line in the road! Whether I needed it or not, he would call out the number of steps I had to negotiate and whether they were uneven or with short or long drops etc, which was very helpful as judgment of these things could be difficult. With poor vision it was often hard to work out if a brass or white strip was just that, or actually marked the edge of a step. I guess I did not usually have too much trouble noticing the road surface unless it was getting dark because my peripheral vision was preserved, but I struggled with subtitles or other printed items on the TV screen. I was glad that Stewart would read these out without me even having to ask. We also enjoy eating out and in restaurants Stewart always asked for a seat with good lighting but not facing the glare of a window for me. This was not so much for reading the menu as he usually had to do that anyway, but more to give me some chance of seeing my food.

You will have gathered from what I have already said that Stewart was remarkably considerate of all my needs, and he never showed impatience with me in my shortcomings. Well, at least, not the ones associated with my eyes! I was glad that he was able to get out as much as possible when the weather permitted to play a round of golf with his 'seniors' group, and I enjoyed hearing the news he brought back as well as his efforts to tell me some of the more suitable jokes without forgetting the punch line! He also managed to find plenty of other things to keep him busy, including being honorary treasurer for several organisations, and giving talks to various social groups around Devon and Cornwall - all potentially providing outside interest for me also.

These activities were important for Stewart because no matter how much couples enjoy doing things together, it is vital for the health of any marriage for each of them to have activities they do on their own which do not involve their spouse. Unfortunately, the AMD was making me increasingly dependent on Stewart to help me do everything outside the home, and although he had always somehow managed to fit a quart into a pint pot as far as time was concerned, I did not want the poor fellow to completely wear himself out!

Eventually, I found I was struggling to recognise people as their faces were just a blur, so Stewart would try to help by telling me their names as they approached. The only trouble was that we were both really bad at remembering names! As they drew ever closer, he often found his mind a blank so would whisper any details about them he could dredge up, hoping it would prompt me to remember - which might well have helped if only I'd been able to hear him!

Sometimes I even found Stewart difficult to identify although I only once seriously mistook someone similarly dressed for him, but fortunately, I saw my mistake before total embarrassment set in. At first, people would often think I was joking if I asked them if Stewart was in the room when they could see him quite plainly, not realising I couldn't. Luckily, I only had to do this if he was not laughing. His hearty infectious laugh gave him away every time! I had only heard such a laugh from one other person, but Stewart's father's ghost would hardly be so noisy!

24. NEW LENSES - TWO FOR ONE!
'The person who says it can't be done should not interrupt the person doing it!'
Chinese Proverb.

My world was not only smaller; it was slow and laborious. Looking carefully became necessary for every action and took much more time. It was easy to feel that very little was being achieved each day. Although he never complained, the Wedding Day 'for better, for worse' promise so easily made at the time seemed to be giving Stewart far more of the latter, and very little, if any, of the former as far as I could tell as my eyesight worsened.

After I had been discharged from the local NHS eye clinic because they thought nothing more could be done for my dry AMD, I started to attempt to teach myself eccentric viewing[21] from a Kindle Book,[22] but was finding it hard work. The Macular Society had me on its waiting list for tuition which they were trying to arrange locally, but it was taking a long time to achieve a mutually convenient date.

I started thinking about external devices that might bend light entering my eye so that it would essentially do the eccentric viewing for me and perhaps cut out my struggles as I couldn't seem to stop trying to look at things the way I used to when my vision was still good. As you can imagine, I had already searched Google for information about dry AMD, but although I had found nothing about any such lens at the time, I decided once more to turn to Google for help.

When I was a GP I had barely heard of the internet, even though I had introduced one of the earliest GP computer systems into my surgery using Abies software and a classification system[23] devised by Dr Jim Read, a fellow GP from Loughborough that Stewart and I had met at the GP training seminars hosted by Abies. I can't help thinking

---

[21] See Related Matters: 'A Sideways Look at Life' in this book for a description.
[22] Macular Degeneration by Lylas G Mogk MD & Marja Mogk PhD, Ballantine Books, 2003
[23] Read Codes became Crown property in 1999, now in process of replacement by integrated NHS SNOMED CT system by Apr 2020.

of the contrast between the ease and simplicity of using computer 'search engines' for looking things up today, and the time-consuming task it used to be in my student and professional years when I had to carry out my own detailed search of several enormous medical tomes. First, I would consult the index in each one, writing down all the possibly relevant chapters and pages on a scrap of paper like some secret code before carefully checking each reference separately to see if it bore any relationship to the information that I was looking for.

In hospital dermatology sessions we constantly (often two of us joining forces to search together) referred to three heavy volumes collectively known as the 'Rook Book' [24]. These books were so expensive that only one set could be purchased when a new edition came out. The newest went to the consultant, and the older editions were handed down the hierarchy from senior to less senior doctors until eventually the oldest set that would otherwise have been scrapped could be kept at home by one of us. I still have mine - the fourth edition - more out of sentimental than any practical value - as the illustrations are unhelpfully in black and white, and only marginally more useful for comparing your patient's skin problems than a chocolate magnifying glass might be in examining them.

As dermatology relies so much on visible appearances, I was surprised to find that I was the only doctor in that 1990s department who took advantage of the recently introduced digital camera to keep track of patient's skin appearances between visits. Even the patient's memory could be biased in some way, and laborious written ddescriptions could not convey as much as a picture which 'is worth a thousand words'.

Now I was benefiting from modern technological advancements again as I returned to my Google search. On this occasion I think I 'googled' the words 'macular degeneration' and probably also included some specific terms like 'bending light' and 'lens systems' but I was not

---

[24] 'Textbook of Dermatology' by Rook, Wilkinson, Ebling, Chapman, Burton, Blackwell Scientific, Oxford (1986)

directed to such an external lens system or another operation I have since heard about that incorporates a mini telescope into the eye[25], but amazingly, I did find help. What actually came up was the London Eye Hospital site[26] and my attention was immediately caught by the phrase: 'The revolutionary treatment for Macular Degeneration'. I discovered that a pioneering British eye surgeon, Mr Bobby Qureshi, had been inspired by the way NASA had corrected a fault in the Hubble telescope, and in collaboration with award-winning optical physicist, Professor Pablo Artal, had managed to adapt and apply this method to a lens system they had devised made of pliable material that could be inserted into the eye through a tiny incision no bigger than 3 mm.

When thinking about advances in the realm of telescopes, the mind tends to conjure up images of extremely large devices like the 250 foot (76m) Lovell Radio Telescope at Jodrell Bank Observatory with which most of us in the UK are familiar. Now in the operation devised by Mr Bobby Qureshi which I would shortly experience for myself I was about to have my outlook and my eye-sight changed by a development at the opposite end of the spectrum. Two minute lenses cleverly constructed from a special material that could be furled up to pass through a tiny incision and then restored to their original state would be carefully and separately positioned inside my eye where they would act like a little telescope.

I wish to stress here that what I had implanted in the spring and early summer of 2015 was not the Implantable Miniature Telescope (IMT) approved by the US Food and Drug Administration in 2010 which is inserted into one eye, and was first implanted in the US and more recently in the UK by CentraSight™ and VisionCare™. In this procedure, a miniature intra-ocular telescope is implanted into one eye only. The implant projects a greatly magnified image onto the retina, actually covering and extending beyond the macula which leads to a gain in visual acuity. However, this improvement comes at

---

[25] IMT - Implantable Mini Telescope CentraSight™
[26] http://www.londoneyehospital.com/treatments-services/iolamd/

the expense of peripheral vision, so that the eye without an implant has to provide this. This means that patients must adapt to using one eye for central vision and the other for peripheral vision, something that does not come naturally. To achieve this, they need to undergo special training This visual rehabilitation usually takes from six to twelve months.

A very interesting account of the IMT™ implant is given in a book by American Jim Hindman[27], the founder of 'Jiffy Lube International' and also the Hindman Foundation which has been set up to find a cure for dry AMD. He had the IMT™ operation in December 2012, and has written a truly inspirational book which tells the story not only of his experience of this operation, but also how he surmounted many challenges, overcoming the hardships of life as a street child to eventually become the founder of several businesses, four of which went public. The theme running through his book and his life is summed up in the phrase: 'Never give up, no matter how hard things get.'

The iolAMD™ implant which was carried out in both my eyes (at different times) differs from the IMT™ in that both eyes are treated in the same way. The magnification produced with the implanted lenses is not so great and therefore peripheral vision is not compromised. Two lenses are inserted. A magnifying lens replaces the body's natural lens (as in a cataract operation), while the other lens is positioned so that it bends the light to project the image onto a healthier part of the macula[28].

With the iolAMD™ implant the eyes can be used normally as before, and extensive visual rehabilitation is not required. Visual

---

[27] 'Was blind, but now I see - Life stories (and lessons) in my fight against Age Related Macular Degeneration' by Jim Hindman.
Sold by Amazon Digital Services, Inc and http://hindmanfoundation.org/.
[28] See: 'How does the iolAMD™work?' in 'APPENDIX 3 - More about Telescopic Vision -iolAMD™ for an image showing how the lenses are positioned, and a more detailed explanation of this process.

improvement will be noticed almost at once or soon after the eye has settled down post-operatively.

25. MAKING CONTACT

'Only those who risk going too far can possibly find out how far they can go.'
T S Eliot

With Mr Saj Khan – the surgeon who operated on both my eyes

On the London Hospital website that I had found on Google there were videos of happy patients reporting the great difference that having had the iolAMD™ implant operation made to their lives. I had read about the procedure in a newspaper article in 2014, but knowing just how long medical developments can take, I had assumed that it was still in the experimental stages. Fortunately for me, I found that the operation was already being offered privately in London and making a great difference to people's lives.

I wasted no time in contacting the London Eye Hospital and made an appointment for an assessment to see if I was suitable for the operation. The four hour initial investigations which took place in their

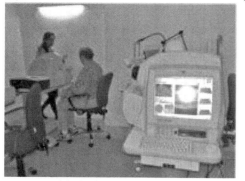

Liz being assessed

Harley Street Clinic were very thorough. First I saw an optometrist, who took my medical history and tested my eyes with the reading charts and visual examinations that would normally be done by a local optician or hospital Eye Department, but they also used several amazing machines that mapped and measured the inside of the eye in various ways.

I then saw the consultant - Mr Saj Khan - who was to carry out the operation if I was suitable, and he made his own thorough examination as well as referring to the earlier findings. We chatted a little about the Corneo Plastic Unit at East Grinstead where he and I had both worked at different times[29]. He confirmed that I had a degree of the condition known as 'Dry Eye'[30] which I had already suspected. I had started to use drops for this although only in a somewhat random fashion, but he stressed how important it was to take this condition seriously.   He advised me to use drops regularly, and even recommended one brand he had found to be effective[31]. This conversation didn't surprise me as I had already heard of his 'passion' for controlling this condition. We also spoke about the dietary supplements that he recommended for people with AMD - all of which are outlined under the 'Dry Eyes' section in this book[32].

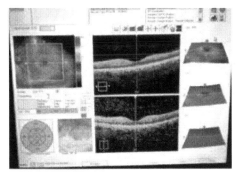 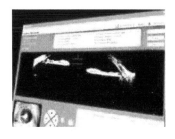

Showing the visual display of two different machines usd to measure the dimensions of the eye.   On the left, showing detail of the retina. On the right, showing the anterior chamber *(ie the area which has as its border the cornea as the outer layer and the iris the inner layer)*

I then had to look through an external lens system that mimicked what the lenses would do when they were surgically inserted into the eye during the operation. I should mention here that although I was having only the left eye operated on at this stage which was visually my worst

---

[29] I worked at the National Eye Bank in the 1980's. See Chapter 16: 'Quests & Bequests'.
[30] See Related Matters IV: 'A Dry Eye in the House?'
[31] Thealoz Duo: Related Matters IV: 'A Dry Eye in the House?'
[32] Related Matters V: 'A a Dry Eye in the House?'

eye, they were already examining and measuring both eyes in readiness for when I would be able to have the second operation. The results were all good and I elected to accept a booking to have my left eye operated on the very next day.

I wrote a Facebook message to my friend who had been very supportive to me in going for this treatment: 13th April. *'Saw eye clinic today. Will do operation tomorrow on worst eye. Slight possibility that my eye proportions are not right for lens system implant so it could fail to sit well and might need removal. Taking the chance on the possible improvement at vast expense!'*

The following day I was feeling anxious as I wrote on Facebook before the operation: *'Very apprehensive now as I contemplate this eye surgery later in the day!!'*

This resulted in several *'Thinking of you'*, *'Prayers with you'* and *'Take courage'* responses which I was so pleased to receive. I was surprised to find just how remarkably encouraging they were. It gave me the feeling that I was being supported in what I was about to experience.

26. THE OPERATION EXPERIENCE
'To the patient, any operation is momentous.'
Joseph Murray

The LONDON EYE HOSPITAL
Harley Street branch *(left)* and lower waiting area in the Wimpole Street Surgical unit *(Right)*

On the day of the operation they repeated several of the previous day's examinations to check that the measurements were consistent.

I was then started on eye-drops to dilate the pupil and anaesthetise the eye.

Because we had elected to have the operation at such short notice we had to go through several formalities to take care of the finance before the operation commenced. This was not an easy task and a bit unsettling for me, knowing that if the total cost could not be paid in advance the operation might not go ahead. For anyone considering this route, make sure you have finance ready for instant transfer if you think you might also opt for an immediate operation.

The next operation two months later (as we had a pre-booked holiday arranged) was much easier as we were able to arrange the finance in advance and take advantage of LEH's easy payment terms. However, we managed to satisfy the requirements well enough for the first operation to go ahead as planned, and so we made the short walk to the London Eye Hospital's Wimpole Street premises where the operation would be carried out.

They were running slightly late, and there were a few patients waiting ahead of us. Stewart and I chatted with several people waiting for their second eye operation, and got some helpful information about the first one and how it had gone, and what they thought of the improvement in their vision since. Drinks were available, and a friendly nurse kept checking up on us, making sure that all the patients were kept 'topped up' with pre-operative eye drops.

While I was waiting the very pleasant anaesthetist offered me an optional relaxing injection which I was not stupid enough to refuse! This clearly loosened my tongue because I reckon that during the operation I must have given Mr Khan my full professional history! At one stage he even had to request that I stop talking as I was moving my eye, and it was fortunate that he did, or else who knows what I might have gone on to say next! The eyes were well anaesthetised by the drops, and after the very advanced Femtosecond laser had been used to destroy my own lens, it was time for the part that everyone hates the thought of, including me! I was told I might feel a little pressure from the 'injection' but I was pleasantly surprised that

155

insertion of the new lenses through the tiny incision was completely pain-free.

In the waiting room we had noticed patients were taking about 40 minutes to return to their seats after leaving for the operation, and it was exactly the same for me as I sat back down beside Stewart in my comfortable reclining chair with a patch and eye-shield over my left eye. I felt great, especially as the worst had been faced and I had proved for myself that it really was painless.

The nurse asked me to stay at the clinic until she was happy that I had recovered enough to walk the short distance to our hotel. This recovery period took about 15 minutes, and while I was waiting she supplied me with a neat little carrier bag [33] with the London Eye Hospital logo on the front. In it were three kinds of drops (steroid, antibiotic, and non-steroidal anti-inflammatory) which I had to use over the next few weeks in various dosages, plus a chart with the times for using the drops, clearly marked, ready for me to fill in. The bottle of sterile water and antiseptic hand-cleansing agent supplied were to make sure I did not introduce infection when I applied the drops, and these were very helpful on the long train journey back to Plymouth. There was also a spare plastic ventilated eye-shield, because although the dressing was due to be removed the next morning, it was important to wear an eye-shield overnight for the following two weeks to prevent accidental trauma to the eyes.

The last item in the bag was a leaflet outlining the post-operative instructions [34] that I needed to follow, and an emergency contact number which I am glad to say I had no need of. Indeed, I felt remarkably well after the operation, and sent my friend a second email to let her know how it had gone: 'Operation between 1610hrs and 1719hrs went well. Now in hotel about to go out to Pizza Express. No food since 0730hrs. Mimicking Nelson with patch!!'

---

[33] See pictures in Related Matters V :TLC for your Eyes - Eye Routines
[34] An outline of these and general lid hygiene will be found in Related Matters V :TLC for your Eyes - Eye Routines

156

At my check-up on the next day the optometrist ran more tests to check that all was well and the lenses were in a satisfactory position. Although it had only been a short time since the operation, I could already tell that my vision was greatly improved, and the optometrist was very pleased. As I would not get a prescription for new spectacles until after my next appointment the following week I got a local optician to remove the lens from my spectacles on the operated side as this correction was no longer valid.

When I next attended the clinic the optometrist was clearly delighted with the results. My visual acuity had already improved from 6/120 to 6/19[35], and as the swelling caused by the operation had now settled I was given a new prescription for separate near and far vision spectacles to take to a dispensing optician. The optometrist said I should not consider bifocals at this stage as I would have enough to cope with learning to adjust as one eye was currently long-sighted and the other short-sighted.

Pre-operation on 13th April, the vision in my left eye had been 6/120. By 11th June it was 6/15, and on 23rd June it was 6/12[36] which was four lines better than the two lines of improvement predicted on the assessment mock-up. No wonder on my arrival I was greeted with the words, "The doctors are very pleased with you." There had been a total improvement of six lines - an amazing result!

On holiday between the operations I soon found that modern clothing, particularly for females, seems to lack enough pockets in which to keep and easily identify all the different spectacles and magnifiers I now needed (Distance, left pocket, Near vision, right pocket etc). Handbags, as any man will tell you, are bottomless pits of long lost objects, and as I normally try to manage without, I usually succeed in leaving a bag behind somewhere when I am forced to use one. I began to wonder if they produced handyman or gardener's tool-belts

---

[35] Nearly 20/60 US
[36] 20/40 US

157

in gold lamé or another attractive fabric as those were the only things I could think of that might have done the trick!

In the end, I found it easiest to keep both pairs of spectacles hanging round my neck, one on a chain and the other on a strand of strong, sparkly knitting yarn that matched most of my outfits. This was both reasonably presentable and practical for identifying each of the glasses, while the two different materials made them less likely to get tangled up. The glasses themselves, however, were rather apt to collect crumbs and drips at mealtimes if they were not removed. I eventually gave up the struggle to manage with two pairs of glasses, because in spite of these measures, I always seemed to have the wrong ones on, and constantly swapping the two made me feel vulnerable to eye trauma as I worried I might accidentally jab my eyes with the spectacle arms. So I went back to wearing my old bifocals with one lens removed as I had done post-operatively while I waited for my new spectacle prescription.

The operated eye was made to work without any visual correction at all. I managed quite well with this, but I have to say that although I could see clearly, there seemed to be a different quality about what I was seeing through the left eye. Right until the end of my holiday I was still saying that I was not sure how I felt about having two eyes like this, although it might also have been something to do with how the brightness and glare were affecting it, but just a week before the second operation everything felt good to proceed and it went ahead on 11th June, two days after our return from holiday. A Facebook entry from 9th June reads: *'Liz Lenton feeling concerned! It would mean a lot to me to know that I would be in the thoughts and prayers of my friends as I travel to London tomorrow for an operation on the other eye on Thursday around 11am.'*

I had a different anaesthetist for the second operation. This time it was a woman who had worked at a hospital in Redhill, Surrey where years previously I had done dermatology sessions – what a small medical world it was turning out to be! Once more I elected to have the relaxing medication, but this time it made me sleep throughout the procedure! Was this by the request of the surgeon to keep me quiet?! I have to say that at neither operation did I feel any discomfort. Afterwards I walked from Wimpole Street all the way to the RAF Club near Hyde Park Corner where we stayed the night. On returning home, my 12th June Facebook entry read: *'Thank you everyone for all your kind thoughts, prayers and good wishes. I am back home now after a pretty successful trip. The first eye has exceeded their expectations and already the newly operated one is doing very well. I am not using any spectacles at all at present and managing pretty well. Will see the clinic again next week, and perhaps get a prescription for specs then. Eyes are different and the first was reading better without correction at all. It is so good to have got to this stage!'*

It is interesting now for me to look back and see how much I was depending on the prayers and thoughts of others. It felt so much better when I knew they were 'with me', rather like the team effort that was needed to get to the top of Cader Idris in my schooldays at DWS.

27. RESULTS
'Beauty is in the eye of the beholder.'
Plato

My Mother with glasses

I have had to get used to my face without glasses again, and at first I did not like it! My mother used to wear 'Dame Edna Everage' [37] style elaborate spectacle frames and one of the things I had needed to adjust to in the ageing process was looking in the mirror and seeing my mother! After my operations I could see those familiar features in ever greater detail every time I looked in the mirror. There was no disguising the fact that I was no longer a spring chicken! But something was missing – it took me a while to realise it was the embellishment of those elaborate spectacle frames!

---

[37] Comedy female character played by Australian comedian Barry Humphries

Imagine my joy when at my first choir practice after my second operation I was able to read my words and music with the naked eye in normal size print just like anybody else, although my ability to do this was still very dependent on lighting conditions. Another delight happened when I was showering. As I reached for the shampoo to wash my hair, I was about to call Stewart as usual to get him to make sure I had got the right bottle and not the conditioner when I found that I could read not only the word 'Shampoo' but also the instructions in small print!

My visual acuities before the operations were only CF (counting fingers) in my left eye, and 6/30 (20/100) on the Snellen's chart in my right eye. At my last check-up with my glasses on I could just about read 6/12 (20/40) with my left eye and 6/19 (20/63) with my right eye. Using both eyes together I was just below the visual standard required to drive, but I have been told that my eyes might still show further improvement as my brain continues to adapt. However, it took a little while to read the charts to my best ability as I had to spend a few seconds focussing on each letter. I would be no good at reading the number plate on a speeding getaway car from a distance!

The right eye required a slightly stronger spectacle correction and took longer to settle, and although it achieved the predicted improvement, it did not quite match the success of my first eye which far exceeded all expectations and, as already mentioned, went well beyond the pre-operative forecast I had been given.

Although pre-operatively the left eye had been my worst eye, when I looked at pictures of the retina I could see there was less density of drusen (the damage caused by dry AMD) in that eye than in the right. As success in the operation is bound to be determined by the quality of the available tissue on which the light is to re-focus, this may account for the difference in visual acuity between the two eyes post-operatively.

I found after my first operation that because I now had one eye that saw better than the other, I developed a tendency to close my weaker eye and use the other when doing fine work so my optometrists advised me to put a patch on the good eye to force the other to work on its own. I followed the same procedure after my second operation to force the newly operated eye to work, and also then had to patch each eye at different times to force them both to work.

In spite of this, I managed quite well without any external correction for my vision for nearly three months while waiting for my bifocal prescription to be made up. Stewart had to keep reminding me when I got frustrated about my vision (usually with difficult lighting conditions) that I was not wearing any spectacles at all! It was as if I had gone back 35 years to the stage when I had just started to need reading glasses! In fact, I wrote virtually the whole text of this book in about 6 weeks without glasses, and recently when I rushed into a supermarket to get a couple of items I was able to glance down the rows of shelves and quickly pick out what I wanted for myself. I even managed to find Stewart who had left me to go to the checkout!

However, the AMD is still there. The operation is not a cure, and I still have a few less sharp areas of vision and continue to need to look slightly to the side of a face on TV if, for example, I want to see if I really fancy the bloke with the nice voice! One thing did worry me though - the face cream that was supposed to sort out ageing skin did not seem to be working any more. I had wrinkles!

28. A MEETING WITH THE MAKER
'Per ardua ad astra.'
'Through struggle to the stars.'
RAF Motto

It could seem a little perverse that I use the RAF motto to head this section which is not about the RAF at all, but I think you will understand why when you have read this chapter.

When I contacted the London Eye Hospital (LEH) to see if somebody could help me make sure I had all my facts about the lenses and the operation right, I did not expect to be offered an appointment with the very busy Medical Director himself, Consultant Ophthalmic Surgeon, Mr Bobby Qureshi. I had been disappointed not to meet him on previous LEH visits, and I was very much looking forward to doing so now, not only because he was the person who had invented the lens system that restored my vision after I had been told it was impossible, but also because I knew from the website that he had attended St Andrews University where I had also studied, although I very much doubted we would have a chance to talk about that.

Stewart and I took the train from Plymouth to Paddington, but, as it looked like rain, we didn't walk as we'd done for my spring and summer appointments when we'd enjoyed winding our way through the quieter back streets, making sure we passed a certain well stocked Lebanese grocer's shop to purchase authentic Turkish delight as a thank-you gift for our cat-sitters. Instead, we took the bus down Oxford Street where the Christmas lights had just been switched on, although it was not yet dark enough to get the full effect. In passing, we caught a glimpse of the attractive window displays at Selfridges, although I was sorry not to see jolly Uncle Holly of my youth welcoming children into Santa's Grotto - a Christmas character that Stewart's father had introduced when he was a manager there in the 50s.

Having been well supplied with coffee and tea on the train, we did not help ourselves this time from the fascinating dispenser in the now very familiar waiting room at LEH which automatically delivered a variety of drinks, chosen by pressing a picture on a small computer screen. After our appointment, I couldn't help thinking that this ingenious drinks machine might also have been designed by the

medical director himself. As we passed the reception desk, the glass bowl filled with discarded spectacles waiting to be sent to LEH's overseas charity caught my attention. It reminded me of the church of 'Our Lady of Ta Pinu' on the Maltese Island

Unwanted spectacles being collected for the LEH Trust

of Gozo, a place of pilgrimage where people left crutches and other objects testifying to miracles of healing.

162

Mr Bobby Qureshi was welcoming and relaxed as he ushered us into a consulting room and introduced himself, "Since I designed the lenses, I thought you would be better off talking to me." He struck me as a man who was easy to speak to and not at all remote or self-important, although he told us quite frankly about his achievements without false modesty. He revealed that there had, of course, been setbacks, but he had dealt with criticism by listening to it carefully as he thought you could always learn something, although he also said he never allowed such things to put him off reaching the goals he had set himself.

Stewart & Me meeting with Mr Bobby Querishi

I need not have worried about briefing myself on the train because this easy-mannered young man (mid-fortyish - so young to me!) knew exactly what I wanted to hear about. He talked quickly as if to give us as much information as possible in the hour we spent with him, and Stewart, who was helping me by taking notes so I could concentrate on what this fascinating man was saying, was soon struggling to keep up. In the end he also got so interested that he gave up note-taking altogether.

What was it that made Bobby Qureshi go into this particular area of endeavour? From a child he enjoyed programming computers to

163

solve problems - they were his playthings - he loved mathematics, deriving great pleasure from solving equations at a stage when most of us would be content with nothing more challenging than noughts and crosses! He had a passion for astronomy, but instead of buying him a telescope his wealthy father gave him the basic tools to build his own. By age eight, Bobby was grinding lenses by hand to make his telescope as good as it could be!

He seemed ideally suited, and possibly uniquely talented, to become the person who would later develop lens systems to solve problems with human vision, but following a medical career was not his original ambition. As he indulged his love of astronomy, gazing towards the stars and identifying different celestial bodies through that first telescope, he became familiar with the world of the sky and wanted to get an even closer look, so he decided that he would become an astronaut. Ironically, it was his eyesight that put an end to that ambition, but I must say, "Thank God," because what a loss he would have been to ophthalmology, especially for AMD sufferers like myself, if his vision had been as exceptionally good as we were rapidly realising his brain was!

We asked about his home and background, and he told us that he was born in England and lived in Windsor and Epsom in his early years, although his family roots were Saudi Arabian. His father started his professional life as a barrister, but changed to medicine and became a cardiologist! There was no lack of money in the family, but neither did there appear to be any shortage of intelligence. All his siblings went to different schools up and down the country, each specifically chosen for them by Bobby's parents, and all of them became legal or medical professionals. Bobby's brothers followed him into medicine, later joining him at Guy's & St Thomas' teaching hospital in London where he did his clinical year after sensibly spending his initial years at St Andrews University. It was at Guy's and Tommy's that he met Mr Saj Khan who would eventually join him at LEH. This was the surgeon who actually performed my eye operations. Bobby's father hoped his son would follow him into cardiology, but once Bobby started working with eyes he was so

164

intrigued by the subject that the die was cast. He decided his future lay in ophthalmology.

However, although he gained considerable experience over a number of years in the NHS, notably at the prestigious Moorfield's Eye Hospital in London, he found the system could be frustrating as there was little opportunity to develop innovative ideas for new and better treatments and devices. Bobby was full of enthusiasm and wanted a chance to put his own ideas quickly into practice as he was convinced they would benefit numerous patients, but this was difficult under such bureaucratic constraints. His philosophy was quite simple. When he encountered patients with eye problems which were currently untreatable, he saw it as his responsibility to find a means to help them.

Fortunately, he had been blessed with financial independence and was willing to use this to obtain the necessary clinical freedom to develop his ideas and put them into practice as soon as possible to achieve success and benefit his patients. What could give a better expression for his talents than to found a totally independent hospital in the area of London best known for private medicine? Accordingly, Bobby Qureshi became the founder and Chief Medical Officer of The London Eye Hospital in 2005, followed by the London Eye Hospital Pharma in 2012.

His ambition was for LEH to become cutting-edge so he could offer the best corrective surgery available to treat various eye conditions. To do this he knew he would require excellent examination equipment, some of which had not even been designed yet, in order to obtain the precise measurements of the eye needed for the innovative operations he had in mind, while the creation of specialised instruments to perform these delicate operations that had never been done before was also necessary.

In addition, he wanted to ensure that the most effective dietary supplements and other pharmaceutical products for eye treatment and eye-care in line with the latest research and findings were made available at LEH Pharma.

Not only was he able to do this in London, but he was also invited to establish a state-of-the-art Eye Hospital in Abu Dhabi by wealthy rulers of Middle Eastern countries. Remarkably, the design of this hospital seen from the air seems to resemble the London Eye Hospital logo which, at first sight, looks like an iris surrounding a central pupil. However, the logo is actually not a pictorial image at all, but a design Bobby produced himself based on a mathematical formula. Plans are also under way for a clinic in Jersey and an eye unit in Shanghai[38].

Stewart and I both sat absolutely spellbound listening to Bobby as he told us about the progression from the first early attempts at using lens systems for AMD sufferers. He explained how each of the older systems had originally been meant to work, what their limitations were, and how he had devised modifications to overcome these problems. He admitted that it had not all been plain sailing, but he was obviously not a man who would give up just because he faced a setback. Each obstacle was just another problem for which there had to be a solution - it was just a case of persevering until he found it.

A fortuitous friendship helped Bobby turn his ideas about what kind of lens was necessary to overcome certain visual problems into reality. He was able to gain the co-operation of Professor Pablo Artal - the first ever European winner of the prestigious 'Edward H Land' award for scientific contributions to the advancement of visual optics – and together they set out to tackle the historical challenges of AMD treatment. Sometimes it was a question of Bobby Qureshi persuading Professor Artal that he could provide a lens to fit the seemingly impossible specifications they needed, but sure enough eventually a suitable lens would emerge.

---

[38] http://s3-us-west-
.amazonaws.com/wdm/designer_uploads/Widgets/BR_EU/2012/12-Dec12-Jan13/BRO-BRE-London+Eye+Hospital-HCG-DecJan13-spreadwidget.pdf

Although there were several 'firsts' for Bobby Qureshi and the LEH, my interest from the point of view of writing this book was naturally the process of developing a lens system for AMD sufferers. Bobby explained that the early attempts to introduce lenses to deal with AMD were rather like the very first cataract extraction operations which required large incisions and several stitches to close the surgical wound which meant they were more prone to operative and post-operative complications and required a much longer time to heal. In comparing these to the operations he now does with only tiny 3mm incisions, the difference is like that between the old style major surgery involved in something like a gall bladder operation compared to the modern key-hole techniques of today.

Bobby had himself used an early development of a double lens system called AMDVIP, the VIP here standing for Visually Impaired Person [39] where the two implanted AMDVIP lenses were made of PMMA (a material similar to perspex), the same substance used for over 50 years in cataract implants. The complications of these operations were also similar to those early cataract extractions, ie, mainly due to infection.

Intraocular telescopic lenses had also been developed for AMD sufferers in the form of the pea-sized miniature telescope or IMT (Implantable Mini Telescope) already mentioned [40] but this could not be inserted through such a small incision.

Using two lenses to act like an intraocular Galilean telescope to refocus the image onto a different part of the retina is a complex technique. One major problem is that people's eyes are of different dimensions, but the distance between the lenses must not vary if optimal clarity of vision is to be achieved. In addition, if the internal dimensions of an eye are too large, it may prevent successful insertion of the lenses altogether.

---

[39] You can still see these devices advertised on the internet by clinics.
[40] In Chapter 24: 'New Lenses -Two for One'

With Bobby's interest in all things astronomical, the news that the Hubble telescope had encountered problems with producing sharp images that turned out to be due to spherical aberration inspired a new and exciting train of thought. Was it possible that the adaptive optics used to correct this fault in the Hubble telescope could be applied in a similar way to lenses for correcting AMD? His hunch turned out to be right, and when the two pioneers achieved success with iolAMD™□, it transpired that the system was also more tolerant of some variation in distances between the lenses.

The new iolAMD™□ lenses developed by Pablo Artal are made from advanced hydrophobic acrylic and contain hyper-aspheric surfaces and unique wavefront characteristics that reduce optical distortions normally associated with high powered lenses as well as creating an increased tolerance of relative lens positioning. Furthermore, as already mentioned, the new lenses are pliable and capable of being furled up and introduced into the eye through a tiny incision, making the procedure less traumatic and less prone to the operative and post-operative complications of older lenses.

During our conversation Bobby touched on other contemporary research solutions providing treatments for AMD; for example, stem cells and 'bionic eye implants', while he also explained the basic concept of Ellex 2 RT™□[41] in simple terms. He thought in the future it might even be possible to use treatment combinations, and is looking forward to greater co-operation between the proponents of these fields.

When he was explaining the new iolAMD™□ EyeMax, he told us about a useful instrument, the MIA (Macular Integrity Assessor), which grades and colour codes the sight ability of various parts of the retina from good to fair to nil. (I had already been examined with this during my initial and later assessments). Observations of post-op patients after iolAMD™□ EyeMax using the MIA indicated that their vision had continued to gradually improve after the operation as the

---

[41] See Related Matters VIII :More Cause for Hope?

brain itself has the capacity to sort out which areas of the macula to use.

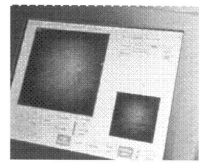

The MIA (Macular Integrity Assessor) that maps the best areas of a patient's vision. Coloured according to best, fair and no vision

In chatting, I mentioned that I wanted the profits from my book to benefit eye charities, and it was then that Bobby revealed his own desire to have trachoma eradicated. This devastating eye disease needlessly causes much misery and blindness in poorer parts of the world due to the lack of safe drinking water supplies and antibiotics. I have since discovered that Bobby has pledged huge sums from iolAMD™□ proceeds to his charity London Eye Hospital Trust which aims to totally eradicate trachoma.[42]

Surprisingly, we even got a chance to compare notes about our student days in St Andrews. After spending his first year in St Salvator's ('Sallie's'), one of the student halls of residence, he bought a house in Hope Street which seems a very appropriate name as 'hope' is something I am trying to impart in this book, and what he also aims to give through his pioneering eye operations. Funnily enough, his house was next door to the student house where Jenn was living when I met her and she invited me to share her uncle's flat. Our 'student prince' also once lived on this same street together with another student, Kate Middleton, who later became his wife.

After this extraordinary meeting with Bobby Qureshi we walked back along Oxford Street admiring the Christmas lights shining in the

---

[42] http://www.dubaiprnetwork.com/pr.asp?pr=91785

darkness, although since my eye operations I can find the dazzling effect of such bright lights quite difficult. I held Stewart's hand as we walked and talked about how inspiring the whole interview had been. We now had a chance to enjoy the close-up view of Selfridges' windows denied from the bus, and somehow it seemed very fitting after our meeting with Bobby that one window housed an intriguing moving model of the universe.

On the train home I was considering what to write about Bobby Qureshi in this book where my own life has been outlined, and I could not help thinking that there could not have been a greater contrast between the two of us. It seemed audacious even to consider myself beside him as he is of a totally different calibre. My career path has been haphazard, governed by circumstances rather than any drive to achieve success in a particular field. My original goals were not set much higher than my medical degree, whereas for him this was just a starting point as he literally reached for the stars.

Bobby has the rare combination of a unique talent and the focus and ability to apply it, and in his case I actually think the term 'genius' is merited. He has a vision of what is possible and pursues it with undaunted enthusiasm. I can only admire him from afar and thank Heaven for him.

29. THE END OF SHELF LIFE

'Ideas have a short shelf life. You must act on them before the expiration date.'
John C. Maxwell

This book, although intended to give hope to sufferers from Age-Related Macular Degeneration, has not just been about that condition. I have also shared much about my life and beliefs; in fact, more than I intended when I started out, but I just could not write without doing so.

The word 'age' in the condition cannot be ignored because we are talking about one of the many things that happen to people as they grow older. To some extent, this has been covered in the chapter 'Sell-by Date' but I did not talk about something we 'oldies' must all think about even if few of us ever mention it, much as we might like to. This subject, although I have seen much of it, especially as a GP and in two of my other jobs - 'Care of the Elderly' and 'Psychiatry for the Elderly', is one in which I am no expert because there are none! This is an event that when I finally experience it, I will be in no position to tell you about it!

I don't know if my elderly readers have ever gone through a phase of questioning the things we made up our mind about when we were younger. Stewart and I have met regularly with a group of friends who are no longer, shall we say, in the first flush of youth. Our ages have varied within 10 to 15 years. This does not seem to matter so much as you get older, unlike when you are children and have little in common with those not your own age. The composition of our group has also varied, and it is not always the oldest who have permanently left us first. That is part of the problem; there is nothing entirely predictable about our exit from this mortal stage - other than knowing that exit there must be! Even when the greater odds against us like more years in the balance or growing infirmity are taken into account, the race to the finish can be won by a complete outsider with no form at all!

In this group we 'debate' various issues over coffee, ranging from current affairs to matters philosophical or theological. It seems that each of us is less sure now of the things we were so clear about in our youth. As we look back on our lives privately, we would like to think they had amounted to something. Have we been right about the paths we decided to follow and the beliefs that underpinned our efforts? Have we really followed through with the things that we profess to be passionate about? Much of our expertise is outmoded and we ourselves feel redundant. It is possibly too late to make significant changes that might impact the world now, however vibrant our ambition to do so remains. What about our deeply held beliefs? These are once more being tested.

Writing this book has helped me. Perhaps everyone should go through some formal written exercise in writing down the stages and changes that have occurred through their whole lifetime. Those who believe that they must balance the good against the evil they have done will have a harder task. I think that those who believe they may have earned themselves another, perhaps better life, will still have uncertainty, while those who believe they live on through their children, be they their biological offspring or their good works, creations or establishments, would not see in what I have told them of my own story any future hope for me at all.

Looking back has certainly made me see how amazingly fortunate I have been against all the odds. In return, wretch that I am, I have done little that amounts to anything. I would like to be able to show something in return, if only for the great kindnesses and, at times, sacrificial help I have received along life's pathway from others. If only I had repaid more into the general pot... but then I never could have done enough. You cannot 'out-give' God himself. For that is who I am convinced that ultimately I am indebted to. Not only for giving me my life here, but for defeating death so that I can fearlessly face whatever... whenever... because, when I look back, like footsteps in the sand I see the mark throughout my life of the 'Good Shepherd'. Why should He cease to be with me now?

'Yea, when I pass through the valley of the shadow of death, I shall fear no evil, For You are with me; Your rod and Your staff, they comfort me. For have not goodness and mercy followed me all the days of my life? So I will dwell in the house of the Lord forever.'
(Adapted from Psalm 23)

Now I have reached the end of my story and what I can tell you about macular degeneration from a personal viewpoint. I will leave you to read the useful information contained in the 'Related Matters' section, and as one pilot of a dual controlled aircraft would say when handing over to the other:

"YOU HAVE CONTROL!"

RELATED MATTERS

'It's not what happens to you, but how you react to it that matters.'
Epictetus

This section is for those who may wish to read something further about AMD and related topics rather than putting off taking it seriously like me because there are few or no symptoms in the early stages of this condition. As I have already stated, I do not profess to be an expert on this subject so all the information in this section consists of things I have discovered for myself and found helpful. Hopefully, you will too!

However, always consult your own medical or optical advisers about what is suitable for you.

Hindsight is a wonderful thing. I now wish I had researched the condition when it was first diagnosed as I could have done a number of positive things to help my vision like taking AREDS medication (see Appendix 4) or taking steps to prevent dry eyes (Related Matters IV) or making sure I protected my eyes against UV/blue light by wearing good wrap-around tinted or reflective glasses (Appendix 5).

I. My Favourite Things - Helpful Devices

'When all else fails read the instructions.' (If you can!)
Ralph Waldo Emerson

I thought it was important to add something about devices I have found helpful in my struggle with failing vision. However, I do not claim to be an authority on the subject and have also been fortunate enough to receive a timely intervention with surgical treatment before I experienced the worst of the end stage of dry AMD. Therefore, I am very aware that you may actually have more experience than I do. However, perhaps I will mention something you have not considered before, or you may be prompted by something I say to seek out more expert or in-depth help, or take the step of consulting a low vision specialist if you have not already done so. The most important advice I can give is that you speak to an expert before you act on anything you read here, particularly if it involves parting with your money.

Incidentally, I have continued to use some of the things mentioned here even since my successful eye operations; for example, to read printing on food packaging where often the list of ingredients and/or cooking instructions seems to be in some sort of competition to find the smallest print possible! Even after an operation you are unlikely to emerge with the good eyesight you had in your teens, and what post middle-aged person is not thankful for a little magnification of very small print now and then? So may I suggest that you do not 'throw away your crutches' just yet!

Also, there is still no cure for AMD yet, so it may continue to progress and deprive you of some of the ground you have gained at a later date. In the case of my operation that could mean further surgery to adjust the lenses to re-focus on a healthier area, although recent advances[43] mean that they can now insert a lens that allows the brain to make its own adjustment so that a better area can be selected without any further operation.

---

[43] See Chapters 30 - 'A Meeting with the Maker'.& Related Matters IX 'More Cause for Hope?'

Television

Like many people, Stewart and I find that we rely on TV to effortlessly update us on the latest news and current affairs, even if the rest of the time we find ourselves endlessly flicking through the countless choice of programmes now available, only to complain that there is nothing worth watching that we have not already seen at least twice. Our video-recorder is of course useful when the only programme we've wanted to watch all week clashes with something else we're doing, but for AMD or low vision sufferers an extra benefit of video recorders or DVD players is that you can also pause or rewind if you haven't been able to see what is happening clearly enough to catch up with the storyline.

If, like me, you suffer from deafness, it can also be helpful to rewind to hear what was said if you didn't manage to catch it first time round. Although we frequently find these days that even when we do that, we still cannot understand what was meant! I must say that there have been plenty of funny moments when I've heard something that simply rhymes with what is being said, sometimes with hilarious results. I was listening without watching the TV news one morning and thought it was talking about 'High Street chains' but it seemed to make no sense at all until I realised they were actually talking about 'high speed trains'! On another occasion, I was puzzled to hear that somebody worked in a 'butcher's' but what had really been said was that they worked in a 'bookshop'!

Stewart did not find his own view of the screen was enhanced when I moved my chair ever nearer to sit almost on top of it or stood beside it to see better, so, in spite of the limitations already mentioned, we decided for once to hang the expense, and buy the largest TV we could manage in our living room without making it look like an ostentatious home cinema.

The one we already had was neither old nor small, so I made the minor sacrifice of allowing it to perch on my dressing table top as it was too large for the TV wall bracket and I could easily use the bathroom mirror for my daily routines which these days are more likely to consist of eye drops than eyeliner. This larger bedroom TV has also helped enormously as we can more comfortably finish our evening viewing in bed, and watch the morning news with our early morning cuppa, while I also use it to test which area around the side of the announcer's face I need to focus on to see his/her facial features more clearl

VISUAL AIDS

CCTV video camera-based devices

Table- top CCTV device

As my eyesight worsened, I started to make more use of a large table-top CCTV video camera-based device lent to me by a sister-in-law that could be used to project an enlarged printed document onto its screen. This useful, albeit bulky, expensive device could be adjusted to show optional colour contrast, while the magnification of the projected image could also be changed. At first, I only used it to help me write in the squares of crossword puzzles, a task that I had been finding quite difficult, but I soon also started using it to help me read the rest of the newspaper, rather than wait for Stewart to read it out to me later. However, the CCTV device really came into its own for reading all the small print detail on documents - the kind that can often land you in trouble if you don't read them when you only find out too late that there is some important exclusion clause 'hidden in the small print'.

This table-top CCTV device had to be plugged into the mains, so, although it could be moved, it was not really 'portable'. As the dry AMD progressed, I also wanted to have something that would help me outside the home so I I invested in two similar, but smaller, battery operated devices, a 'mini' portable pocket-sized one that helped me read things like labels when shopping, and a slightly larger device with a handle that could convert to a stand. Unfortunately, neither was any use in helping me read my music in the choir because they only focused on a small area at a time, and it was far too awkward to move them along and still keep up with the pace of the music.

One noticeable change when you start getting symptoms from AMD is how much longer it takes you to do everything. Life moves into the slow lane as you struggle to do everyday routines. Selecting matching ear rings from your jewellery box is difficult enough, but putting the little keepers on them the right way round can be a real battle, while you may spend ages looking for a missing kitchen tool only to discover that it has been in the drawer with the others the whole time. If you are like me, you may also need to take extra care that your food is deposited in your mouth and not down your front so that you do not end up wearing it because you may not notice that you are!

Some people with advanced vision loss go to great lengths to organise their whole wardrobe so that outfits with colours that go together and any accompanying matching or contrasting accessories are kept on the same hanger or close to hand to minimise the difficulties that can be caused when getting dressed.[44] Of course, doing this has the added advantage of making sure you do not select a pair of navy blue trousers to wear with your black jacket! Mind you, even before I had any AMD symptoms, my boss asked me one day whether it was a new fashion to be wearing a pink earring in one ear and a blue one in the other! Many an RAF officer has been caught out wearing brightly coloured socks instead of black uniform ones because he got dressed in the dark when leaving for an early morning duty rather than disturb the wife by putting on the light on. Even though such mistakes are common among people with normal vision, it somehow matters more to avoid making them when you

---

[44] More helpful tips like this can be found in: 'Was blind, but now I see: Life stories (and lessons) in my fight against Age-Related Macular Degeneration' by Jim Hindman. Sold by Amazon Digital Services, Inc.

have visual problems, but try not to let things like this stress you unduly, and, if you haven't already done so, learn to laugh at yourself!

Perhaps I should say here that possibly the best equipment I was advised to acquire when I started to suffer the effects of dry AMD was a sense of humour! The old adage applies here: 'Laugh, and the world laughs with you. Weep, and you weep alone.'

Enlargements and Magnifiers

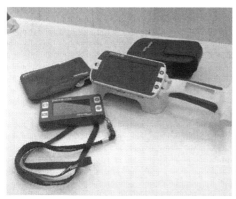

Portable Mini sized Devices

Various simple magnifiers the large one has a light built in. and the small black item is a clip on light. The dome shaped magnifier has a measuring scale built in.

It must seem pretty obvious to everyone that magnifiers are essential, but not all of them are equal and it is important that you seek advice about purchasing these if you require anything other than a small degree of magnification.

Next to attempting to develop that all-important sense of humour, my most useful piece of AMD equipment was the folding pair of magnifying lorgnettes mentioned earlier[45], but as they were more of an 'antique' and designed to be used by anyone for simple magnification needs, they would not necessarily be so suitable for those with low vision eye problems.

---

[45] Chapter 21; 'Music and Choir.'

Magnifiers not only come in all shapes and sizes but also different magnification strengths, and often need to be held at a specific distance away from you and what you wish to examine to work properly. It can all be rather complicated and so it is better to seek advice from a low vision specialist if you have need of very strong magnification or require magnification for a specific task. One useful magnifier device even fits on to your existing spectacles, rather like some sunshades, and is very helpful as it frees up your hands to do other things. Magnifiers also come with or without lights, with or without stands, and with different types of handles. This means you can generally find something that will ease the performance of particular tasks such as reading or sewing, playing the piano or helping you see where you are going when out walking. When purchasing a magnifier, the first thing you need to ask yourself is: *'What do I want to use it for?'* You may even find that you come away with an assortment of devices to meet different purposes. Well, nobody said that having AMD was going to be easy on your purse, particularly if you do not qualify for any assistance which is another subject to seek expert advice on.

However, before I leave the subject of magnifiers I must not forget binoculars. It may seem to be stating the obvious to say that binoculars can 'amplify' your vision, although this is actually at the expense of your field of view which is then smaller, but some people find it very useful to have a pair handy to gain greater clarity on small details; for example, if you want to look at something on the opposite side of the road. I was prompted to mention their usefulness after a trip to the theatre where they really were essential, even better than the old coin-in-the-slot opera glasses still found in some theatres.

As well as making use of the text enlargement facilities on computers, Kindles, iPads, etc, you can find enlarged versions of print books in libraries, while many public places like restaurants, museums and churches also offer helpful large print versions of items like menus, catalogues, orders of service, hymn books and programmes, although you may need to ask for them.

I have already mentioned in Chapter 21: 'Music and Choir' how useful I found it to have my music copied onto the largest size paper even if I later had to cut it up to make the pages more manageable, and this is equally helpful for any type of document you need to read aloud or learn by heart. I made use of this technique when I played the part of an ancient storyteller at a social gathering we held in our house last Christmas Eve. I had large print prompting sentences pasted in strips inside my 'story book'. Serious musicians can obtain software online[46] that can enlarge any sheet music in a matter of minutes, while there are other special devices to help you read things written on a notice board, blackboard or presentation display at a distance. You can also find many different sizes and types of telescopes, binoculars and monoculars designed to help you maximise your vision for specific tasks, sports, hobbies or entertainments.

Electronic Devices: Kindle, E-Readers, tablets

I am so glad that, in spite of having no grandchildren to help us, Stewart and I have launched ourselves into the world of digital technology, albeit to a limited extent. We have each used the technology for slightly different applications, so that when things go 'pear shaped' we can sometimes help each other out as the other will often have already experienced a similar problem and found a solution.

If you have not used these types of devices before or lack confidence, I would recommend that you enrol on one of the many 'Computers for the Elderly' courses held in various venues like colleges or schools because this technology is really helpful to those with low vision, as well as providing many other enjoyable advantages such as looking things up on the internet, online shopping, and keeping in contact with people by email or social media which is a real lifesaver when you can't get out so much.

---

[46]http://www.largeprintmusic.com/

The non-computer literate may find some things that I say here rather confusing and possibly off-putting, although I would recommend persevering as the benefits offered are very real, and the 'gobbledegook' of 'computer speak' will begin to make sense much quicker than you think. I know when I first launched into the world of computers, long before I had my visual problems, I got completely out of my depth at first and relied heavily on my more computer literate friends, but I soon discovered that the assistants in computer shops or manning telephone computer help-lines were very used to dunces like me who didn't know a 'pixel' from a megabyte' and didn't seem to mind my idiotic questions.

They don't bat an eyelid when, for the third time, they have to take you through the simple task of turning your computer ON! You are unlikely to be the first more mature person they have come across who is a total beginner, even if it is like 'mother's milk' to the younger generation. I found that a good salesperson, especially when the shop or department was not too busy, was more than willing to explain things. Tell computer sales people exactly what you want to use the equipment for, and then they can advise you on what you really need and talk you through the basics. After all, they want a sale! However, if you do decide to invest in a computer or laptop or any other electronic device, don't be rushed into buying anything before you are ready.

I would also like to encourage you to ask the salespeople if any help is available to teach you how to get the most from your device. I know that 'Apple' stores in the UK have free hour-long workshops for people of all experience levels, offering topics that range from basic computer skills to more specialist subjects like editing photos online or creating the perfect spreadsheet. They even have an 'accessibility' class specifically for people with disabilities, including poor vision. However, all classes and workshops need to be booked in advance which can be done online or in store. Apple also have an online help facility where you can book a phone appointment with an advisor or alternatively opt for an 'online chat' where you type your questions and they will type a message back.

Many electronic devices can be modified for use by the visually handicapped. For example, on the Control Panel on a Microsoft system you can select 'Ease of Access' image (©Microsoft) This directs you to 'Quick access to common tools' where you can:

• Start magnifier

• Start an on-screen Keyboard

• Start Narrator (which will read text aloud in your choice of voice, volume, or speed).

• Set up High Contrast.

Below the 'Quick access' section there are a whole host of other options that can be useful for those with various difficulties or disabilities.

On an Apple system, under 'System Preferences' (cog wheel-like icon (© Apple) in the row of icons on your Mac or amongst the display of icons across the screen of your iPad or iPhone) there is an 'Accessibility' icon[47] (© Apple) that can be clicked to take you to where helpful modifications can be made. Under the headings along the side: 'Display', 'Zoom', 'Voiceover', 'Description' (where audio descriptions can be selected where available); 'Captions' (subtitles for the deaf); 'Audio' (where a screen flash can be selected instead of an alert sound); 'Keyboard' (where modifications like 'sticky keys' or 'slow keys' can be selected to help those with less manual dexterity); 'Mouse & Keyboard' (allowing changes to be made to the pointer and keyboard control of it); 'Switch Control' (giving you control of the computer through use of one or more switches, eg; mouse, keyboard, gameboard, etc) and last, but not least, a 'Dictation' option that allows you to pre-select a means of switching on the dictation facility which shows its readiness

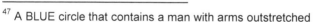

to accept dictation by a small microphone icon appearing on your screen (see image © Apple). The 'Accessibility' function on my Apple Mac has a very good 'Voice-Over'

---

[47] A BLUE circle that contains a man with arms outstretched

facility that explains very simply how to use it. For example, it tells you exactly where to find the place on your screen you need to click. If you experience any difficulties, ask your own computer dealer as all computers will have an application that does something similar.

Larger magnification of letters and other screen items can often be achieved by pressing the command key as well as the plus (+) key for larger text, or to reduce size, press the minus key (-). iPad users can achieve a similar result, either by using the fingers to 'stretch' text or tapping the screen with 3 fingers to enlarge and two fingers to decrease. There are also all sorts of other possibilities that your 'Apple' or other dealer will be only too happy to show you.

Specialised software programmes can also be purchased to help those with visual disability get full use from their computers. A useful YouTube video with a demo on adaptive software for visually impaired users demonstrates screen reading software like JAWS and ZoomText which can also act as a screen magnifier up to 26x magnification, the Kurzweil 3000 text reader where you can choose the voice and speed of reading, and Dragon Naturally Speaking speech recognition software which will type words as you say them[48]. (The video in this footnote is really worth a look.) At the RNIB research library (which is open to all) you can also access computers with JAWS and Zoomtext software fitted if you want to try them first.

Another good resource is the RNIB website[49] which is really worth a visit for those seriously interested in purchasing accessibility software. It outlines and compares several different commercial options and gives an idea of price which will obviously be updated but to give some idea, January 2016 sample quotes are as follows:

Magnification software for Windows

- **SuperNova Magnifier** starts at £275 from Dolphin Computer Access www.yourdolphin.com.

---

[48] https://www.youtube.com/watch?v=_YpNrOkW0Mw
[49] http://www.rnib.org.uk/information-everyday-living-using- technology-computers-and-tablets/paid-accessibility-software

- **MAGic** costs from £295 from Sight and Sound.

- **ZoomText Magnifier** costs £375 from a number of suppliers, including RNIB.

Screen reading (speech output) for Windows

- System Access for use with Microsoft Word, Outlook, Internet Explorer, Adobe Reader and Skype can be purchased for £270 from Computer Room Services.

- Dolphin Screen Reader (formerly known as SuperNova Reader) starts at £575, and a trial version is available from Dolphin or your local Dealer. http://yourdolphin.com/product?id=3

- Window-Eyes costs from £525 excluding VAT from AbilityStore or Computer Room Services.

- A JAWS trial is available for download. The full version costs from £659 excluding VAT from a number of UK suppliers including RNIB and Sight and Sound.

Combined speech and magnification options for Windows and Mac OSX are also available, although the Mac OSX software is not as elaborate as the software available for Windows, perhaps because MAC computers already have built-in accessibility aids as outlined earlier. In addition, you can get simplified computer interfaces for people who have never used a computer. These start at £60 for Simplicity Envelope while Ordissimo sell laptops starting at £499 and a tablet for £399 with their own software designed for blind or partially sighted people already installed.

On the subject of cell-phones, I find the small size of the iPhone, especially its keyboard, makes it of limited use to me. It's a bit frustrating when it's in *'portrait'* mode as I have to aim my finger at the key next to the one I actually want, so I always opt for *'landscape'* where the individual keys are marginally larger. However, I have to admit that the modern smartphone is very impressive in its capabilities which are similar to the iPad, and it's also very easy to carry in your pocket or purse.

On the other hand, I find I use my iPad almost constantly when I travel. It has an excellent camera, the keyboard is a more practical size, and the display and lettering can be easily enlarged. There are also several accessibility features for those with poor vision, similar to its larger relative, the Apple iMac.

A well known characteristic of growing old is a dislike of change, and since I have had AMD I find this even more difficult, especially when it comes to computing. I like to know that when I switch on the screen, things will turn up exactly where I expect them to be, and for this reason my heart sinks every time I am invited, or eventually forced, to accept the latest update, because this often means that the display changes and is quite different from the one I am used to. Pressing a word at the top right-hand corner might have previously meant you could 'edit' something, whereas the latest update may replace it with what looks like the same word but actually performs a different function such as 'exit', meaning that you get a totally unexpected and usually undesirable effect.

However, in spite of difficulties adapting to some upgrades and changes, I would not be without these modern gadgets. They are particularly good if poor eyesight prevents you driving and limits your ability to get out and about as they will keep you entertained and occupied during the long house-bound hours. You can enjoy a shopping trip online, 'meet' friends through social media, or listen to the latest music or 'must read', while the amount of information you can access at your finger tips is addictive.

Even so, when you are writing anything you do need to be sure you select your preference for either UK or US English as everyone knows that Americans and Brits have a common language separated by spelling. You should by now have gathered that I try to select UK spelling, but I need to keep a watchful eye on it thereafter because, like most people, its mischievous computer gnomes favour, or should I say 'favor', the Americans, and tend to revert back when you are not looking! 'Spell Check' is also really good for low vision as it highlights inappropriate letters, although sometimes it will rather unhelpfully insert a completely different word. The other thing to be wary of is predictive text or automatic correction where sneaky 'computer gnomes' creep up unnoticed and start writing words from their own gnome language!

Some computers and iPads have a facility for dictation and also reading back. I find the dictation facility useful in avoiding the sometimes laborious task of finding the right keys on the keyboard, and also noticing when the wrong one has been accidentally selected, or when predictive text has substituted something 'behind your back' and written gibberish as a consequence. I have just had a good example of predictive text doing something I did not intend. At the start of this very passage when I planned to write *'I find the dictation facility useful,'* I found that the word *'family'* had been substituted for the word *'facility'*. Mind you, dictating to the computer can also have its own pitfalls, and it requires careful checking. One day when I was dictating an e-mail, I wanted to say that I hoped so much writing would not be straining my eyes, whereas my iPad wrote of my concern for 'my guys'!

My friends got used to strange words on e-mails and Facebook where *'Spell Check'* or *'Predictive Text'* had substituted things I had not been able to read or noticed when they changed. Some of my favourites were my name *'Liz'* coming out as *'Lizard'* and wanting to write about *'Do's and Don'ts'* but having it appear as *'Dos and Doughnuts'*. People understandably got confused when I wrote I was a *'factor'* rather than a *'doctor'* but I rather liked the image conjured up when I wrote that my friend had to stick to *'fairy free'* products instead of *'dairy free'* products.

Another choir friend was perplexed when I wrote her an email headed: 'Choir Lunch Dimfau'. The last word had her really guessing and me too as she wrote back quoting it out of context. All was solved when I told her that the letters would be on the keyboard close to the ones I intended to type and she wrote back in triumph that the odd

186

word should have been 'Sunday'! But what would you make of a hastily written email that informed her that 'I sn fpumh rp rhr xpmvwty' (*Translation*: I am going to the concert!)?

To check what you have written, it can be very helpful to make use of the computer's own reading facility. If you go to the *'System preferences'* or *'Settings'* section on my computer, it allows you to select the voice you wish the computer to use when reading anything to you. There are about six different voices, male or female, with a variety of qualities and each one has its own name. I found 'Alex' was the most pleasant and I could understand him quite easily. He reminded me of the voice on the iPad known as 'Siri' - perhaps he is voiced by the same actor!

'Alex' is useful in reading back to me what I have written, because he reads everything including the stray words remaining after cutting and pasting or repeated words beside each other. He also has a stab at reading any nonsense words that have arisen from spelling mistakes or that *'Predictive Text'* has mischievously inserted. He might at times have unusual pronunciation, but he manages to get remarkably life-like expression into a descriptive passage. He was quite funny when he read back my chapter about my selection for the RAF medical cadetship scheme, obviously knowing more of the serviceman's liking of the occasional sundowner than 'Battle of Britain' history because he read that I had gone to RAF Big Gin Hill! Oh yes! These robotic voices become quite personified, but I hadn't realised quite how much until last year on Valentine's Day when I told my iPad 'Siri' that I loved him and he replied, "Do you?" I then ventured: "Do you love me?" and his reply was: "I'll have to get back to you on that!"

A friend of mine was using her iPad in the car to navigate the route for her husband. Apparently, you can just say, "Siri, take me to X", and he obliges with map-reading instructions. On this particular occasion the couple noticed that they had returned to a particular cross-road they had already passed so she shouted in frustration: "Siri, are you drunk?" to which he replied in a shocked tone: "Who, me?" Even funnier was when my husband and I were out in a new car and he had to do an emergency stop. He called out some expletive, and a disembodied voice somewhere in the car said disapprovingly: "Pardon?" We had forgotten that the new car had some sort of *'Voice Command'* facility!

While on the subject of gadgets that talk to you, I must mention 'Talking Books' which can be borrowed from the RNIB and most public libraries. It is certainly worth looking into just what you can get from your local library as if you explain your needs and visual difficulty to your librarian, either by phone or by calling in person, you will find that they will be most helpful. Many libraries have a good e-book service through internet access at the library and also online from the library website. I have a library card with a bar code that I swipe when I physically borrow books or DVDs, but there are also numbers on it that connect you to their online services. I can use this online connection to download e-books, listen to audio books or even listen to music. It's certainly a very useful service if it is no longer easy for you to get out.

Love it or reluctantly use it, these are exciting times with many useful break-throughs in technology that will benefit the visually impaired. I have just read about 'Blitab®', an iPad for blind people advertised as the world's first tactile tablet for blind people with full page refreshable braille display, while I also heard that Wikipedia, the online encyclopaedia, has teamed up with KTH Royal Institute of Technology to develop something similar to Wikipedia using speech for readers with reading difficulties or who are visually impaired.

Audiobooks, Talking Books, eReaders

As their name suggests, these are various forms of audio material including MP3s, cassettes, CDs and DVDs - in fact, every audio format available - which allow you to listen to things being read to you. A search online will provide details of just where they can be obtained, ranging from commercial sites to various charities that provide them free of charge to the visually handicapped. In the UK one such charity is the already mentioned RNIB, while another called 'Listening Books' provides audio books by internet streaming and postal service to anyone who has a disability or illness which makes it difficult to hold a book, turn its pages, or read in the usual way. They have audio books for both leisure and learning and you can choose from a library of over 4,000 titles either recorded in their own digital studios or commercially sourced. Of course, audio books are also commercially available to people without handicaps who find them useful to listen to when doing other activities such as housework, gardening, walking, driving, etc.

Kindle devices also have a facility which will read its contents to you. If you press the 'Aa' key it directs you to a menu where you cannot only change the print size, but also select a setting to enable the Kindle to read any book you choose. Make sure you remember to switch it off again in the same place under 'Aa' where you switched it on as otherwise it will not stop, even when you turn the Kindle off. However, this might be useful if you want to fall asleep while being read to; presumably, it just continues until the book is finished or the battery runs out!

Computers and iPads can also have Kindle applications installed so you can read your Kindle books on them. This is so much easier when you are travelling as you've then got everything conveniently in one place, and can leave your Kindle at home. My Kindle reading device was a godsend to me as it easily carried a great many books including the Bible, although it might be quite a while before it becomes acceptable to swear an oath by: '...taking the Kindle in your right hand and saying after me..' I was even able to where I first read how essential it is to develop a sense of humour with this condition.

Keyboards

Keyboards with large keys can be obtained, but beware as the cheapest will sometimes have an atypical arrangement of keys that only display dollar signs, although, somewhat annoyingly, the pound signs, though not visible on the keypad, are apt to turn up unexpectedly when you press another key altogether! However, these keyboards are absolutely fine if you have the kind of mind that can adapt to the differences and remember to press " when you want @, but not vice versa unless you enjoy surprises!

I managed to find a cover for my neat little 'Apple Mac' keyboard with sections in different colours that helped me navigate the keyboard, and provided better contrast than the grey letters printed on silver keys. I must say that 'Apple' does seem to favour grey on white or grey on silver for almost everything they produce at present which looks very smart, but is not helpful to the likes of those and me with low vision.

Monitor Screens

I found it a mistake to follow the same principle I used with my TV because if you get the largest monitor screen possible the line of writing, especially in emails, extends too far out to the sides of the screen to be read easily without moving your own position. I found that a smaller screen with a large setting for text and icons worked much better, although you can still only see a portion of the whole display at one time, and have to scroll around to see the rest if you want to build up a complete picture of what is there. At least the text is in smaller line widths so you can focus on what is in front of you without having to move your head to the side as well as vertically when trying to read a page of text. A word of warning, however, as whenever you are exposed to these screens, whether small or large, and also TVs and many types of modern lighting, you are actually exposing your eyes to blue light which can also have harmful effects[50].

Credit and debit cards and online shopping

Online shopping became more important to me as a convenient way to shop once driving was out of the question. *'You Shop - We Drop'* is

---

[50] See Appendix 5

190

a clever slogan. *'Find it Fast and Ferry without Fuss'* is mine, if not so slick! Unfortunately, I don't have shares in it and nobody is paying me to say that the huge firm (beginning with an A*****) that sells everything from books to baby clothes has become my favourite in terms of convenience, simply because they keep a record of my credit or debit card which means I do not have to go through the slow and tortuous process of entering all the numbers and card details every time I make a purchase.

Other sites as well as A***** offer a good visual display and description of their goods along with helpful customer feedback. However, although essential for modern existence, I often find credit and debit cards most frustrating with the long numbers that have to be read from the card and then entered accurately on a line to complete a purchase. There are just too many chances you will get that heart-sinking red error warning telling you that you have 'goofed' which makes you feel like a fraudster or a prize idiot! I am sure companies like the one I almost mentioned above get far more trade just because they save your card details which makes the whole process much easier and simpler, thanks to their 'purchase with one click'.

Unfortunately, many cards are not 'low vision' friendly. Perhaps they assume that if we are half blind we are able to read braille. One of my credit cards one year had silver lettering on a grey card, but when I spoke to someone in the issuing bank they simply remarked that I was not alone in pointing this out. I am afraid that I probably went against all security advice as I asked someone to write down the numbers of all my major cards in large script! Doing this at least lowered my chances of getting the numbers wrong when typing them online or reading them out if choosing to purchase by phone. No wonder that I usually get Stewart to take over once I have selected my items for purchase.

As I write this, especially the part about security, those wretched pin numbers, passwords and usernames come to mind. I don't know about 'low vision' friendly, but they are certainly not 'elderly person' friendly. I doubt if even an ageing 'Mr Memory' could cope with the multitude of them that seem to be required today. Are they all necessary? Every online business seems to want them. Sometimes I wonder if they really want my business.

We are told that the best way to remember passwords is to use the first letters of a memorable sentence, but I have yet to find a way of remembering my creations for longer than a few minutes unless I write them down. This reminds me of the mnemonic used by medical students to remember the cranial nerves, the first letters of which I can write to this day - OOOTTAFAGVAH - but I was younger then, and the sentence by which they are remembered is rather salacious![51]

II. A Sideways Look - Eccentric Viewing
'To see what is in front of one's nose needs a constant struggle.'
George Orwell

It was the same Kindle book on macular degeneration[52] previously referred to that first informed me about a technique to improve vision for people with AMD called Eccentric Viewing (EV). Detailed information on how to do this can be obtained from the Macular Society and also Low Vision Clinics, but I am also mentioning it here to give you a rough idea of what it is about, although I am far from being an expert!

In AMD the central area of vision is affected, and therefore it helps to look slightly to one side of an object while looking out of 'the corner of your eye'. Eccentric Viewing uses this technique to allow people suffering with AMD to bypass the area damaged by the condition, and make use of their peripheral vision which remains intact. When my husband trained as a pilot they also used this technique in night flying. It allowed them to make better use of the specialised retinal cells called rods[53] which are used in night vision and are in plentiful supply

---

[51] Oh,Oh,Oh, To Touch and Feel A Girl's Vagina, AH!
[52] Macular Degeneration by L Lylas, G Mogk MD & Marja Mogk Ph D, Ballantine Books, 2003
[53] See Appendix 1

outside the macula which contains mainly cones[54]. So if you are a frustrated fighter pilot at heart, you can at least now enjoy the thought that in using EV to improve your sight you are employing the same technique that you would have used as a fighter pilot to maximise your night vision.

In looking to one side of an object, I found that I could catch sight of it with greater clarity; for example, people's faces on TV now appeared to have distinctive mouths and noses rather than just being a blur. My trouble was that as soon as I saw this, I would by habitual reflex look directly at the image to see it more clearly. Then, of course, I was back to using central vision and the clarity I had momentarily glimpsed would disappear. I have been practising finding the place on the side of, for example, a TV announcer's face where I can see his or her facial features more clearly without changing my focus, and then trying to hold that direction of gaze while I examine these details without moving my eyes or head – not easy! It is really preferable to use a still picture to give you time to do all this without frustratingly finding that the picture has now changed to a basket of fruit or some other thing. However, it makes good use of the time spent watching the TV news yet again while waiting for the next programme to come on!

You may have noticed that I said: ...'find a place ... where I can see his or her facial features clearly', and this is because as you look all around the face or another static object, you will find some places are more blurred than others and do not show the features in the central area clearly. This is because we all have one or more blind spots (scotoma) in our field of vision that show up as black or empty areas. These are the areas where our vision is at its worst and when learning EV you will be shown various ways of identifying where yours are. You need to know this in order to know how to move them out of the way. It may sound illogical but you do this by looking towards them because they will move along with your line of vision.

---

[54] See Appendix 1

193

There are various methods taught to identify where scotoma and areas of best vision are. One requires the help of a patient partner who sits in front of you with their knees placed against yours, and then holds up a card selected from a box with a very clear letter printed on it. The partner needs to hold it so that it is strictly equidistant between you as you face each other squarely. Using a different card each time so that you have no clues to help you anticipate what you might see next, he or she then tests how well you can see each card by going methodically around in a circular fashion until the circle is complete, and then doing the same with another circle inside the previous one, ie, with a shorter radius each time, taking careful notes of where each card can be seen and where it cannot. It may be easier to start with the four basic positions - above, below, left and right - and then fill in the gaps between.

People who have no partner for this purpose can get some idea of where their blindspots and best vision areas are by drawing a large clock face with a central point. Even if you cannot see the central point when you position it, you can focus your eyes where you know it must be by holding it at eye level. Don't put it too close, but where you have some chance of seeing the whole disc. Looking at the central point, or roughly where you know it should be, try to see 1 o'clock, then 2 o'clock and so on for each time until you get back to where you started. You should then have a map of where you see clearly, where it is blurry, and where you have no vision at all. Obviously, where you can see clearest is the place where you should direct your gaze in order to see an object. In other words, if I see the facial features of my TV announcer more distinctly when I direct my gaze towards the twenty past or the figure 4 position on a clock-face, then this is the direction I must look at to be able to see anything better. This holds true for whatever I am looking at. If someone hands me a photograph to look at, I need to direct my gaze toward the bottom right where the figure 4 would be situated on a clock where I will then 'out of the corner of my eye' see the picture as clearly I can. If someone with AMD drops something on the floor, a careful observer might notice them turning their head slightly as they go to retrieve it. This is because they are using their 'side vision' or EV to see better.

Certain parts of a letter, as described below, help to distinguish it from similar letters, so I make sure that I concentrate on this part using EV, even if I have to move my eyes or my head or even the printed material itself in order to see that particular part of the letter with my best position or 'preferred retinal locus' (PRL).

One exercise in learning how to find and use your PRL involves getting a large bold printed letter about 4 inches high and ideally moving about 5 to 10 feet away from it, (or to where you can still see it). Looking systematically all round that letter until you find a place or places where you see the letter clearly, then practise holding it in view as long as possible. It's a good idea to do this for about 5 -10 minutes daily. EV is not easy but don't give up and it will eventually become second nature[55].

The same approach can be used for any letter. By carefully looking eccentrically all round each letter you may find that what you thought was a 'P' is really an 'R'. You need to focus on the right lower quadrant of letters like 'B','P' and 'R' to tell them apart, especially as 'B' can be easily confused with 'S' or even the figure '8'. You also need to pay careful attention to the bottom of letters such as 'N' 'M' 'W' 'V' & 'Y' to differentiate them, while you will quickly work out other letters that are easy to get confused such as 'O' and 'Q'.

Certain styles of writing (fonts) are more complicated than others, and some can be very difficult to work out for the AMD sufferer. Seeing the 'Q' beside the 'O' reminds me that when I was at school we were taught to write a capital 'Q' so it resembled a large and elaborate figure '2'. I cannot even find a way of reproducing this on my keyboard, but if you know anyone over 90 who can still see and write well they will probably be able to reproduce it for you. If we were to use it today, it might solve the confusion with 'O', but then we'd probably get it confused with '2' so it wouldn't really help!

---

[55] http://lowvision.preventblindness.org/library/low-vision-rehabilitation/self-training-in-eccentric-viewing/

This is just a simple introduction to EV, but if you are interested I suggest you ask a macular or low vision society group how you can have more training in this technique. As you have probably already realised, this is a slower reading method which requires effort and if your short term memory is not good you can imagine easily losing the plot! But even though you will need to persevere, most people with AMD find it is well worth it to improve their reading skills.

Here is a game you might like to play which will show you what I mean. I have written some groups of letters below that can easily be confused by the AMD sufferer. See which portions of them - above, below, right or left - look the same if you hold a piece of card over the rest. Then see which side needs extra attention to help you distinguish them. The example I have chosen includes the letter '**P**' which is an old friend of mine as it was this letter in huge size that I could not see when the optician asked me to read it before I had my operation. I thought she had held up a blank screen to tease me when I used my left eye, although with the right eye I could just make out

 the curve at the top of the '**P**' when I moved my eyes around it. The shape reminded me of part of a steering wheel, possibly because my mind was dwelling on the driving that I knew I would have to say 'Good-bye' to. Covered up so only the tops show, these letters look identical, but if you look just at the bottom right area, they are completely different.

EV Exercise

Write each of the following groups below in large letters on a piece of card or paper with a felt-tip pen, (or computer print them) and then use another strip of card to cover them in various ways, noting where they are alike and where they can be seen to be different as in the previous example.

N   M   W   V   Y
X   K

```
T  I    J L
C G    O Q
O D U
E F    B P R    F P R
```

Now, write down the lower case letters in the following groups in the same way, and again look at which part(s) of the letters you will need to pay attention to in order to tell them apart. Some forms of 'a' (a) are more like 'o' whereas the 'a' below is more like 's'.

```
i l j    f t l    m n u    c e o a s
v w y    b h p    h n r       g q
```

III. Seeing ghosts - Charles Bonnet Syndrome (CBS)
'No ghost was ever seen by two pair of eyes.'
Thomas Carlyle

Charles Bonnet syndrome is the name given to worrying visual hallucinations that occur in people with loss of vision including some who have AMD. However there is no need to be alarmed because although it may seem a bit frightening the first few times it happens, it is harmless. I mention it simply because anyone who has never heard about it may be troubled if it happens to them, and will often not speak about it in case people think they might be suffering from a mental illness.

Although the precise mechanism behind CBS is not known, I find it helpful to think of it as the visual equivalent of 'phantom limb' where a limb has been amputated but the owner can still feel it! In CBS the part of the brain that received images from the eye no longer has any stimuli to process, but it continues to do what it has always done and starts 'seeing' things - but in this case they are not real!

They may occur frequently or infrequently, and last for varying amounts of time, while what is seen differs widely from person to person with some people seeing several different kinds. These images can be complex - anything from patterns to familiar objects, faces or animals, or even lights, although bright or flashing lights should always be reported medically as it can be a symptom of retinal detachment. However, if you stop to think about them, you should have no problem in realising that CBS hallucinations are recognisably not real.

There is no treatment for CBS but it is important to mention these visual phenomena to your doctor as they can sometimes happen when you are below par for some reason and may signal an infection or disorder in your general health. As hallucinations tend to occur in situations of inactivity when your brain is less engaged and/or dim lighting, it may help to dispel them if you:

- Stand up and move around which may cause the hallucination to vanish.

- Move your eyes or blink them rapidly.

- Get involved in an activity to distract your brain.

- Increase the lighting. Seek the company of others

- Try putting the radio or TV 'ON'.

One recent study has shown that doing an eye movement exercise may also help. When the hallucination starts, look from left to right about once every second for 15 to 30 seconds, without moving your head. The best way is to stand about 1.5 metres away (5 feet) from a wall and then move your eyes between two points, one on the left and one on the right with about a metre (3 feet) between the two. You need to keep your eyes open while doing this. If it persists, have a rest for a few seconds and then repeat the exercise for another 15 to 30 seconds. If the hallucinations haven't stopped or got any less after four or five periods of doing this, the exercise is probably not going to work this time, but that doesn't mean it isn't worth trying again when you next get one as many people find that doing this helps.

IV.   Dry Eye in the House? 'Dry Eye Syndrome'
(keratoconjunctivtis sicca (KCS))
'Eyes that do not cry, do not see.'
- Swedish Proverb

The cornea in a healthy eye is lubricated by a film of tears, but this process tends to become less efficient with age and also some health conditions. In Dry Eye Syndrome (DES) too little tear lubrication is produced or the tear film evaporates too quickly. This can mean the eyes become inflamed (red and swollen) and irritated, but dry eyes can also be present without you really noticing.

Symptoms of 'Dry Eye Syndrome'

The symptoms of Dry Eye Syndrome usually affect both eyes. They may include:

- feelings of dryness, grittiness or soreness that get worse through the day.
- red eyes.
- eyelids that are stuck together when you wake up.
- itchy eyes.
- temporarily blurred vision which usually improves when you blink.
- watery eye(s).

Contributing Factors

As we age there can be a tendency to produce less lubricating fluid (tears), especially if you also have certain dermatological or general medical conditions. Women, especially post-menopause, are more prone to the condition. Some medications are also implicated in causing dry eyes. These may include antihistamines, antidepressants, and beta-blockers, while you may find that surgery, especially laser surgery, can also trigger the condition.

Environmental factors

Environmental factors such as sun, wind, dry climate, hot blowing air or high altitude can cause a drying effect in eyes, and be a

199

contributory factor in causing tears to evaporate. Our living and working conditions can also increase eye dryness which is exacerbated by factors like central heating and the multiplicity of devices with screens that most people have in their home, eg, smartphones, tablets and computers. Although dry eyes are generally considered an issue for the elderly, more young people are now developing this problem because of excessive screen use, eg, on smartphones.

Some Helpful Remedies for Dry Eyes

• When you spend a long time watching a computer screen it is easy to forget to blink. often enough which results in poor lubrication – a good way to remember is to blink every time you hit the Return or Enter key.

• Avoid dryness from central heating by using a humidifier.

• Use eyedrops on a regular basis.

• Take 200mg of a good quality Omega 3 supplement by mouth, eg, PRN Omega.

Using Eyedrops
Eyedrops to combat this condition are in plentiful supply an include Hypromellose and Artificial Tears, although these last two are thought to be less efficient these days. Speak to your pharmacist or eye specialist for advice. I use Thealoz Duo which was recommended by the London Eye Hospital. It is preservative free, phosphate free, isotonic and pH neutral making it suitable for all Dry Eye sufferers including wearers of contact lenses, and is available from A*****.

I find it useful to keep a bottle of eye drops by my computer and also in my bathroom so I can use them whenever my eyes feel dry - which is often when I wake up to visit the bathroom during the night. The dosage is not restricted - and definitely not a case of 'less is more'! Medical advice is that overuse is better than underuse – a good rule of thumb is at least 4 to 6 times a day.

Useful equipment for 'Dry Eyes' - Microwaveable eye compress

Tired or uncomfortable eyes can also be helped by using drops for dry eyes. A trick that I learned from a dermatologist colleague who had severe eczema was to kee p any used tea-bags in the fridge, and when the eyes feel tired (or itchy because of the eczema) gently place the tea bags on the closed lids as you rest for a while. This forms a simple and soothing compress. Hot compresses are also useful for managing Dry Eyes and you can read more about this in Section V: 'TLC for your Eyes'.

V. TLC for your Eyes - Eye Routines

'Keep your eyes wide open before marriage, and half-shut afterwards.'
Benjamin Franklin

Pre-operation Lid Hygiene and Care for Dry Eyes (lack of tears)[56]
Cleaning procedure

Perform twice daily for one week, then once daily at bedtime. Take cottonwool balls or pads and soak in warm water. This should be as hot as you can tolerate - test temperature by touching the cottonwool ball on the inside of your upper arm before using it on your eyes. Place a cottonwool ball on each closed eye for 3 to 4 minutes - keeping them warm by periodically soaking in warm water. (For dry eyes generally, a clean face flannel can be used, but cottonwool balls or pads are more hygienic pre-operation.) Alternatively, you can purchase an 'EyeBag'[57] which you heat in the microwave for about 30 seconds and then rest on your eyes (check it's not too hot first, in the same way as the cotton wool balls)

---

[56] See Related Matters IV: 'Is there a Dry Eye in the House?'
[57] © The Eyebag Company Ltd 2014. See illustrations in Related Matters IV: 'Is there a Dry Eye in the House?'

Following the heat treatment, take cottonwool balls as required, using different ones for left and right eyes and replace with fresh ones as necessary. Place a small drop of baby shampoo (Johnson's 'No Tears' formula) on each ball, squeezing them gently between your fingers to lather slightly. Then, in turn, gently but firmly rub along the closed eyelids from the inside (near nose) to outer side to remove all flakes. Repeat 3 - 5 times. When done, rinse your face with clean warm water.

Above left – Post operative take away pack and some of the contents
Above middle - Post operative eye drops and dosage chart from eye pack
Above right – Baby shampoo and swabs (Actually make up remover pads) for eyes and drops. Also a black eye patch to work newly operated eye while covering the other (See Chapter 29 for results)

Post-operative Care

The following advice was given to me on a leaflet after my operation.
HOSPITAL LEAFLET
(Discharge Advice by the London Eye Hospital)

On discharge from hospital your eye will be covered with the shield. Keep this in place until the following morning. The effect of your local anaesthetic could last for 2 to 6 hours. During this period you may have a droopy lid, double vision or a bloodshot eye. This is normal. The following morning start your eye-drops. Do not rub or apply pressure to the eye.

Special eye-care precautions

1. Each morning, carefully wipe away any secretions with a cotton ball dipped in cooled boiled water. Use single strokes and wipe away from the nose to the outer edge of the eye, discarding the cotton after one use. Repeat as necessary. It is vital to keep it clean at all times, thus reducing the risk of infection. Wash and dry your hands before and after touching your eye to avoid infection.

2. Wear the eye shield at night for two weeks with no exceptions. Nail varnish remover on a cotton ball can be used to remove the sticky tape residue each morning from the cheek and forehead.

3. The following day, when the eye shield has been removed, you may wear dark glasses to protect the eyes from glare.

4. Resume your normal diet.

5. You may sleep on your back or either side, but not on your front.

6. You may bathe or shower, but do not get water in the operated eye during the first three days after surgery. Someone may wash your hair for you as long as the operated eye does not get wet.

7. You may use eye makeup two weeks after surgery.

8. Reading and TV are permitted.

9. Driving can be resumed as soon as you feel comfortable.

10. Sexual intercourse may be resumed two weeks after surgery.

11. Light walking may be resumed immediately if you feel like it. More strenuous sports activities such as jogging, swimming, bowling, tennis and golf may be resumed four weeks after surgery depending on your progress. If your work, exercise habits or other activities are usually strenuous, please check before resuming them

12. For the first two weeks do not bend over with your head hanging down. If you need to pick something up, kneel or ask someone to pick it up for you.

13. Avoid constipation/straining which could cause the eye to bleed. Have a high fibre diet and see your GP if constipated.

It will take several weeks for your eye to completely heal. Your vision will gradually improve over time. Do not be alarmed if your vision is not improving as fast as you had hoped. Each eye is unique and heals differently.

VI. Driving Mad or Mad to be Driving?
'You know, somebody actually complimented me on my driving today. They left a little note on the windscreen, it said 'Parking Fine'.'
Tommy Cooper

In the UK legal requirements for driving are quite specific, unlike the USA where they vary considerably from state to state. Even after the operation you may find your reading is not quick enough to read signposts and road signs which is alright if you know an area but problematic if driving along unfamiliar roads. In fact, driving well known routes that require no signpost reading might have stopped

203

you noticing your vision had fallen below legal driving requirements in the first place!

The standards of vision for driving are stipulated by the DVLA. You must be able to read (with glasses or contact lenses, if necessary) a clean car number plate made after 1st September 2001 from 20 metres. Reading car number plates at twenty paces is quite a skill, and I am convinced that a great many drivers on our roads, even without diagnosed visual problems, are in blissful ignorance that they cannot actually do it. I'm not even sure how useful it is unless you have an ambition to become an ideal witness for spotting get-away cars. However, it is the test required by law in the UK, and any 'bobby' stopping you is entitled to see if you can do it. At least it will be on a stationary car, although I don't know if there is any time limit. If so, that could be a drawback for AMD sufferers as it can take quite a while to focus well enough to distinguish letters and numbers on number plates.

You must also meet the minimum eyesight standard for driving by having a visual acuity of at least 0.5 (6/12 UK = 20/40 US) measured on the Snellen scale, using both eyes together or one if you have sight in only one eye (glasses or contact lenses may be worn). Another requirement is that you must also possess 'an adequate field of vision' to be passed as fit to drive which can only be properly assessed by a vision specialist.

Once you have a diagnosis of AMD you will find that whenever you visit opticians they become obsessive about your field of vision as treacherous blind spots can creep up on you without you noticing. Disappointingly their concern over your field of vision may even increase once they know you have had an operation for AMD because earlier operations used very strong lenses to achieve greater magnification which, unfortunately, reduced the field of vision. This is not usually the case with the iolAMD™ implant such as I had, but your optician may not be familiar with it, and so be extra cautious.

It is a legal requirement in the UK that you declare to the DVLA if you have any medical condition that could affect your ability to drive which, of course, includes AMD. Upon such a declaration an assessment is then made and, depending on the results, you will either be told that you can continue to drive or you have to surrender your licence until you are pronounced fit to drive again.

As I was about to have an operation to remedy the situation, I originally decided that I could avoid these formalities and didn't need to inform the DVLA that I had fallen below the visual requirements because of AMD as I wouldn't be driving again until I could meet the official standard so there was no question of me breaking the law. Unfortunately, soon after my operations when my eyesight was still not quite up to this standard my driving licence was due for renewal. I realised my vision would probably not improve in time for me to answer 'yes' to the question: 'Can you meet the visual requirements?' on the licence renewal application form so I phoned the DVLA who were very helpful. They advised me to surrender my driving licence right away as otherwise they would have to decline its renewal. If they did this, it would mean I would have to take another driving test to get it back as well as submitting to examination by an optician of their choice, whereas by voluntarily surrendering the licence I would only have to do the latter.

Living as we do virtually off any bus routes, once I'd surrendered my driving licence I had to think of other ways to get about without always relying on Stewart. I looked longingly at electric bikes to take me up those steep Devon hills, but that was before we had several weeks of continuously rainy weather and in any case Stewart said that he would worry about me going through our local very narrow lanes which, although they had passing places, often offered only poor visibility of oncoming traffic.

Next, my mind turned to how country folk got around in the past, but while I could see a cart taking the place of my little Smart car in our garage I could not work out how I was going to house a horse or even a donkey in our garden. Anyway, I was finding two cats to care for quite demanding enough, and I somehow didn't think owning one or two horses would really suit my lifestyle. It is bad enough looking for a car parking space in Plymouth, let alone a suitable hitching post for equine 'transport' while attending choir practice. Thoughts of Peggy the stampeding milk float horse from my youth came too readily to mind! Well, if returning to the past cannot help me, perhaps the future will as I see that they are now trying out driverless cars!

One possible problem related to driving for AMD sufferers is that you may have learned to adapt to your loss of central vision by looking off centre to get a clearer image,[58] but your instinctive reaction when you see something 'out of the corner of your eye' will be to look at it using central vision as formerly, only for it to completely disappear due to the loss of central vision. As you will appreciate, this could have serious consequences as anything which compromises reaction time when driving carries life or death implications.

This may be worrying if your vision is declared good enough to drive once more and you find yourself back on the road because it is impossible to know if you are NOT seeing something because it is in a blind spot. If things are not seen clearly at least you are aware of their presence, but if you do not see them at all there is no way of telling if you have not seen something unless another person travelling with you in the car tells you, or alternatively, you hit it! That is somewhat drastic! As the regulations say, it is wise to get an optician to test your visual fields. A positive result should give you more confidence, but even then frequent checking will still be necessary as AMD is progressive. Another way to gauge if you might have a problem in this area, or alternatively, boost your driving confidence, is to test your driving skills in a simulated scenario - such as you will see in 'Driving Simulators' below.

Driving Simulators

Some important research in Boston, MA using state of the art driving simulators to assess the effects of central vision loss and blind areas in the visual field of drivers with AMD has been looking at potential

---

[58] See Related Matters II: A Sideways Look at Life - Eccentric Viewing (EV)

problems in their ability to appropriately avoid pedestrians[59]. The results of two published papers (2013 and 2015) suggest any degree of binocular central field loss causes possible delay in a driver's ability to detect moving hazards quickly enough to take safe, corrective action in time.

The study found late reactions usually occurred because pedestrians were entirely or partially obscured by the driver's blind area. Drivers would notice the pedestrian using peripheral vision, but then try to look directly by reflex, causing the blind area to obscure them.

The use of simulators seems to me to be a good way for a person with AMD to assess their fitness to drive or perhaps demonstrate to someone who should not be driving the dangers of trying to do so. Alternatively, simulated driving could serve as a useful confidence building exercise before going out on the road for someone whose vision has been improved by surgery.

These tests are not universally available in the UK although simulators are used by organisations like the Institute of Advanced Motorists (IAM). I remember as a student, even before I learned to drive, trying my hand on a very realistic simulator that the Dundee police were using as part of an information display on driving. You gained points for reacting to things like a child playing with a ball beside the road or a mother walking along with an unrestrained toddler beside her. You were supposed to spot them as potential hazards, and if you did not, points were deducted. I did pretty well at that, but my general difficulty with nerves in examinations was what also let me down in driving tests – that, and in Malta, my refusal to hand over a suitable 'envelope' when I presented the official paperwork which meant they failed me before I even had a chance to show off my driving skills. I hadn't even touched the steering wheel!

---

[59] 'Driving with Central Visual Field Loss II: How Scotomas Affect Hazard Detection in a Driving Simulator' by P Matthew Bronstad, Amanda Albu, Alex R. Bowers, Robert Goldstein & Eli Peli was published on September 2nd, 2015 in the scientific journal PLOS ONE.

VII. Is This for Me?

'You must look at facts, because they look at you.'
Churchill

As I explained initially, I wrote all this to give others hope, so you may think that this is a strange title to include, but it is a question I have often been asked and the answer is not always as straightforward as you might expect. My mother would no doubt remark, "At last, old age has taught you that you may have to take 'No' for an answer!"

Perhaps the first time I had to personally struggle with a similar hard choice was when Stewart told me it had to be my decision whether to take up the offer from Robert Edwards to have another go at IVF after their success with the birth of the first 'test-tube baby' (See Chapter 15: Test Tube Babies). It was a hard one as we had both longed passionately for a child of our own, but the complications with my work commitments and the potential problems of an 'elderly' pregnancy, even though some people today have IVF as old as 60, meant that eventually I realised I had to say 'No'.

Returning to possible obstacles that you might need to think about when considering the iol/AMD procedure that I had, the first hurdle you must face is the long assessment process before any surgery is agreed by the London Eye Hospital and you can even check the likely improvement that might be achieved by it with an external lens mock-up. This assessment alone has a price tag, so it is worth thinking it through carefully and perhaps even ringing LEH to rule out any obvious reasons that would prevent you from being considered.

Besides cost, the main things to think about are:

1.   Am I up to it physically and in generally good health?

As much as you would like the potential benefit to your eyesight and however simple the operation may be, only you know how you feel physically and whether you might find the additional stress of such an eye operation too much to cope with.

208

At present, the procedure is only available in the UK at the London Eye Hospital, so this could mean quite a bit of travelling if you do not live near London, and possibly overnight accommodation in London as well. You will need to consider the extra effort involved, and how you will make the journey between your accommodation and the hospital when you attend the assessment consultation, the surgery itself, and any follow-up appointments. These take place at about one week after the operation, one month later, and three to six months after that. There will also be a shorter journey on the day of your operation between the Harley Street Outpatients where you will initially be seen and the Surgical Unit in Wimpole Street. This is not far and I was able to walk this distance, but if you cannot, you might need a taxi. Also, don't forget getting to and from your home and coach or train station or airport if you choose to travel by public transport.

You must decide if this amount of travelling presents a problem for you. I have spoken to a healthy active 83 year old who happily made a four hour journey back home by train with her husband right after her operation, although she did stay the previous night near the hospital for her early morning appointment. If the frequency of visits is a problem, some of them may be negotiable in exceptional circumstances, depending on how your eyes are after the operation, and whether any follow up can be delegated to a local eye consultant if you can find one willing to liaise with LEH to do this.

There may also be other factors to do with your general health that already impose lifestyle limitations, and the benefits from having the operation may not be enough to justify going ahead. If this is the case, excellent reading devices such as CCTV readers may still give a good level of help[60] so, if you have not already done so, seek out a low vision consultant who will offer helpful suggestions to suit your personal needs.

---

[60] See Related Matters : 1 - A Few of my Favourite Things - Helpful Devices

2. Do I really need this right now?

Crazy as this may sound, you could be better off delaying the operation. You do not need to have it as soon as dry AMD is diagnosed just because it is available. If you are managing adequately as you are, this is a good reason for not subjecting yourself to any surgical risk, however small, for the time being. It is not possible to predict when symptoms will start to appear in dry AMD, if they ever do, because the disease has not read the text books and it may affect you differently. Don't forget, you can always change your mind later if the condition does progress.

On the other hand, although it may be a tricky decision, once symptoms become intrusive or if the condition is already into 'end-stage dry AMD' - ie, causing enough problems to make you willing to try anything that might help, the sooner you go for an assessment the better while the remaining retina is still healthy enough to give the best chance of operational success. For that reason I would say that if you can afford it, have no health issues and are experiencing worsening symptoms, don't delay in going for an assessment to see if you are suitable.

Things to remember.

Be realistic!

If you could not paint a masterpiece before the operation, you are unlikely to be able to do so afterwards! Are your expectations reasonable? For example, if you are told at the assessment that your reading ability will probably be two chart lines better, but you've pinned your hopes on at least three lines to allow you to drive again, do not bank on getting a better result than predicted as you will only feel disgruntled if it doesn't happen. And definitely do not have the operation on the strength of reading instruction No.10 in the post-operative instructions 'Sexual intercourse may be resumed two weeks after surgery'![61]

---

[61] See Related Matters; V. TLC for Your Eyes - Eye Routines.

Results cannot be absolutely guaranteed

Never forget that, as one of my professors often said, 'Medicine is not an exact science.' Predictions of outcomes may be just off the mark of what is actually achieved in both directions. I was told that I could put all thoughts of the operation restoring my vision to driving standards out of my mind, and yet I am almost there with only one of my eyes falling just short of the official requirements, and the possibility of gaining still more improvement as I have been told my brain may still continue to adapt. Realistically, I am not going to bet my last dollar on this happening, but if it does it will be a bonus. Even without that coveted driving standard, I am happy because I can now read many things that I could not before the operation, and as dry AMD is a progressive condition I must be a country mile better off than I would have been without the surgery.

On the other hand, if you do decide to look at reviews online it doesn't take long to realise that some operations have had disappointing, if not disastrous, results. It is worth reading such reports if only to make you aware of the right questions to ask about what could be an outcome in your case, while also remembering that people rarely feel the same urgency to report good results.

Another important practical thing to be aware of is that even though your vision will have improved after the operation, you may still be slower at reading. I find that when I have a patient optometrist who gives me enough time, I can improve considerably on my initial chart reading score, although as I have already explained, needing extra time does not always fit in well with favourite activities like choral singing and driving.

You may also be slowed down in other things you want to do. For me, it means allowing more time for cooking as I repeatedly struggle to find my place in the recipe, or decipher the correct oven temperature amongst the mass of information in tiny print crammed on small packets of prepared food. At choir practice I am useless at reading new music unless the beat is 'Lento' and when I can't read the words I

211

often have to resort to making vague sounds that I hope will be mistaken for the real thing.

Every operation carries risk

It is in your surgeon's interest to eliminate as much risk as possible, but unexpected things can still happen. Today, we are so used to having amazing procedures carried out with no problems at all that we forget that a few people, and only a few, do get the terrible outcomes that you will be cautioned about and wish you did not have to hear before every operation. Please ask your surgeon before you book the operation what the risks are, and what the likelihood is of them happening to you. It is also a wise precaution to be clear about what happens in the event of something not turning out as planned, especially if there would need to be another operation to correct this. If this is the case, make sure you find out at whose expense this will be done.

However, there are some risks relating to your health in general that you may be able to minimise, including doing everything possible to avoid infection. You should obviously declare any health issues, whether you see a connection with your eyes or not, and also do what you can to keep weight and blood pressure down by eating healthily and taking adequate exercise. Inform the hospital of all medications, prescription or otherwise, that you take and ask about stopping any anticoagulants etc, before the operation. It is important to keep well hydrated by drinking plenty of non-alcoholic fluids, and also to keep your eyes lubricated with drops as instructed by the hospital.

It is in your interests to play your part in reducing the risks of infection as much as you can. Lid hygiene pre-operatively is important and you will find a procedure for this outlined under 'Eye Routines'.[62] The hospital gives good clear guidance on what to do, and the little post-operative 'takeaway' bags contain hand steriliser and sterile water to help you. Making sure you always wash your hands, as you

---

[62] Related Matters V: TLC for your Eyes.

will read on notices in every hospital and most public toilets, may seem too basic to mention, but it is SO essential. Get into the habit of washing hands before and after anything that might affect your eyes. It should precede tasks like lid hygiene routines, putting in drops, removing a dressing, touching the eye or retiring for the night, and washing hands is also a sensible precaution after actions like wiping your nose, touching animals or travelling on public transport etc.

Also, do remember to have sunglasses available for use both before and after the operation. Choose a pair with good protection at the side, not only to prevent any glare from the sun, but also to stop painful grit getting blown into the eyes. They are especially necessary just after your operation, but also before it when you make the journey to the LEH Wimpole Street surgical unit after pre-operative eye-drops have been inserted at the Harley Street premises as these dilating and anaesthetic drops make your eyes much more vulnerable to glare and injury.

VIII. Causes and Contributions
'The body politic, as well as the human body, begins to die as soon as it is born, and carries in itself the causes of its destruction.'
Jean-Jacques Rousseau

Age - being over 50. Macular degeneration is most common in people older than 65, but the risk of it increases every decade after age 50.
Remedy - too drastic!
Race - macular degeneration is more common in whites (Caucasians) than in other races.
Remedy - artificial colour does not work!
Family History of Macular Degeneration - you are at increased risk of developing AMD if you are related to someone who has or had the condition.
Remedy - choose your parents wisely!
Smoking - smoking cigarettes not only increases your risk of macular degeneration, but also many other conditions and costs you money you could spend on better things.
Remedy - quit smoking! If you are finding this difficult, think about getting professional help to quit.

Light & Sunlight - the harmful effects of ultraviolet (UV) rays are well known, but blue wavelengths from the sun can damage the macula as well. AMD sufferers generally require increased lighting in the home so you need to be aware that certain types of artificial lighting can also emit blue light.

Remedy - bear this in mind and get advice about devices that provide extra illumination, and what kind of eye protection is best to wear. *(See Appendix 5: Light and AMD)*

Cardiovascular Disease - diseases that affect the heart and blood vessels (cardiovascular disease), especially high blood pressure, may also contribute to the risk of AMD.

Remedy - some improvement may be made using the recommendations below. If you have a family history or already have a problem, strictly follow your doctor's advice.

Failure to Adopt a Healthy Lifestyle - in this section I am grouping several conditions together because they are related.

a) Obesity - as with smoking, being seriously overweight increases your risk in many conditions eg, cardiovascular. It heightens the chance that early or intermediate macular degeneration will progress to the more severe form of the disease quicker. It also predisposes you to developing type 2 diabetes which is not good as diabetes carries its own risks for retinal eye problems.

Remedy - take regular exercise and keep weight within recommended limits.

b) Unhealthy Diet - a poor diet high in saturated fat and sugar with few fruits and vegetables may increase the risk of macular degeneration.

Remedy - follow the guidelines in the next section. *(Related Matters IX: Healthy Eating for Better Vision)*.

Briefly, your diet should include:

• Lots of fruit and vegetables - aim at 5-10 portions daily.
• Whole-grain breads and cereals that have lots of fibre – probably half of your daily grains and cereals should be 100% whole grains (take care to avoid sugars and refined white flours commonly found in bread, cakes and some cereals).

- Healthy fats and oils. Omega-3 essential fatty acids which are found in fish, flaxseed oil, soya beans and walnuts can help to prevent dry eyes. Eat fish or seafood twice weekly or take flax oil every day. These measures will help you avoid undesirable saturated fat.
- Proteins. These are found in lean meats, fish, nuts, legumes and eggs, but check that your cooking methods do not add saturated fat. Eat fish or white meat in preference to red meat.
- Water in plentiful amounts to stay hydrated. Non-sugary, non-alcoholic beverages can be included.

c) **High Cholesterol** - cholesterol is a lipid (meaning a fatty substance) which is required by the body, but too much cholesterol can lead to a risk of cardiovascular disease (including angina, heart attacks and stroke). It has also been implicated in contributing to AMD.[63]

There are different types of blood cholesterols or lipids and you may have heard about good and bad cholesterol. There are two main types of cholesterol:

- Low density lipid (LDL) also known as 'bad cholesterol'
- High density lipid (HDL) or 'good cholesterol'.

Another common lipid in the body is triglyceride (TG) which is derived from dietary fat coming from both animal (including dairy) and vegetable sources in our food. Triglycerides circulate in our blood where they provide a calorie source wherever energy is required, or alternatively, if the immediate energy needs of the body have been satisfied, they will be stored by fat cells for later use. After a fatty meal, blood triglyceride levels are raised for a few hours, but persistently high blood triglycerides are linked with an increased risk of health conditions including heart disease.

For good health there must be a balance between the different lipids, and it is the relationship between total cholesterol (LDL+TG) and

---

[63] An article published online in the journal Cell Metabolism (2nd April 2013): 'Cholesterol build-up links atherosclerosis and macular degeneration' by Jim Dryden referred to a study at Washington University School of Medicine in St Louis which suggested that drugs prescribed to lower cholesterol may also be effective against macular degeneration because both AMD and atherosclerosis have the same under-lying defect:-the inability to remove build-up of fat and cholesterol.

HDL, expressed as total cholesterol divided by HDL that is important, because it is thought that HDL (good cholesterol) may have a protective effect against heart disease.

The supposed protective effect of HDL has caused some people to look for a means of artificially raising blood HDL, but recent research at Cambridge University has shown that for some people HDL cholesterol[64] is not always 'good cholesterol' as people with a genetic predisposition to have high levels of HDL are also at greater risk of heart disease as the HDL cholesterol loses its ability to protect them.

Remedy - the first thing is to get your blood cholesterol measured. A 'spot' or finger-prick test will give a rough guideline, but if it is raised you will need to have a proper blood test that can give a breakdown of the different cholesterol and triglyceride levels (known as a 'lipid profile'). This will normally be done at your doctor's surgery, and if levels are high they will usually arrange follow-up tests, especially if there is any personal or family history of cardiovascular complications.

A diet low in saturated fats and dairy produce, together with exercise and other measures advised in this section, should help maintain or even lower your cholesterol, but there are some people who, even if they don't have a familial condition called hypercholesterolaemia (where a very high cholesterol is inherited), cannot reduce their blood cholesterol by dietary measures alone. In such cases medication called 'statins' is often prescribed to do this. Some people also advocate the use of certain butter substitute spreads and drinks with commercially added plant statins. *(For more dietary advice, see the next chapter)*

---

[64] In an article published in the journal Science (11 Mar 2016), Zanoni et al, found that some people with exceptionally high levels of HDL-C carry a rare sequence variant in the gene encoding the major HDL-C receptor, scavenger receptor BI. This variant destroys the receptor's ability to take up HDL-C. Interestingly, people with this variant have a higher risk of heart disease despite having high levels of HDL-C.

IX. Healthy Eating for Better Vision
'If it came from a plant, eat it; if it was made in a plant, don't.'
Michael Pollan, In Defence of Food: An Eater's Manifesto

Eating a healthy balanced diet with a wide variety of foods but avoiding saturated fats is considered beneficial for improving eye health and your health in general. Make sure you include:

Lots of Vegetables and Fruit
The antioxidants in fruit and vegetables protect against oxidation which contributes to AMD. Dark green leafy vegetables like spinach, kale, mustard and collard greens contain high levels of lutein, a critical antioxidant. Brightly coloured fruit and vegetables also contain antioxidants, eg; red grapes, peppers, sweetcorn, oranges, cantaloupe and mango. Try to include as much fresh produce as you can in a variety of colours to get a wide range of vitamins in your diet. Aim for over 5 and possibly up to 10 servings a day.

Fish - especially oily fish
Fish contains Omega-3 which seems to be a critical nutrient for the heart and eyes so try to include fish at least 2-3 times a week. If you cannot tolerate fish, an Omega-3 supplement should be taken. A word of caution here, however, because a number of supplements taken for various conditions these days already contain Omega-3 so it is important to read the labels and check that your total daily dose does not exceed 3g (or 3 x 1,000mg capsules) daily.

White meat is better than red meat
A thirteen year study carried out by Dr Elaine Chong and her colleagues at the University of Melbourne in Australia[65] monitored diet and its effects on the vision of nearly 7,000 middle-aged men and women and found that people of middle-age and over who ate red meat a minimum of ten times a week were 47% more likely to develop symptoms of age-related AMD than those who ate red meat 5 times a week or less. Interestingly, the research also found that people who ate chicken (instead of red meat) roughly 3 times a week, rather than

---

[65] The research was published in a 2009 issue of the American Journal of Epidemiology.

those who ate chicken only once a week, reduced their risk by 57%. The message seems to be to eat more chicken if you want to reduce the risks of AMD!

Limit Your Fat Intake

The amount of saturated fats in the diet is the important issue. Saturated fat comes from animal products - beef, lamb, pork, lard, butter, cream, whole milk and high fat cheese, but can also be present in some plant oils including coconut oil, cocoa butter, palm oil and palm kernel oil. Replace these with healthy fats like olive oil or avocado, and always check the labels on processed foods and baked goods which may also contain saturated fat.

Following the above advice should mean your weight and cholesterol levels will tend to look after themselves unless you have a medical problem with maintaining blood cholesterol at recommended levels, in which case your doctor will prescribe cholesterol lowering agents. *(More about cholesterol will be found in Related Matters VIII: Causes and Contributions).*

Spices and Herbs

If you enjoy spices and herbs in your food, you may like to try adding rosemary[66] and saffron as both these plant substances have been attributed with AMD helping properties. Rosemary is also said to have other health giving benefits, including - music to the ears of us 'oldies' - the ability to improve memory, while saffron capsules taken in a dose of 30 mg/day (15 mg twice per day) was shown to be as good and cause less side effects than donepezil 10 mg/day (5 mg twice per day), a common current treatment for mild to moderate Alzheimers disease[67]. *(For AREDS recommended dietary supplements, see Appendix 4: Vitamins and Dietary Supplements.)*

---

[66] Reporting in the journal Investigative Ophthalmology & Visual Science, a team of scientists from Sanford-Burnham Medical Research Institute led by Stuart A Lipton, MD, PhD discovered that carnosic acid, a component of the herb rosemary, protects your retina from degeneration and toxicity. November 2012.
[67] Psychiatric Research Center, Roozbeh Psychiatric Hospital, Tehran University of Medical Sciences, South Kargar Street, Tehran 13337, Iran. s.akhond@neda.net January 2010.

X. More Cause for Hope?

'To be without hope is like being without goals, what are you working towards?'
Catherine Pulsifer

If you have been told you cannot have an operation like the one I had (iolAMD) because you have undergone previous cataract surgery, you may be interested to know that Mr Bobby Qureshi and Professor Pablo Artal have also devised a lens implant system for people who have had a cataract extraction. This is what it says about it on the LEH website:

'Previous cataract surgery? IolAMD-EyeMax™ [68]

Many patients develop macular disease years after previous cataract surgery and until now, haven't had the possibility of improving their vision or slowing the effects of its degeneration. The new iolAMD EyeMax™ lenses have unique qualities that mean they can be implanted in patients who have previously undergone cataract surgery and have subsequently found that their vision has deteriorated due to macular disease.

How do the iolAMD EyeMax™ lenses work?

The EyeMax™ lenses are made from a pliable material, and are Inserted into the eye via a tiny incision that is so small that there is usually no requirement for sutures. The lenses are placed in front of the patient's existing intraocular lens, which were implanted during previous cataract surgery. These wide-angle lenses project gently magnified, higher quality images to a large proportion of the back of the eye, so the patient gets edge-to-edge vision with improved clarity. The brain takes information from this image and uses the best parts to make up a picture. Unlike traditional lenses, the wide-angle technology used in iolAMD EyeMax™ can provide images of superior quality, enabling the brain to create a higher resolution composite result which should result in improved vision'.

---

[68] http://iolamd.com/previous-cataract-surgery-patients.php. *Quoted with permission.*

219

The really clever part about this operation, is that there are built-in safeguards against the effects of the progression of the macular degeneration process. I read on:

'Insurance against future progression

The wide-angle iolAMD™☐ EyeMax lens projects images both in the fovea (centre of the retina) and at the eccentric (not central) areas. This means that if the macular condition progresses, the patient's brain could continue to take images from where they are still available at the back of the eye - potentially maximising their vision into the future.'[69]

My understanding from the short video on the website is that the EyeMax™ lenses consisting of two components are inserted in front of the existing replacement lens implanted during cataract surgery. One lens is angled backwards towards the patient's existing iol (cataract replacement lens) while the other is angled forwards through the pupil. Both lenses feature advanced wavefront geometry which improves tolerance to variations in lens placement and also reduces distortions in a similar way to the original 'Hubble' iolAMD lenses.

The typical monofocal iols normally used in cataract replacement operations produce sharp images in the central area of vision where the macula is located. However, many patients with AMD already have significant blindness in this area, and cannot therefore be helped by any improvements there. To cope with this, most will have learned to adapt and got used to automatically focussing peripherally, ie, outside the central area, but then another problem emerges because this is outside the area that a monofocal lens would improve. EyeMax™ overcomes this by providing a larger area of focus so the brain itself is able to process signals from the best area(s) to build up an optimal composite picture by using signals received from each eye. In other words, the brain possesses a phenomenal capacity to adapt in selecting and processing the best area(s) of the macula

---

[69] Please contact info@iolAMD.com for more information

outside the diseased fovea centralis[70]. This provides an optimal image if the fovea itself can no longer do so, and moreover, the brain will continue to do this as the AMD progresses for as long as any useful retinal tissue remains.

In future routine cataract operations Mr Qureshi plans to replace the lens that has the cataract with a lens similar to the EyeMax™ which offers the benefit of wide-angled projection together with a gentle magnification. If these patients then go on to develop AMD later, the corrective lens implanted in the earlier cataract operation will allow the brain to continue selecting the best possible image from the non-diseased portions of the macula without further surgery.

To envisage this, it might help to picture a cinema with a wide screen projection. The new lens has the ability to focus the light over a wide area in the same way that the film you are watching gets projected onto a wide screen. In the case of the eye, this area is all around the damaged area of central vision caused by the AMD and includes the whole of the rest of the macula. This ensures that any parts of the macula that are capable of being stimulated by the light will be sending signals to the brain which will then select the best signals from all those it receives to interpret as a picture.

When I had my operations in 2015 I was told that if my AMD progressed and started affecting the new area which currently receives the light re-directed to it by the implanted lens causing my AMD symptoms to return, the lens could be moved slightly to use a different healthier area of macula. Yet just a few months later in December of that year, the EyeMax™ lens was developed and Bobby Qureshi himself told me that he would no longer do that, but would simply insert one of these newer wide-angled lenses! This would ensure that as the degeneration process continued there would always be enough areas for the brain to select from as long as it was necessary to do this. Furthermore, EyeMax™ is not exclusively for

---

[70] The natural area of focus in the centre of the macula which gives the sharpest image. Appendix 1

people who have had cataract surgery, so surgeons are now able to choose between two corrective lenses for the AMD patient, according to what would be best for the individual concerned. In March 2016 I was pleased to see a report on the 'Patient UK' website about an 88 year old man who has had an EyeMax™ lens implanted in one eye and is doing so well that he will shortly have the other eye similarly treated.

Perhaps one of the best causes for hope is that there are people like Mr Bobby Qureshi and others mentioned in this chapter who are totally committed to finding a better way forward for those of us with AMD and other eye problems. I have no 'insider knowledge' and no special qualifications to write about these specialised areas, while the people engaged in this important work are generally far too busy to respond to enquiries so answers are more often gleaned from press releases and websites. However, in keeping with the heading of this chapter, I shall endeavour to describe some interesting developments I have discovered that offer yet more hope for AMD sufferers.

Injection for dry AMD

In the Autumn 2015 UK Macular Society 'Sideview' magazine my attention was drawn to a recruitment drive for patients with dry AMD willing to participate in the third stage trials of an injection treatment for this condition. This injection has shown encouraging results in its preliminary stages so it has now been extended to a multi-centred, multi-national trial to further evaluate the results, any potential side effects, and whether certain individuals have a genetic predisposition to respond well to the treatment.

The drug lampalizumab is injected into the eye at 4 to 6 week intervals. Professor Andrew Lotery of the Department of Ophthalmology at Southampton University, who heads up the trial in the UK, explained the process: 'Lampalizumab has already been most shown to reduce damage caused by Geographic Atrophy[71] by 20% in

---

[71]Geographic atrophy (GA), an advanced form of dry AMD

cases, and for some patients with a specific genetic biomarker by up to 44% in early stage trials.

These are significant reductions which, if replicated in this larger study, will revolutionise the way we treat the condition and mean that patients are no longer condemned to blindness when diagnosed. The two-year project will see nearly 2,000 patients enrolled onto one of two multi-national studies. Two-thirds of the patients will receive a 10 mg dose of lampalizumab by intravitreal (into the vitreous of the eye) injection every 4-6 weeks and the other third will be treated with sham injections".[72]

The final results and conclusions will not be available for some time as the trial will run over two years but patients with dry AMD will be eagerly awaiting the outcome, especially as it appears that in the case of injections for wet AMD the earlier they are given, the better the results will be.

Ellex Retinal Rejuvenation Therapy (2RT®)

'Shutting off the thought process is not rejuvenating; the mind is like a car battery - it recharges by running.'
Bill Watterson

The Ellex website[73] provides an encouraging introductory heading followed by the following statement:

'2RT: A New Hope for AMD Patients: 2RT® is a breakthrough laser therapy which has the potential to positively influence the lives of millions of people suffering from retinal disease, including AMD. It is a gentle 'cold' laser treatment capable of delivering a three-nanosecond pulse exclusively designed to target selected individual cells within the retinal pigment epithelium (RPE). It is not accompanied by any heat generation and so collateral damage to the nearby light sensitive retinal cells and other intra-ocular structures is eliminated'.

---

[72]http://www.uhs.nhs.uk/AboutTheTrust/Newsandpublications/Latestnews/2015/
Southamptoneyeexpertstrialnewdrugtoreducesightloss.aspx
[73] www.ellex.com/products/treatment/2rt-parent/retinal-rejuvenation/amd-treatment/

In an attempt to picture the manner in which the 2RT® treatment works, I like to think of the targeted cells swelling up and disintegrating whereupon 'scavenger' cells clear up the remains. At the same time, a repair response is stimulated in the RPE so that cells around the targeted areas move in to repair and recolonise the deficit left by the disintegrated cells, while the bottom layer of the retina, Bruch's membrane, becomes permeable again to fluids, allowing nutrients to flow into the area once more. Another benefit according to the research is that '2RT® also stimulates a natural immune response of the retina, resulting in drusen clearance and restoration of natural metabolite flow to the retinal environment.'[74]

A great deal of research has been going on in Australia[75] and other centres including St Thomas' Hospital, London[76] into treatments using 2RT® and, more recently, a study was commenced at Moorfields Eye Hospital, London looking at the effectiveness of 2RT® to treat various conditions of the retina including those caused by diabetes such as Diabetic Macular Edema (DME) which is a form of diabetic retinopathy.

To the non-specialist reader at least, the 2RT® system appears to have some outstanding advantages:
• Non-painful to the patient.
• Non-collateral damage because no heat is generated.
• It can be used early in the disease to prevent progression.
• There is some 'cross-over' of benefits to the non-treated eye.

Of the above, I find its use in early AMD perhaps the most encouraging. Theoretically, this means it could be used in that falsely

---

[74] Jobling et al., "Nanosecond Laser Therapy Reverses Pathologic and Molecular Changes in AMD without Retinal Damage," The FASEB Journal Vol 29, no 2 (February 1, 2015): 696–710, doi:10.1096/fj.14-262444
[75] On early dry AMD - at the Centre for Eye Research, Australia (CERA) by Professor Robyn Guymer, MB, BS, PhD, FRANZCO.
[76] On CSME - Prospective, open-labelled pilot study conducted in 2012 to investigate the safety and efficacy of 2RT® in the treatment of CSME. Patients with newly diagnosed DME underwent 2RT® with pulsed energy 78 µJ to 131 µJ, with the number of shots dependent upon patient extent of edema and leakage on FFA.

reassuring lull between initial diagnosis and the time when the patient first begins to notice actual symptoms. In my case, for example, it could have been given at any time in the period between 15 years ago when ophthalmologists and opticians first diagnosed my AMD and around five years ago in 2011 when I started to get symptoms. Even had it been used as late in the disease as five years ago, I might have avoided or delayed some of the worst visual impairment and resulting problems.

However, this statement is entirely hypothetical as this treatment had not been invented when I was first diagnosed, and does not seem to be widely available today - certainly not for early AMD at any rate - and although reports seem encouraging, it has obviously not gained the necessary widespread or NHS approval to be readily available. This may be because even longer follow-up studies are needed to ascertain whether the effects are only short-term improvements in retinal health and whether they actually can prevent or delay the eventual development of later stages of AMD.

Stem Cell Research

It's no use going back to yesterday, because I was a different person then.'
Alice in Wonderland, Lewis Carroll

What are stem cells?

You may already know that the cells of every organ in the body are different. From reading detective mysteries you will be familiar with the idea of tracing what substances are and where they come from by their microscopic appearance. If a medical student is faced with a small piece of red fleshy tissue and cannot tell with the naked eye whether it is, for example, a piece of spleen or liver, examining the cells under the microscope should remove any doubt as to its origin, providing the medical student has been working hard enough on his/her studies!

This is because liver tissue has some microscopic characteristics that spleen tissue does not, and vice versa. In fact, every organ in the body has its own specialised cells which develop in a specific way to

225

carry out the function of that particular organ. However, they all start from basic cells that take on the characteristics appropriate to the tissue they are destined to become part of as they mature.

As part of the 'repair kit' for every tissue in the body, there is a reserve of stem cells which are basic cells that have not yet developed into specialised cells for different parts of the body. When they receive a biological signal, they start to develop and replace 'time expired' or otherwise damaged cells in order to maintain the necessary numbers of healthy cells needed for each individual tissue to function. Indeed, stem cells associated with a particular tissue have already become slightly specialised or 'bespoke' for the organ they will become a part of.

Embryonic stem cells, as their name implies, are derived from a human embryo of just a few days old, and therefore are not yet 'biased' towards any organ. Thus, they are considered the best option for research into artificially stimulating the generation of new cells in body tissue, eg, the retina.

The retina is composed of different cells specialised to perform different tasks. There are two different light-sensitive cells, rods and cones[77], which transmit signals back through the nervous system to the brain which then interprets them, enabling us to see. These cells are located close to the Retinal Pigment Epithelial (RPE) cells located near the blood supply which help nourish the photoreceptor cells. RPE dysfunction is found in AMD and Retinitis Pigmentosa, and is also involved in diabetic retinopathy.

In September 2015 a BBC headline announced: 'First patient treated with stem cell therapy for wet age-related macular degeneration.' It continued, 'The trial will test if it is safe and effective to transplant a type of eye cell called retinal pigment epithelial (RPE) cells, grown from stem cells in the lab, to restore sight in people with severe visual loss from wet AMD. The cells are used to replace diseased ones at

[77] See Appendix 1:The Eye

the back of the eye using a specially engineered patch. The patch is inserted behind the retina in a surgical operation which lasts 1-2 hours.'

This research is being carried out by retinal surgeon Professor Lyndon Da Cruz from Moorfields Eye Hospital and is co-directed by Professor Pete Coffey of the University College London Institute of Ophthalmology. At the time of the news report a woman had been treated a month earlier by inserting a patch of these RPE cells into her retina and they appeared to be still present as expected, with no complications observed. The plan was to recruit limited number of patients to this trial over the following 18 months and then follow their progress over the subsequent year. The original patient was due to be re-examined in December 2015 to assess how much vision she had been able to recover through this process, but the results will not be published until other patients in the trial have been assessed.

If successful, it is hoped that this treatment will not only restore sight for the group of selected patients with severe wet AMD, but also be a useful remedy for many other kinds of macular disease, including dry AMD. It is impossible to predict how these injected cells will function long-term, or whether they will actually develop into fully working retinal cells capable of replacing the activity of cells lost by disease or degeneration, but, theoretically at least, this again appears to give cause for hope in the future. On 5th January, 2016 The Daily Telegraph website displayed a video of Professor Lyndon Da Cruz explaining the new technique[78]. He predicted that it will take about 5 years to fully assess this research before it has any hope of becoming available as a treatment.

Objections to stem cell use

Some people are uncomfortable with stem cell use, generally because they hold deeply held religious beliefs or support certain

---

[78] http://www.telegraph.co.uk/news/health/news/11896593/Doctors-take-big-step-towards-a-cure-for-age-related-blindness.html

moral values which cause objections to the use of stem cells in this way, particularly if the stem cells in question are derived from human embryos.

However, many who feel qualms over this procedure have no objections to using stem cells derived from adult human tissue, and proposals have been made based on the alternative option of using a patient's own skin cells as a possible source. Unfortunately, these do not have the great potential possessed by embryonic stem cells which have not yet been designated for any particular tissue. Another benefit of the embryonic stem cells is that they are free from the risks that might possibly be encountered in using cells that are already 'old'.

Other people have concerns about risks associated with the possible introduction of viruses or other unknown factors when the cells are embedded, while there are also fears about the unknown risks of adverse developments of the cells long-term, eg, risks of causing cancer to develop, particularly in the case of stem cells derived from the patient's own tissue. Unfortunately, even if the stem cell trials do produce successful results, it is still not possible to pronounce that a cure for AMD has finally been found as there is no guarantee that the newly produced cells will not also eventually succumb to the ravages of AMD.

Gene research

A lot of research is currently taking place into the genetics of AMD to try and identify which genes are present in people with AMD and other retinal diseases, and what their influence on eyesight might be. This may give clues to help channel the future direction of research for possible cures.

In December 2014 an article in 'Medical News Today' by Catherine Paddock PhD[79] announced: 'Macular degeneration research gets a boost from large gene study.' It stated that an international study

---

[79] www.medicalnewstoday.com/authors/catharine-paddock-phd

published in the journal 'Nature Genetics' had significantly expanded the number of genetic factors known to be involved in the development of AMD. Researchers from the International AMD Genomics Consortium collected and analysed genetic data from 43,566 people of predominantly European descent and found 52 common and rare variants linked to AMD. First co-author Jonathan L Haines, a professor of Genomic Studies at Case Western Reserve University in Cleveland, OH, observed: *"These variants provide a foundation for genetic studies of AMD going forward."*

Before the new study scientists knew of 21 regions of the genome containing sequences of DNA whose variations might affect the risk of developing AMD. The new study brings that number to 34. Professor Haines concluded: *"The next step is to investigate what the variants are doing to the genes and how they affect gene function. Do they turn them on, or off? Do they interact with other genes spurring a series of events along a pathway that leads to AMD?"*

In April 2016 the BBC[80] announced some promising results from research with gene therapy, published in the New England Journal of Medicine from a study of 14 patients in the UK and 18 in the US, Canada and Germany over the past four and a half years. They injected genes into the cells of the retinae of patients with retinal disease resulting in encouraging reversal of some of their visual loss. More work needs to be done, but at this stage the scientists concerned are daring to hope that this could lead to a permanent cure of some retinal conditions.

Other Routes to Better Vision

'You are going to do some bionic snooping, my dear!'
Oscar Goldman in the 1976 film 'The Bionic Woman'.

To make blind eyes see again seems to have been the elusive dream of countless people from many fields of endeavour for generations, and for a long time it seemed this was just the stuff of fantasy fiction and Sci-Fi movies. Yet, more recently, encouraging progress has

---

[80] http://www.bbc.co.uk/news/science-environment-36101786

been made in a number of ways that have succeeded if not quite in making blind eyes see, at least in giving some kind of 'vision'.

Although it is right at the other extreme of the age spectrum being considered in this book, I shall just mention something about premature babies because it comes close to the goal of 'Making blind eyes see'. With advances in care of the newborn came the ability to sustain life in the tiniest of human bundles, sometimes weighing under 1lb (453.59g), but this was often done at the cost of their eyesight as their retinas would then fail to develop properly, leaving them blind. However, for a number of years now skilled surgeons have been able to operate microscopically on their minute retinas to give them some vision, even if not perfect sight, thanks to the advances in micro-surgical techniques.

External Gadgets

Modern technology has enabled huge leaps forward in the search to restore vision. New types of electronic gadgets are now emerging that can be worn to help the blind and partially blind receive information about the world around them in various ways. There are clever technical devices rather like cell-phones in appearance, or even adapted from them, that can be activated in different ways, eg, by visible or invisible (infra-red) markers placed on pathways or objects around the home that give off vibrations so the blind person knows they are there. Such devices can also tell people with sight problems whether they are on the 'correct path', rather like an airliner's Instrument Landing System (ILS) which informs the pilot whether the correct 'approach path' is being followed as the aircraft comes in to land at an airport.

Of course, what I have just described makes use of sensory systems (the sense of hearing or touch) to replace part of the eye's function. However, in recent times we have also been privileged to see some function restored to blind eyes themselves by light being redirected to fall on the retina once more, or stimulating the retina in various ways. In some cases this will allow just a very basic degree of vision where shapes can be distinguished, but in others a considerable amount of detail can be seen.

Clearing a Light Pathway to the Retina - Surgical Techniques

Perhaps the most obvious example of allowing light to fall on the retina again and thereby restore vision is the simple cataract extraction operation in which the clouded cataract hindering the light from falling onto the retina is removed. Until the pioneering work of eye surgeon Harold Ridley, patients had to resort to wearing very thick spectacle lenses to replace the body's natural lens. Harold Ridley observed that WW2 fighter pilots' eyes did not suffer any rejection reaction to penetrating injuries from cockpit 'glass' in contrast to ordinary glass splinters and went on to implant the first intra-ocular replacement lens (IOL) in 1950. For the first thirty years after this landmark achievement IOL's were not universally approved or commonplace after cataract surgery, but eventually they became the norm to replace thick spectacles and were later also developed to help sufferers from dry AMD[81] by redirecting light to fall on a healthier part of the retina.

A similar clearing of an obstruction to vision has also been achieved through corneal grafting which involves replacing a cornea 'clouded' by disease or damage by excising it and grafting on another cornea from a donor in its place.

Another intriguing way for light to reach the retina once more was reported in October 2013 by the Daily Mail. What caught people's attention was the extraordinary heading: 'HOW A TOOTH CAN RESTORE SIGHT!' It went on to relate the curious experience of a man whose eye had been damaged by trauma many years previously. He regained his vision when a small plastic lens was implanted by extracting one of his teeth and fixing it inside his non-functioning eye in a curious operation known as Osteo-Odonto-

---

[81] See Chapter 30: A Meeting with the Maker'

Keratoprosthesis (OOKP).[82] Fortunately, this patient's retina had not been damaged in the accident which caused his sight loss, and the use of his own tooth avoided any rejection issues that might have occurred with material taken from somebody else. The OOKP operation was carried out at the Sussex Eye Hospital in Brighton by Mr Christopher Liu, the only person in the UK then performing it.

Improving the Retina itself - Stem Cells and Gene Therapy

I have already outlined the possibilities that stem cells offer by stimulating replacement of the retinal cells themselves, but gene therapy is another interesting avenue of research. New studies using gene therapy to transform normal nerve cells into light sensing cells, capable of performing the function of the photoreceptor cells (rods and cones) in the retina, are currently being carried out in animals, but it is hoped that the research will shortly expand to humans.

Another curious operation which falls into this category was reported in 'The Independent'. The technique developed by Zhuo-Hua Pan of Wayne State University in Detroit is part of a new field called optogenetics which transplants algae or other micro-organisms that respond to light or create molecules to do so into nerve cells, making them capable of receiving light.[83]

This is not the only form of gene therapy that has been used, and virus mediated (AAV adeno-associated virus) gene therapy has already helped considerably in the treatment of a rare genetic retinal condition known as Leber's Congenital Amaurosis (LCA). It is outside the scope of this book to explain this in detail, but promising results were substantiated in three centres in 2008 leading to a great deal of optimism about the possibility of treating different forms of

---

[82] In 1996 the first OOKP UK operation was televised as a BBC 'Tomorrow's World' programme. However, this was not a new technique as OOKP was invented by the late Benedetto Strampelli over 30 years ago. See: Strampelli B (1963) Keratoprosthesis with osteodontal tissue. Am J Ophthalmol 89:1029–1039 and B. Strampelli (1964) Tecnica E Risultati Della Osteo Odonto Cheratoprotesi. SOI Proc XLIII, pp 288–291.
[83]From The Independent:Andrew Griffin @_andrew_griffin Tuesday 19th May 2015

non-inherited and inherited blindness. This includes wet AMD which has been the subject of AAV gene therapy research undertaken at the Lions Eye Institute in Australia.[84] It is hoped that this will eventually result in a single treatment for this condition rather than repeated intra-ocular injections. The Ellex 2RT® cold laser therapy described earlier also comes into this category as the aim is to produce healthier retinal cells.

'Artificially Stimulating the Retina - Bionic Eyes'

In July 2015 The Daily Telegraph announced a 'World First' in Manchester, when an 80 year old pensioner suffering from advanced AMD was fitted with a bionic eye[85]. Consultant ophthalmologist Paulo Stanga at Manchester Royal Eye Hospital explained that the bionic eye had already been used successfully for people suffering the condition retinitis pigmentosa, but he wanted to find out if it would also work for people with AMD. He further stated that he was very pleased with the results so far, and was looking forward to treating more patients by this method.

In this operation an electronic device is implanted in the patient's retina and the patient wears spectacle frames incorporating a video-camera. Video recordings are sent to a video-processing unit worn on a belt or strap which then formats the information, sending it back to the glasses where it is transmitted wirelessly to the implant in the eye. Pulses of electricity pass through electrodes that sit on the retina which stimulate the healthy cells so they send electrical signals to the brain via the optic nerve just like the normal eye, resulting in a sensation of vision comparable to that experienced by people with normal sight.

---

[84] Safety and Efficacy Study of rAAV.sFlt-1 in Patients with Exudative Age-Related Macular Degeneration (AMD)'. US National Institutes of Health. Retrieved 1st June 2012.
[85] http://www.telegraph.co.uk/news/science/science-news/11753949/Bionic-eye-fitted-to-British-pensioner

This Manchester pensioner is the first person in the world to have both artificial and natural vision combined, and he also has the dubious advantage of being able to see with his eyes closed. So, in future, beware of assuming that the person wearing bulky spectacles, who appears to be asleep, can't see you, because he may actually be watching everything you do!

The heading of Sebastian Anthony's article on 22nd February 2013 was exciting: 'The first real, high resolution, user-configurable bionic eye'. [86] It described a procedure carried out in Germany at the University of Tübingen where a device called the Alpha IMS retinal prosthesis was implanted onto the patient's retina which was able to be stimulated by light entering the patient's eye.

It was completely self-contained, unlike other 'bionic eye' devices that rely on some form of external camera, and in contrast to the camera based devices, the person with the implant could look at something just by moving their eyes rather than their whole head. The Alpha IMS can be connected to your brain via 1,500 electrodes, providing unparalleled visual acuity and resolution. The clinical trials reported a huge degree of success with participants being able to distinguish between small items, facial expressions, signs on doors, and whether the wine in a glass was red or white!

On 5th January, 2016 the BBC reported: 'At Oxford's John Radcliffe Hospital a clinical trial is taking place in which six patients who have had little or no sight for many years are having a cutting-edge 'bionic eye' implanted in an attempt to give them some sight and independence back'. [87] The patient interviewed had quite severe blindness caused by retinitis pigmentosa which destroys the light sensitive cells in the retina, but apparently had some basic vision restored and could distinguish shapes.

---

[86] *http://www.extremetech.com/extreme/149106-the-first-real-high-resolution-user-configurable-bionic-eye*
[87] http://www.bbc.co.uk/news/health-35220615

The device replaces the light-sensitive retinal cells in the eye and is connected to a tiny computer that sits underneath the skin behind the ear. When it is switched on using a magnetic coil applied to the skin, signals travel to the optic nerve and on to the brain. The patient was able to control the stimulus she received with an external controller and, with practice, her interpretation of the signals was expected to improve. The consultant speaking about the implant also spoke of its improved design, meaning that devices would now last for around 5 years rather than 18 months as formerly.

Some people believe future developments for successfully treating AMD and other types of retinal disease lie in further developing such electronic retinal implants, particularly as they may be able to get round the problem of using retinal cells which could themselves eventually succumb to progressive AMD.

Future treatments may possibly involve the use of a combination of the methods outlined above or other research yet to be made known. I personally find it encouraging to know that all these pioneering developments have been going on when so many of us had been given the depressing news that there was no treatment for dry AMD. Year by year it seems there are many more advances that continue to solve the problems and improve the quality of life for those who suffer from diseases of vision.

APPENDIX 1 - The Eye

To explain what is meant by the process of macular degeneration, let me take you back to school to explain the basic biology of the eye. I will try to keep it simple and you can follow it by referring to the diagram on the next page which illustrates the anatomy of the eye.

You may know that the eye has three layers making up its 'shell'. The outermost layer is the **sclera** or 'white of the eye' - a tough coating or housing that gives the eye a degree of protection. The sclera continues in front of the eye as a transparent layer known as the **cornea**. If this were not transparent, we would not be able to see as light could not penetrate the eye.

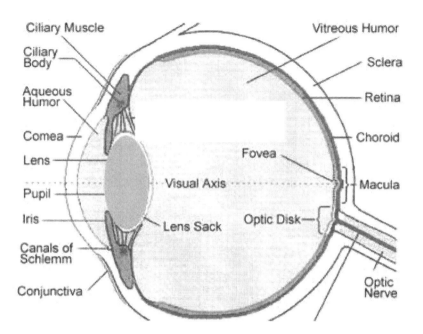

Beneath the sclera is a layer called the **choroid** that contains blood vessels that nourish this part of the eye. Inside the choroid is a light sensitive lining called the **retina**. When light falls on this, it stimulates special light sensitive nerve cells (**rods** and **cones**) that send messages to the brain via the **optic nerve** so we are able to see an image of what our eye is looking at.

The bulk of the centre of the eye, the '**vitreous chamber**', contains a gel-like substance called '**vitreous humour**' which helps the eye keep its shape.

The '**anterior chamber**' is positioned in front cf the lens below the **cornea,** and the '**posterior chamber**' below the lens. They contain '**aqueous humour**' which is a fluid that keeps this area nourished and well lubricated.

The light enters the eye through the **pupil** which is a gap similar to the aperture in a camera, and this is surrounded by the **iris** which you will recognise as the part which gives the distinctive colour (blue, brown, hazel, etc) to a person's eyes. The pupil is located in the centre of the iris. The iris is a circular muscle that contracts or dilates to make the pupil (aperture) smaller or larger, thereby controlling the amount of light entering the eye.

This light coming through the pupil then meets the lens which, just like the lens in a camera, focuses the light to the place where the picture of what is being seen is sharpest. The human eye is designed so that, ideally, the sharpest image will fall on the surface of the retina. If we carry the analogy of a camera further, the retina is similar to the film in a camera - a light sensitive area that must receive the light in order for the whole structure to work.

In a person who is short-sighted (**myopic**) the sharpest focus falls slightly short of the retina *(See Fig 1),* while in a long-sighted person (**hypermetropic**) it falls slightly behind the retina *(See Fig 2).* Both these lens faults can be relatively easily corrected by wearing an external lens to remedy the vision problem in front of the eye (better known as spectacles or contact lenses!). Convex lenses are used for long-sighted correction and concave lenses for short-sighted correction .

Fig 1

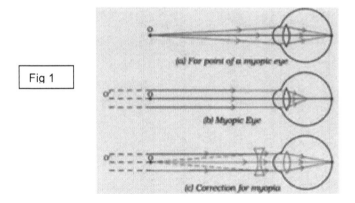

(a) For point of a myopic eye

(b) Myopic Eye

(c) Correction for myopia

Presbyopia (age-related loss of refraction) is a type of long sightedness (hypermetropia) caused by age. In this condition the eye starts to find difficulty in focussing on objects that are near to it. It is like the situation in long-sightedness *(fig 2)* where the light rays are directed to focus behind the retina.

237

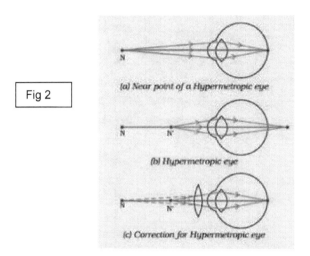

(a) Near point of a Hypermetropic eye

(b) Hypermetropic eye

(c) Correction for Hypermetropic eye

Fig 2

The lens of the younger eye has elasticity enabling it to focus objects at varying distances because the shape of the lens can be adjusted through the contracting or relaxing action of the **ciliary muscles** and their **suspensory ligaments,** a process known as **accommodation** which gives the image a sharper focus. For example, if an object is close, the lens will become fatter and more convex to get the sharpest focus on the retina. In the ageing process the lens of the eye becomes stiff and less elastic, losing this ability to change shape to precisely focus light on the retina, and it becomes necessary to add an extra convex lens in the form of spectacles or contact lenses in order to achieve a sharp focus on the retina once more. If with the lens in its normal resting position you can still focus on objects in the distance you are long-sighted. In other words, your near point is further away *(fig 2)* and you may need to hold your newspaper at arms-length!

I mentioned that there are two kinds of light-sensitive cells in the retina. The **cones** are most useful when the level of lighting is high so they are used mainly in day vision and are also involved in colour vision. The other cells are called **rods.** Rods are used in low levels of illumination as in night vision. However, there is an area on the retina that is especially sensitive to light and has the greatest density of the light sensitive cells called cones. This is known as the **macula** and the lens system of the eye is designed so that the light focused by the lens goes right into the centre (**fovea**) of this area. It is this part of the eye that is subject to degeneration in the condition known as **Age Related Macular Degeneration (AMD).**

In a person with AMD there is a loss of central vision so that the cones, which also help to see colour, lose their ability to function as photoreceptors. However, the peripheral vision remains intact, but that is produced largely by the rods. It will not give such sharp images as those produced by the fovea, the clearest area of vision of the macula, and colours may not show up so clearly, but learning how to use peripheral vision is a very useful skill for AMD sufferers (see Related Matters II: A Sideways Look at Life.)

APPENDIX 2 - Age-Related Macular Degeneration

(Please note that this section is included for your convenience but is not written by an ophthalmologist. As new treatments are continually being developed you are advised to consult your own eye-care professionals for the most recent information relating to this condition).

The picture on the right below indicates how a person with AMD might view the scene on the left *(from LEH website)*[88].

In considering Age-Related Macular Degeneration (AMD) it is important to know that there are two distinctive types with different

---

[88] The RNIB have an iTunes app that provides further information and a simulation of the vision that AMD sufferers have at various stages of the disease
https://itunes.apple.com/gb/app/rnib-amd/id657382683?mt=8

causes, and therefore the treatments will also be different. As the name Age-Related Macular Degeneration suggests, this is a problem of advancing age and the condition in either form is rare below the age of 50. However, as the years progress the chance of having AMD increases so at the age of 90-plus some degree of the condition is very likely.

At the present stage of medical knowledge, there is no cure for either type, although there are now some treatments available that can help in various ways, either by slowing the disease's progression or providing a way for the patient to cope in spite of the disease, some of which are described in the 'Related Matters' section of this book.

Both kinds of AMD may occur in the same patient, and both can affect either eye or both eyes in the affected person. Usually both eyes will eventually become affected, at least in the case of dry AMD, but often the eyes may be at different stages of the condition. In other words, the disease may be more pronounced in one eye than the other, and therefore vision will be worse in that eye.

Dry Age-Related Macular Degeneration (dry AMD)

As a person ages **drusen** grow in a layer of the retina known as the **Bruchs membrane**. Drusen are small yellow or whitish deposits of lipids, a type of fatty protein that actually interferes with the ability of the retinal cells to function as photoreceptors. As they grow, they push their way up through the retina and are clearly visible on the retina's surface when the back of the eye is viewed as part of an ophthalmic examination. When more than just a few drusen are seen, this is the stage where dry AMD is said to exist. The size of the drusen and how many there are within a given area (ie, their density) are important indicators of the disease. If the drusen are small, hard and well spaced, there is less cause for concern. Problems are caused by a greater density of the larger, softer drusen.

The drusen actually cause atrophy of the nearby retinal cells so that they cease to function, shrink and die. This shrinkage can be measured on examination of the eye using Optical Coherence

Tomography (OCT). This is a non-invasive imaging test that uses light waves to take cross-section pictures of the retina. The shrinkage (or atrophy) shows up as thinning in that area, a process called 'geographic atrophy' which is another name sometimes used for dry AMD. If you use the analogy of a lawn, this atrophy is rather like the effect you get if somebody puts weed killer on parts of a nice green lawn. Soon afterwards dead and dying patches where everything is brown and withered will appear. When there are increasing numbers of drusen, especially the large soft ones, they gradually start to interfere with a person's vision until eventually the condition can no longer be ignored.

This is the stage when dry AMD becomes symptomatic. In other words, you begin to realise that what the ophthalmologists told you was happening at the back of your eye, possibly some years before, is actually now affecting your ability to see! The drusen alone, unless in large amounts, do not constitute dry AMD, but their presence does flag up the need for regular eye checks to make sure that AMD is not developing. In other words, drusen can occur in the absence of dry AMD, but in dry AMD drusen will always be present.

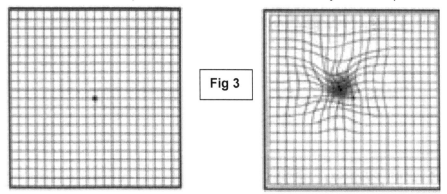

Fig 3

**On left is what an Amsler grid normally looks like and
On right how it might look to someone with MD**

There is also a small possibility that wet AMD may occur in a person with dry AMD although it only affects approximately one in every ten dry AMD sufferers. This is no consolation if you happen to be that one, and as there is as yet no way of predicting who the unfortunate ones will be, it is important to check your vision regularly using the

Amsler grid chart, and report any sharp decline in vision without delay, (see Fig 3). Other measures to help keep your eyes healthy include beneficial lifestyle modifications and taking AREDS 2 approved supplements *(see Related Matters: IX Healthy Eating & Appendix 4).*

If you do have an operation for dry AMD, it is important to remember that this is not a cure and that the underlying AMD will still be progressing. Normally, dry AMD tends to advance fairly slowly, but there are no hard and fast rules, and, once the symptoms become noticeable, vision will sometimes deteriorate fairly rapidly to end-stage dry AMD, causing natural fears that you may now also have wet AMD. The only way you can be sure is to have an eye clinic examination. Usually the onset of wet AMD tends to be much more dramatic. (See next section.)

Wet Age-Related Macular Degeneration (wet AMD)

Wet AMD is quite different from dry AMD because in wet AMD the loss of vision is caused when tiny new blood vessels grow out from the layer of blood vessels just below the retina, pushing between the cells and leaking blood or tissue fluid into the eye. The alternative name for wet AMD is neovascular AMD (literally 'new blood vessels') which is very appropriate as these blood vessels growing in the eye are completely new. If bleeding does take place, it leads to a very serious and rapidly destructive state of affairs resulting in sudden dramatic loss of vision.

The current preferred treatment involves injections into the eye at intervals using a substance that inhibits the growth of these new blood vessels. This has replaced the laser treatment formerly used as the tendency towards a recurrence of the leakage is much reduced. Wet AMD is currently responsible for 90% of all blindness in people suffering from macular degeneration.

Extract from Macular Society UK on wet AMD treatment

'*There are several drugs which are currently used to treat wet AMD. They are all a class of drug called 'anti-VEGF'. VEGF is short for 'Vascular Endothelial Growth Factor'. It is the substance in the body which is responsible for the development of healthy blood vessels.*

In wet AMD too much VEGF is produced in the eye, causing the growth of unwanted, unhealthy blood vessels. Anti-VEGF drugs block the production of VEGF and stop the development of the blood vessels. Lucentis is currently the drug used most often in this country. Its medical name is ranibizumab. Lucentis is given as an injection into the eye. Don't be alarmed – the injections are much less frightening than they sound! Most people need between 6 and 8 injections a year.

Another drug, Avastin (bevacizumab), is sometimes used to treat wet AMD. It is the most commonly used drug in countries such as the USA, but its use here is controversial. Avastin is an anti-VEGF drug used to treat cancer. Research suggests it works as well as Lucentis for wet AMD. However, it was not licensed for use in eyes and some doctors questioned the safety of Avastin as an eye drug. It was used in some areas because it was much cheaper than Lucentis. A new drug, Eylea (aflibercept) was coming into use in 2016. Eylea is also an anti-VEGF and is injected into the eye. Trials suggest that it is effective for longer than Lucentis and so may mean fewer injections are needed. It will be some time before it is clear how long it lasts, so patients may still need to have frequent check-ups to make sure their wet AMD is under control.

A few patients with AMD may be offered laser treatment. A light sensitive drug is injected into the patient's arm. The drug travels to the eye where it is activated by a laser beam, shutting down the abnormal blood vessels. Most people need two to five treatments. The treatment is only suitable for people with particular patterns of damage to the retina.

Diet may also play a role in AMD (See Appendix 4) *and many experts recommend a diet high in antioxidants, or sometimes a dietary supplement. Further trials into dietary supplements are underway.'*

APPENDIX 3 - More about Telescopic Vision - iolAMD™

'Enthusiasm is a telescope that yanks the misty, distant future into the radiant, tangible present.'
Anonymous

I was excited when I first read on the London Eye Hospital website:[89] *'This ingenious iolAMD lens uses technology developed by NASA to fix the Hubble Telescope. Mr Bobby Qureshi, Medical Director of the London Eye Hospital, joined forces with Professor Pablo Artal to create the iolAMD lens using this technology, which can be inserted during a straight forward cataract operation.'* I was very interested to see a coloured version of the image of how the lenses worked with the following explanation:

How does iolAMD work?

'The iolAMD lens uses technology that was developed after NASA scientists noticed that images from the Hubble Telescope were out of focus and fuzzy. To counteract this they developed an advanced solution using minute changes (adaptive optics) that successfully reduced the effects of distortion, and compensated for imperfections. In the ten minute iolAMD procedure, two tiny lenses made of pliable material are inserted into an incision of less than 3mm. The two iolAMD lenses work together to act like a telescope, gently magnifying the image entering the eye and diverting it to a healthier part of the retina. This section of healthier retina receives the image, taking over the role of the macula and can provide the iolAMD patient with significantly improved vision. Depending on the visual potential remaining in the eye, an iolAMD patient could regain the ability to drive, read or see faces, significantly improving their quality of life.'[90]

---

[89] http://www.londoneyehospital.com/treatments
[90] http:/ http://www.londoneyehospital.com/treatments-services/iolamd/   All material and diagrams reproduced with permission of the London Eye Hospital

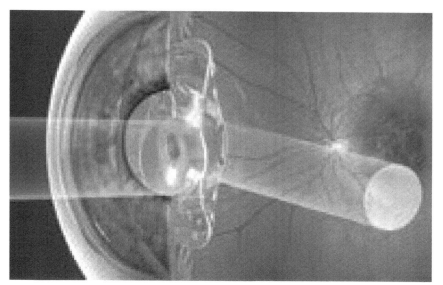

**Diagram illustrating the bending of light entering the eye in iolAMD to
redirect it to a different part of the retina**
Copyright: London Eye Hospital (By kind permission)

For those who like a bit more detail about the science behind the procedure I have also copied the following information from the 'physician's' part of the LEH website[91]

'In the iolAMD procedure, 2 advanced hydrophobic acrylic IOLs are placed inside the eye using modern surgical techniques. The magnification achieved is around 1.3x which allows for bilateral implantation, so that whilst visual acuity is improved, visual field is maintained. The iolAMD lenses contain hyper-aspheric surfaces and unique wavefront characteristics that reduce optical distortions normally associated with high power lenses as well as creating an increased tolerance of relative lens positioning.'

An excellent new video explanation of AMD and its surgical treatment can be found by visiting the website below.[92]

---

[91] http://iolamd.com/what-is-iolamd.php
[92] http://iolamd.com/how-iolamd-can-help.php

APPENDIX 4 - Vitamins and Dietary Supplements

The following is an extract from The University of Michigan Kellogg Eye Centre website: 'Dietary Supplements and Age Related Macular Degeneration':

'In 2013 the National Eye Institute (NEI) published the results of the Age Related Eye Disease Study 2 (AREDS 2) clinical trial, which followed the original AREDS study in 2011. The first AREDS study found a 25% reduction in the risk of developing advanced age-related macular degeneration (AMD) over a five year period in individuals with intermediate AMD, or advanced AMD in one eye if they took a specific formulation of antioxidant vitamins and minerals.

AREDS 2 attempted to improve on the original formulation and found that individuals taking the original AREDS formula with lutein and zeaxanthin but without beta-carotene (vitamin A) may have a slight reduction in the risk of developing advanced AMD. In addition, the formulation without beta carotene may have a lower risk of developing lung cancer in former smokers.'

Recommendations

Although the AREDS 2 clinical trial data was not strongly conclusive, it provided enough evidence to suggest taking the formulation quoted below.

Dietary Supplements
Vitamin C: 500 mg
Vitamin E: 400 IU (international units)
Zinc: 25 to 80 mg,
Copper: 2 mg,
Lutein: 10 mg
Zeaxanthin: 2 mg.

Unfortunately, in spite of specialist age-related eye studies indicating the benefits of these dietary substances they are not available on the NHS, and therefore you must buy the tablets 'over the counter' at your own expense. However, do be careful when buying dietary supplements for the eyes as a great many commercially available products that claim to improve your vision do not contain the correct AREDS 2 formulation.

Although not part of the original AREDS recommendation, some AREDS 2 supplements will also contain Omega 3 because of its potential eye-health benefits. However, if this is the case, care must be taken not to exceed the recommended daily dose (which is 3 gms) because Omega 3 is in many other proprietary supplements and you may not always be aware that something you are taking for the good of your joints, heart, skin or brain may actually contain various omega oils. Many people also take pure Omega dietary supplements because we have all been persuaded that they are good for us, especially if we do not eat oily fish. Omega oils can also influence other medication such as the anti-clotting agent Warfarin - so although these dietary supplements are available without a prescription, it is wise to consult your doctor or pharmacist before starting to take them.

If you dislike taking tablets you can now even buy a chocolate bar containing the AREDS formulation called The 'EyeBar' by Altacor.

Breaking News: AREDS and AREDS2® preparations eg, MacuLEH Light – a prescription only AREDS based vitamin and mineral health food supplement - were approved for inclusion within the UK drug tariff from 1st March 2016.[93] However, at the time of writing, it would appear that not all Primary Care Trusts are allowing their doctors to prescribe them on the NHS.

APPENDIX 5 - Light and Looking after your Eyes

Lighting for AMD sufferers is a complicated subject and not all who market lighting products understand the implications for AMD. Therefore, my advice is to consult a low vision specialist before you

---

[93] https://londoneyehospitalpharma.com/healthcare-professional-site-our-products/

purchase additional lighting to help your condition as they will give you informed advice on the best lighting to protect and maximise your vision. This is especially important if you are taking any medication that might have photosensitising properties of which there are a surprising number, including some commonly used by those over 50.

The most suitable type of lamp is one that gives 'natural light' and avoids the harshness or glare of some lighting, eg, fluorescent tubes.

LIGHTING RECCOMMENDATIONS

• **Ott-Lite** – Dr John Ott developed this pioneering high contrast, low glare 'natural daylight' lighting more than 50 years ago.
• **LazLight** – The goose-neck design of this lamp allows you to focus light exactly where you want it. The LazLight was specifically designed for people with low vision and macular degeneration. It is not an ordinary reading lamp, but a serious lighting tool. Its dimmer switch means light can be precisely adjusted to suit the user's specific needs.
• **Berryessa Designs** – desk or table lamps using safe cost-effective long-lasting LED technology to emit light that is not damaging to the eyes. Ask for the AMD 50% discount on the Junior design.

HELPFUL LIGHTING HINTS

• Use lamps that can be angled to help direct the light.
• In floor-lamps with adjustable lamps, direct the light over the shoulder of the eye with the best visual acuity.
• Position lamps near frequently used appliances and install lights under cabinets to give good illumination on kitchen work surfaces. Provide extra lighting in stairs and hallways where lighting can be poor.
• Install motion sensor lighting for outside entrances and garages.

LIGHT THERAPY LAMPS

Light therapy lamps are often used in treating SAD (Seasonal Affective Disorder, more commonly known as 'winter blues') but should be approached with caution as research shows some do not filter the short blue visible light which is thought to increase the risk of developing AMD.

However, there are alternative options now available such as the low intensity Lo-LIGHT lamp using GreenLIGHT technology developed by Sunnex Biotechnologies which does not advance the onset of macular degeneration or damage the retina and so can be safely used by patients suffering from SAD or sleep disorders.

SUNGLASSES and TINTED LENSES

Sunglasses are supposed to protect your eyes from the sun but many versions allow some direct sunlight to enter your eyes from the top and sides of the frame which is not helpful if bright light causes you problems. However, there are some designed specifically for people with AMD with features like side panels and a ridge at the top of the glasses so that all the light is filtered, while designs include wrap-around shades for total protection or designs that can be worn either on their own or over your normal prescription glasses. When choosing sunglasses, lenses with amber, brown, or orange tints are preferable as they block blue light more efficiently.

Reputable manufacturers of sunglasses for people with AMD include:
- **NoIR:** the N-Series filters provide excellent glare protection with large side shields and top lip.
- **Solar Shields:** fit over your normal glasses to offer 100% protection from UVA/UVB rays.
- **Cocoons Low Vision:** incorporate special absorptive filters that are specially designed to help increase visual acuity for people with low vision. They can be worn alone or over normal prescription glasses.

BLUE LIGHT

Sources of blue light include the sun, digital screens (TVs, computers, laptops, smart phones and tablets), electronic devices, fluorescent lighting and some LED lighting. It is a largely unrecognised hazard, but prolonged exposure to blue light may cause retinal damage and contribute to AMD. People with AMD find that yellow/amber-tinted lenses that absorb blue light, and others which have a blue reflective surface are helpful to wear instead of the usual clear lenses in their normal spectacles because these coloured lenses are soothing and will also protect eyes from further damage by blue light. I find both yellow lenses and blue reflective lenses particularly useful when working at my computer.

With growing evidence that both UV and blue light damage the retinas of people affected by, and at risk of, retinal disease, everything possible needs to be done to avoid aggravating the condition. Some optical companies offer blue-light and UV blocking technology which is particularly useful for anyone who spends a lot of time in front of the computer screen. They include Nikon (SeeCoat Blue UV) and Essilor (Crizal Prevencia) which offers a clear lens that selectively filters harmful UV and blue light.

COMPUTERS

When working at a computer for several hours at a time, eye strain can be a real problem causing dry and watering eyes, aching around the eyes, a stiff neck and headaches. Looking at a screen for long periods often means you may forget to blink enough to maintain eye lubrication. To protect yourself from the effect of dry eyes caused by this, use lubricating drops and blink frequently. Another way to minimise the problem of computer screen eye strain, is to follow the 20:20:20 rule. Every 20 minutes, take a 20-second break and look at something 20 feet away.

GLOSSARY

AAV (adeno-associated virus): AAV is a small virus which infects humans and some other primate species. AAV is not currently known to cause disease, and creates little immune response. This makes it an ideal vector (carrying agent) for use in gene therapy.

AAV therapy: A type of virus-mediated gene therapy considered beneficial in treating patients with eye diseases including the rare genetic retinal disease Leber's Congenital Amaurosis and AMD.

Accommodation: The process by which the eye adjusts in order to focus so it can produce a clear image of an object even when seen at different distances.

Adaptive optics: A telescopic system that improves image resolution by compensating for distortions.

Aflibercept: The medical name for the newer anti-VEGF drug Eyelea which may require fewer injections to inhibit growth of unhealthy blood vessels in wet AMD.

Age-Related Macular Degeneration (AMD): AMD is a painless eye condition most common in people over 50 years of age and is the leading cause of irreversible blindness in the developed world. It affects the macula area of the retina, and leads to progressive loss of central vision (what you see when you focus straight ahead). It comes in two types - dry and wet.

Amsler Grid: A grid of intersecting vertical and horizontal lines developed by Swiss ophthalmologist Marc Amsler to monitor a person's central visual field. In patients with macular disease the lines of the grid may appear wavy or disappear altogether in some places.

Anterior chamber: This is located in front of the lens below the cornea. It contains aqueous humour, a fluid that nourishes and keeps the shape of the eye.

Antihistamines: A drug used to treat allergic reactions such as hay fever, pet allergies etc. A side effect of this medication is that it may cause Dry Eye Syndrome.

Antioxidants: Antioxidants are man-made or natural substances that may prevent or delay some types of cell damage. Fruit and vegetables are good sources, and also dietary supplements such as AREDS 2 formulated to improve eye health.

Anti-VEGF (Anti-Vascular Endothelial Growth Factor): A type of drug used to block Vascular Endothelial Growth Factor (VEGF), the substance in the body responsible for developing blood vessels

Aqueous humour: This 'watery' fluid maintains the shape of the front of the eye, nourishes parts of the eye that lack a blood supply, and removes waste. It is produced in the posterior chamber by the ciliary body located just behind the iris and circulates through the pupil to the anterior chamber. Poor drainage of aqueous humour may raise pressure inside the eye and lead to glaucoma.

AREDS: Age Related Eye Disease Study: A major clinical trial at the National Eye Institute, Bethesda, USA researching macular degeneration and cataract, the two main causes of vision loss in older adults, to find ways to improve vision for those affected.

AREDS supplements: A nutritional vitamin and mineral supplement containing high doses of antioxidants recommended by AREDS. The AREDS formulations cannot prevent AMD, but may delay progression of advanced AMD and help retain vision longer if you have intermediate AMD or advanced AMD in one eye.

Artificial Tears: Eye-drops previously used to treat Dry Eye Syndrome.

Atrophic or Geographic Atrophic Macular Degeneration: Alternative names for dry macular degeneration.

Atrophy: a wasting away, degeneration, decline or decrease of the body or of an organ, part or tissue, eg, through disease or disuse.

Avastin® (bevacizumab): A cheaper anti-VEGF drug used somewhat controversially in injections to block growth of unhealthy blood vessels in the eyes of wet AMD sufferers.

Beta blockers: A type of medication (eg, drops) for treating conditions like angina, high blood pressure, heart failure and glaucoma that may also cause dry eyes as a side effect.

Beta-carotene: Beta-carotene is an orange pigment found in most fruit and vegetables. The body converts it to vitamin A which we need for healthy skin, our immune system and good eye health and vision.

Bevacizumab: See Avastin®

Biopsy: A small tissue sample removed from the body and examined under a microscope to look for abnormal cells, eg cancerous.

Bifocals: Glasses or contact lenses divided into two parts. The upper half is for looking at things that are far away, while the lower half is for reading or looking at things close to you.

Binocular central field loss: Loss of vision in the central field experienced when using both eyes.

Bionic eye: An experimental visual device intended to restore functional vision in those suffering from partial or total blindness.

Blepharitis: Inflammation of the eyelids which become red and swollen while the eyes may also feel sore and gritty. Treatment is normally through an ongoing programme of lid hygiene.

Blue light: Sunlight contains both UV and blue light, but many modern devices including computer screens, tablets, smartphones, flat-screen televisions and LED lights also emit large amounts of blue light. Blue light reaches deeper into the eye and its cumulative effect can cause damage to the retina while it has also been implicated in the development of AMD. One solution is to wear amber-tinted glasses which are highly effective in blocking blue light.

BMA (British Medical Association): Professional body representing and advising UK doctors and medical students in all areas of medical practice and training.

Brutes membrane: Transparent inner membrane of the retina that separates the pigmented layer from the choroid's layer of blood vessels.

Carcinoma: Cancer that begins in skin or tissues lining or covering body organs. Examples of carcinoma sites include the breast, colon, liver, lung, pancreas and prostate.

Cardiology: Branch of medicine that deals with diseases and abnormalities of the heart.

Cardiovascular disease (CVD): Diseases affecting the heart and blood vessels. Studies have linked cardiovascular disease to major eye diseases including AMD, retinopathy and glaucoma.

Casevac: An abbreviation of Casualty Evacuation which involves the transportation of a wounded or ill person, usually by air, from a military area to an area where medical care can be provided.

Cataract: A clouding of the lens in one or both eyes that leads to decreased vision. Cataracts are very common in older people

Charles Bonnet Syndrome (CBS): A condition involving vivid visual hallucinations that seem real, usually (though not always) experienced by older adults with later-life vision loss.

Cholesterol: Substance made in the body by the liver but also found in some foods. It plays a vital role in how every cell works and is also needed to make Vitamin D, some hormones and bile for digestion. There are two main types of cholesterol: low density lipid (LDL) or 'bad cholesterol' and high density lipid (HDL) or 'good cholesterol'. Raised cholesterol levels in the blood can cause atherosclerosis (hardening of the arteries) which has been linked to the risk of developing heart and circulatory diseases, (including heart attack & stroke), and possibly macular degeneration.

Choroid: Layer of blood vessels beneath the sclera which contains blood vessels that nourish the eye.

Ciliary body: The structure in the eye that releases a transparent liquid (aqueous humour) within the eye. It also contains the ciliary muscles which help your eyes focus on things (accommodation).

Ciliary muscles: Muscles that contract or relax to change the shape of the lens of the eye, thus allowing images to come into sharp focus on the retina.

Concave lens: In a concave lens (also called a negative lens or a diverging lens) the outer surfaces curve inward so light rays passing through it diverge (spread out). Concave lenses are used to correct short-sightedness.

Cones: Light-sensitive cells situated in the macula that are mainly used in day vision and also help us see colours. There are about 3 million cones in the human retina. In AMD cones lose their ability to act as photoreceptors.

Conjunctiva: The mucous membrane (moist surface) that coats the exposed front of the eyeball and lines the inside of the eyelids.

Convex lens: In a convex lens (also called a positive lens or converging lens) the surface bulges outwards in the centre making it thicker at the middle so light rays passing through it bend inward and converge (focus) on a spot just beyond the lens known as the focal point. Convex lenses are used to correct long-sightedness.

Cornea: The transparent layer in front of the eye.

Corneal grafting (keratoplasty): Removal of a cornea 'clouded' by disease or damage which is then replaced by grafting a healthier cornea from a donor in its place to improve vision.

Dementia: Dementia is a general term for a decline in mental ability caused by the permanent damage or death of the brain's nerve cells (neurones) which is severe enough to interfere with daily life. Symptoms include impairment of memory, judgment, language, complex motor skills and other intellectual functions.

Dermatology: Branch of medicine concerned with the diagnosis, treatment and prevention of diseases of the skin.

Dermatologist: A doctor who specialises in treatment of diseases of the skin.

Diabetes: A long-term metabolic disease where blood sugar levels are abnormally high. Type 1 diabetes requires injections of insulin to control blood sugar, but Type 2 diabetes which usually occurs later in life can often be controlled by diet alone or with tablets. More than 4 million people in the UK are affected by diabetes which may cause blindness if diabetic retinopathy develops.

Diabetic Macular Edema (Oedema) (DME): A complication in diabetes where the retina becomes swollen due to fluid leaking from blood vessels in the macula. Affecting up to 30% of long-term diabetics (20+ years), it causes blurred vision, and, if left untreated, may result in moderate visual loss.

Diabetic retinopathy: A common complication in diabetes that occurs when high blood sugar levels damage the blood vessels in the retina at the back of the eye. If untreated, it can cause blindness.

Dispensing optician: Gives general eye advice and fits and supplies spectacles to suit the wearer's visual, lifestyle and career needs.

Distortion: In eyes, the term distortion is used to describe any type of visual impairment that prevents you seeing properly. As well as occurring through problems inside the eye, causes may also originate outside the eye, eg, migraine and stroke. Vision distortion may affect one or both eyes and all or part of your visual field, and takes many different forms, eg, blind spots, black spots, straight lines appearing wavy, blurred or double vision, flashes of light, floaters and halos. In some cases visual distortion may be a sign of underlying illness or serious visual problems which may even lead to permanent blindness, so always consult a vision specialist. In a lens, eg, a spectacle lens, none is so perfectly shaped that it does not bend lines outwards or inwards from the centre of the image, an effect also called distortion.

Drusen: Small yellow or white deposits of fatty protein that cause atrophy and interfere with the ability of the retinal cells to function as photoreceptors. As they grow they push up the retina and can be seen on its surface during optical examinations. Their size and how many are in a given area (density) can be important indicators of AMD progression. Small hard well spaced drusen are less harmful than large soft clusters which can affect vision. Dry AMD is said to exist when a number of drusen are visible on the retina's surface.

Dry Eyes (Dry Eye Syndrome): A condition caused by lack of lubrication in the eye. It is more common in older people.

Dry Macular Degeneration (dry AMD): Dry (Age-related) Macular Degeneration - also known as 'Geographic Atrophy'- is a common eye disorder in people over 65 that results in blurred or reduced central vision caused by thinning of the macula. It tends to progress fairly slowly, but vision may deteriorate quite rapidly in the final stages. Wet AMD may also develop.

Eccentric vision EV (Preferred Retinal Loci: PRL): A technique used by people with central vision loss where the person looks slightly away from the subject in order to view it peripherally with another area of the visual field.

Eczema: Irritating inflammation of the skin characterised by sore itchy patches.

'Elderly Prim': Medical slang for 'Elderly Primigravida' used to refer to a woman at least 35 years old in her first pregnancy.

Ellex Retinal Rejuvenation Therapy (2RT®): A gentle 'cold' laser treatment capable of delivering a three nanosecond pulse that targets individual cells within the retinal pigment epithelium (RPE) without damaging the light-sensitive retinal cells or other intra-ocular structures. It also stimulates the retina's natural immune response, resulting in drusen clearance and the restoration of natural metabolite flow in the retina.

EyeBag®: Developed by consultant ophthalmologist Mr Teifi James in 2004, this reusable warm compress can be heated in a microwave to improve the symptoms of Dry Eye Syndrome and blepharitis.

Eyelea (aflibercept): A newer anti-VEGF drug injected into the eye which helps slow down the growth of unwanted unhealthy blood vessels in wet AMD. Trials suggest it may be more effective than Lucentis and therefore require fewer injections.

EyeMax™ lenses: EyeMax™ lenses consist of two lenses, one convex that is angled outward and one concave which curves in toward the patient's own lens. These are inserted into the sulcus (the space below the cornea and above the lens) via a tiny incision made in the front of the eye. The wide-angle EyeMax™ lens projects images both in the fovea (centre of the retina) and the eccentric (not central) areas so the brain can create a high resolution composite result, thereby improving vision. If the macular condition progresses the patient's brain can still take images from the back of the eye, so vision is maximised for much longer than previously (see also: iolAMD™).

Femtosecond (FS) laser: A femtosecond laser is an infrared laser which produces very short intense pulses lasting only a few quadrillionths of a second = 0.000000000000001 seconds.

Floaters: Floaters are small pieces of debris that float in the eye's vitreous humour and cause spots in your vision. Often resembling specks or cobweb strands, they are generally harmless, but seek medical attention if they suddenly increase in number as this may indicate a more serious vision problem.

Fluorescein Angiography (FAG): Medical procedure in which fluorescent dye is injected into a vein in the arm or hand which then travels to the eye and highlights the blood vessels in the back of the eye. A special camera then takes a series of pictures which will reveal any blood vessel abnormalities in the retina. The test detects signs of wet AMD in patients who may already have dry AMD.

Fovea (fovea centralis): The central area inside the macula that produces the clearest vision. It is this area that deteriorates in AMD.

Gastroenterology: The study, diagnosis and treatment of disorders of the digestive system.

Genome: The complete set of genes or genetic material containing the characteristics of a particular cell or organism. It is like a biological blueprint or pattern.

Gene Research: Research that uses human DNA samples, genetic testing or genetic information.

Genetic biomarker: A DNA sequence identified as possessing certain characteristics, e.g. causing or being present in a specific disease. Useful for creating genetic maps that help treat diseases.

Geographic Atrophy: An alternative name for dry AMD.

Glaucoma: A condition of raised pressure in the eye that can cause damage to the optic nerve which, if untreated, may lead to blindness.

Gynaecologist: A doctor who treats medical conditions and diseases that affect women and their reproductive organs.

HDL (High Density Lipid): 'Good cholesterol'.

Histology: The study of the microscopic structure of tissues, eg, to identify cancer cells.

Hubble Implant: See iolAMD ™.

Hypercholesterolaemia (familial hypercholesterolaemia: FH): Approximately one in 200 people has FH, an inherited condition caused by a gene defect that means cholesterol levels are higher than normal from birth.

Hypermetropia: The condition of long sight.

Hypromellose: Eye-drops formerly used to treat Dry Eye Syndrome.

Immunologist: Immunologists have specialised knowledge of the immune system and treat patients with immune system disorders.

Infrared (IR): Infrared light has longer wavelengths and lower energy than visible light and cannot be seen with the human eye.

Intravitreal injection: An injection made into the vitreous, a jelly-like substance at the back of the eye. Such injections are now a common procedure in eye disease treatment, particularly for injecting Anti-VEGF drugs like Lucentis and Avastin.

IOLs (Intraocular lenses) IOLs are synthetic, artificial lenses surgically implanted following removal of the eye's natural lens when it ceases to function properly. IOLs artificially recreate the ability to focus lost by the patient.

iolAMDTM (Hubble Implant): iolAMD™ is the world's first micro-incision, injectable telescopic implant developed by consultant ophthalmic surgeon Dr. Bobby Qureshi and optical physicist Professor Pablo Artal adapting technology used by NASA scientists to correct fuzzy images transmitted by the Hubble Telescope. Qureshi and Artal developed a hyper-aspheric (flatter than spherical) lens, using two in combination to gently magnify and direct vision to the healthiest part of the macula. iolAMDTM can greatly increase quality of life for AMD sufferers as it restores lost vision, allowing patients to see faces, read, and, in some cases, even drive.

Ion: An ion is an atom or a molecule in which the total number of electrons does not equal the total number of protons so that it becomes electrically charged. Metal atoms form positive ions, while non-metal atoms form negative ions.

Iris: This circular muscle gives the eye its colour, and controls how much light enters the eye by contracting or dilating to make the pupil smaller or larger.

IVF (In vitro fertilization): IVF is a complex procedure used to help women with fertility or genetic problems conceive a child. During IVF mature eggs are collected (retrieved) from the woman's ovaries and fertilized by sperm in a test tube (in vitro). The resulting embryo is later implanted into the woman's uterus.

Keratoconjunctivitis sicca: The Latin name for Dry Eye Syndrome, also known as Dry Eyes.

Keratoplasty: An alternative term for the corneal graft procedure.

Laser treatment for wet AMD: A light-sensitive drug injected into the arm travels to the eye where it is activated by a laser beam which shuts down the growth of abnormal blood vessels. Most patients require 2-5 treatments but it is only suitable for people with particular patterns of damage to the retina.

LDL (Low density lipid): Also known as 'bad cholesterol'.

Leber's Congenital Amaurosis (LCA): A rare genetic retinal condition.

Lens: Just like a camera lens, the lens in the eye focuses the light on the surface of the retina at the point where the image is sharpest. A man-made lens is a transparent piece of glass or plastic with at least one curved surface.

Lipids: A group of naturally occurring molecules that includes fats, waxes, sterols, fat-soluble vitamins (such as vitamins A, D, E and K), monoglycerides, diglycerides, triglycerides, phospholipids and others. They are found in drusen.

Lucentis (ranibizumab): An anti-VEGF drug injected into the eye which helps slow down growth of unwanted unhealthy blood vessels. Most wet AMD sufferers require 6-8 injections per year.

Lutein: Commonly known as 'the eye vitamin', lutein is an antioxidant found in yellow and orange pigments that occur naturally in vegetables such as spinach, kale and orange peppers. It is also found in high concentrations in the macula, and research suggests it may help to block blue light and thereby reduce the risk of macular degeneration (AMD). Used in AREDS formulation.

Lymph node: A small, bean-shaped structure (sometimes incorrectly called a 'gland') found throughout the body (eg, in armpit, neck and groin) that conveys fluid (lymph fluid), nutrients and waste material between body tissues and bloodstream. Lymph nodes are part of the immune system filtering out foreign particles and cancerous cells, and can become swollen when infection and/or cancer is present.

Lymphoma: One of a number of cancers that affects the immune system by attacking the infection-fighting white blood cells called lymphocytes found in lymph nodes, spleen, bone marrow etc, causing them to behave abnormally.

Macula: Area on the retina with the highest density of cones. It is particularly sensitive to light.

Macular degeneration: See Age-Related Macular Degeneration (AMD).

Mammogram: A mammogram is an X-ray of the breast, often used as part of a breast cancer screening programme.

Mastectomy: The medical term for surgical removal of one or both breasts. A mastectomy is usually carried out to treat or prevent breast cancer.

Metabolism: The overall balance of chemical processes in the body needed to sustain life. It consists of two parts; anabolism - a building up process, and catabolism - a breaking down process.

Metabolite flow: A metabolite is a substance involved in metabolism. Movement of metabolites through the body is called metabolite flow.

Monofocal: A monofocal lens has just one focal point - either in the distance or close up. For people wearing glasses, this means another pair is needed to provide the other focus, eg, either for reading or looking into the distance.

Myopia: The condition of short-sightedness.

Neovascular AMD: An alternative name for wet AMD - the name appropriately means 'new blood vessels'. In neovascular AMD

259

abnormal blood vessels grow underneath the retina which can leak fluid and blood and may cause swelling and damage of the macula.

Nephrology: A branch of medical science that deals with diseases of the kidneys.

Non-steroidal anti-inflammatory eyedrops: Widely used in ophthalmology to reduce eye inflammation, pain etc.

Obesity: A medical condition where excess body fat has accumulated to such an extent that it may have a negative impact on health, leading to reduced life expectancy and/or increased health problems. Research suggests obesity may increase the risk of developing dry AMD and also speed up its progression.

OCT: See Optical Coherence Tomography.

Omega-3: A group of essential fatty acids which benefit the heart and eyes. It is found in fish, particularly oily fish, but may also be taken as supplements. Studies suggest Omega-3 may help protect adult eyes from macular degeneration and Dry Eye syndrome.

Oncology: The study and treatment of cancer.

Ophthalmologist: Ophthalmologists diagnose, treat and prevent disorders of the eyes and visual system. As they can also perform eye operations, they are both surgical and medical specialists.

Optical physicists: Scientists interested in how to control light.

Optic nerve: The optic nerve connects the eye to the brain. Light entering the retina creates impulses that travel along the optic nerve to the brain which then translates the signals into images.

Optical Coherence Tomography (OCT): A non-invasive imaging test that uses light waves to take cross-section pictures of the eye.

Optogenetics: Biological technique using light to control cells in living tissue (typically neurons) that have been genetically modified so they can act as channels for light-sensitive ions.

Optometrists: Previously known as ophthalmic opticians, these are primary healthcare specialists trained to examine the eyes to detect defects in vision, signs of injury, ocular diseases or abnormality and also certain underlying general health problems. In the UK optometrists must be registered with the General Optical Council, the profession's regulatory body. When choosing an optometrist, look for the letters FCOptom or MCOptom after their name which means the optometrist is a fellow or member of the College and adheres to high standards of clinical practice.

Orthopaedic: The branch of surgery broadly concerned with the skeletal system (bones and joints).

Osteo-Odonto-Keratoprosthesis (OOKP): Also known as 'tooth-in-eye' surgery, this technique is used to restore sight where the anterior chamber structures have been irreparably damaged but the retina is still functioning. A small plastic lens is inserted into one of the patient's teeth which is then fixed into the eye so light can pass through the lens onto the retina, thereby restoring sight.

Pathologist: A branch of medical science primarily concerned with the examination of organs, tissues and bodily fluids in order to make a diagnosis of disease or cause of death.

Peripheral vision: Side vision produced by photoreceptor cells called rods which are mainly located outside the macula. In AMD sufferers, peripheral vision is not affected so some vision will always remain. It is also used in the technique called eccentric vision (EV).

Peritonitis: Inflammation of the thin layer of tissue lining the inside of the abdomen. Peritonitis requires prompt medical attention as it can lead to severe, potentially life-threatening infection throughout the body if left untreated.

Phantom limb: Phantom limb syndrome causes a person to feel sensation and even pain in an amputated limb as if it is still present.

Photons: Tiny particles of light energy far too small to be seen individually. The information photons provide is converted by the photoreceptor cells in the retina into electrical signals that our brain can interpret and convert into visual images.

Photoreceptor cells: There are two types of photoreceptor cells in the human eye, rods and cones. They pick up photons from light transmitted onto the retina and use them to pass signals to the brain.

Physiology: Physiology seeks to understand how living things work. Human physiology studies how our cells, muscles and organs work and interact.

Posterior chamber: Situated between the lens and iris, the aqueous humour flows from here through the pupil to the anterior chamber.

Preferred Retinal Loci (PRL): See Eccentric Vision.

Presbycusis: Age-related deafness. From the age of 65, 30-35% of adults experience some hearing loss, particularly at high frequencies.

Presbyopia: A type of long-sightedness caused by ageing where the eye finds it difficult to focus on objects that are near to it.

Primigravida: A woman experiencing pregnancy for the first time.

Psychiatry: Psychiatry concerns the study, diagnosis, treatment and prevention of mental disorders.

PTSD (Post-traumatic Stress Disorder): Exposure to very stressful events leads to this mental health condition of extreme anxiety.

Pupil: An aperture which works like a camera lens to allow light to enter the eye. It is the black part in the centre of the iris.

Ranibizumab: The medical name for the drug Lucentis which is injected into the eyes of wet AMD sufferers to hinder growth of unhealthy blood vessels.

Retina: The light-sensitive lining inside the choroid. When light falls on this lining it stimulates the rods and cones which send messages along the optic nerve to the brain. The brain converts these messages so that we see images.

Retinal detachment (amotio retinae): This happens when the retina peels away from its underlying layer of support tissue at the back of the inside of the eye. Symptoms include flashes of light, a sudden dramatic increase in the number of floaters, a dark shadow at the edge of your vision which you cannot see round or through and blurred vision. It should be treated as a medical emergency.

Retinal pigment epithelium (RPE): The RPE is a single layer of pigmented cells located just outside the retina. It is attached to the choroid, a layer filled with blood vessels that nourishes the retina, and its functions include transport of nutrients, ions and water and the absorption of light entering the retina.

Retinitis pigmentosa (RP): Retinitis pigmentosa destroys the light sensitive cells in the retina and is one of the most common forms of inherited retinal degeneration disease.

Rods: Rods are light-sensitive cells in the retina that help us see in low illumination. There are about 100 million rods in the human retina and we use them mainly in evening/night vision. In AMD it is the rods that continue to allow use of peripheral vision.

SAD (Seasonal Affective Disorder or 'Winter Blues'): SAD is a type of depression that recurs on a seasonal basis.

Saturated fat: Saturated fat is a 'bad' fat found in relatively high amounts in many meat and dairy products including full fat milk, cheese, butter, cream and many processed foods. Many studies link saturated fats to high cholesterol levels in the blood which is a risk factor for developing coronary heart disease.

Sclera: The white of the eye.

Scotoma: A scotoma is a blind spot which may be at the centre or around the edges of your vision. Everybody has a naturally occurring 'blind spot' but new ones can be a sign of underlying health problems such as AMD or glaucoma.

Snellen scale: Snellen's eye chart with differently sized letters read from a distance of six metres away is used to test vision. Using this method, normal visual acuity is 6/6 which means you can read either the bottom or second bottom line of the chart. The first number given is the distance in metres from the chart while the second refers to the number of lines you can read. The largest letters on the top line correspond to 60 so if you can only read the top line your Snellen score is 6/60.

Statins: A type of drug prescribed to help lower cholesterol.

Steroid eye-drops: Steroid eye-drops mimic a substance produced naturally in the body called cortisol. Used to reduce inflammation in eye disease and prevent scarring after eye injury or surgery.

Sulcus: Space below the cornea and above the lens where IOLs are often sited.

Suspensory ligament of the lens: A series of fibres that connects the ciliary body of the eye with the lens and holds it in place.

Suture(s): A stitch or row of stitches holding the edges of a wound or surgical incision together.

Thealoz Duo Preservative-free: Eye-drops used to treat Dry Eye Syndrome recommended by London Eye Hospital.

Toxoplasmosis: An infection caused by a parasite which may be transmitted via poorly cooked food that contains cysts or exposure to infected cat faeces. In a few infected people, toxoplasmosis may also cause eye problems.

Triglycerides: Triglycerides are a type of fat (lipid) found in blood. Food is converted by the body into calories and those not needed for immediate energy requirements are converted into triglycerides which are stored in fat cells. Hormones release triglycerides for energy between meals, but problems arise if calories in excess of those burned off are regularly eaten, leading to high levels of triglycerides which can increase the risk of heart disease.

UV (Ultraviolet) light: Ultraviolet light is a form of radiation not visible to the human eye - it's the part of sunlight that gives you sunburn if you're exposed to it for too long. Too much exposure to UV rays has been linked to cataract formation and retinal degeneration in the eye.

UVA rays: Harmful longwave ultraviolet rays contained in sunlight which can cause eye damage, including cataracts.

UVB rays: Harmful shortwave ultraviolet rays contained in sunlight implicated in causing eye damage, including cataracts.

Vascular Endothelial Growth Factor (VEGF): A substance in the body responsible for development of healthy blood vessels.

Visual acuity (VA): Visual acuity is your central vision, ie, the ability to see details clearly. It is commonly measured by reading differently sized letters on an eye chart.

Visual field: This is the area of sight around the edge of your vision that is visible when you look straight ahead.

Vitreous humour: A gel inside the vitreous chamber at the centre of the eye. The vitreous humour helps the eye keep its shape as well as absorbing any shocks to the eye. It also ensures that the retina is properly connected to the back wall of the eye. Light passes through the vitreous humour on its way to the retina.

Wavefront geometry: Geometry that analyses the 'wavefront' of light reflected off the retina when light enters the eye or artificial lens. Lenses such as the EyeMax™ lenses feature wavefront geometry which improves tolerance to variations in lens placement and reduces distortions, thereby maximising vision.

Wet Macular Degeneration (wet AMD): Wet AMD (also known as 'neovascular AMD') is caused by tiny blood vessels that grow out from under the layer of blood vessels beneath the retina, pushing out between the cells and leaking blood or tissue fluid. Wet AMD is a serious matter. It may happen very rapidly and vision loss is often sudden and severe. Current treatment involves injections into the eye at regular intervals of various anti-VEGF drugs which inhibit the growth of the new blood vessels, eg, Lucentis and Avastin. Only about 10% of dry AMD sufferers end up with wet AMD. The condition is responsible for 90% of all blindness.

Zeaxanthin: An antioxidant similar to lutein found in many vegetables and marigold flowers. Believed to protect the eye and reduce the risk of AMD by absorbing damaging blue light, it is used in the AREDS 2 formulation.

USEFUL CONTACTS

RNIB Helpline: Tel: 0303 123 9999 available Monday to Friday 8.45am to 5.30pm.
You can also email helpline@rnib.org.uk
The RNIB Helpline offers support, advice and products to help you remain independent. Specialist advice workers are always ready to listen, and offer a variety of support for your individual needs. They also ring back a few weeks later to find out how you're getting on and see if there is anything else they can do to help. The RNIB Helpline can:

- Give you free information about your eye condition and available treatments.
- Direct you to people, services and organisations which can help, both locally and nationally, including voluntary groups and support from social services.
- Let you know about financial benefits, concessions and grants you may be entitled to.
- Recommend products to make everyday life easier (available from RNIB online shop and other centres).
- Offers a library service of over 40,000 titles in braille, Moon, giant print and audio.
- Gives advice on employment, training and education opportunities.
- Provides housing information to help you stay in your own home or move elsewhere.
- Supports you through counselling services or by offering a listening ear.

RNIB website www.rnib.org.uk/ This is a really helpful user-friendly site with a wealth of information from basic facts on the eye and eye diseases to research tools. I can promise an interesting and informative browse as well as practical help and suggestions. You can also receive your information in Welsh, Hindi or Urdu languages.

MACULAR SOCIETY UK www.macularsociety.org
National charity for Macular Degeneration which has over 21,000 members. Offers helpline, counselling, training, support groups and help with rehabilitation alongside fundraising to find a cure.

LEH (London Eye Hospital)
www.londoneyehospital.com
Tel. UK: 0808 612 2021. Overseas: 0044 207 060 2602
London Eye Hospital in Harley Street is a private hospital and a world leader in ophthalmology, offering expert treatments for all eye conditions, including groundbreaking EyeMax™ lenses for AMD sufferers.

The London Eye Hospital Pharma
http://londoneyehospitalpharma.com/
LEH Pharnma have created a new range of advanced eye vitamins and mineral health food supplements researched and formulated by the London Eye Hospital. Available to buy at LEH.

Moorfields Eye Hospital NHS Foundation Trust
 www.moorfields.nhs.uk/Tel: 020 7253 3411
Moorfields is a Postgraduate Teaching Hospital and an international centre for ophthalmic care.

NHS Choices
Health A-Z - Conditions and treatments
www.nhs.uk/Conditions/Pages/hub.aspx
Find high-quality information on more than 800 health conditions and treatments, searchable by A-Z or body map

Patient (Trusted medical Information and support)
http://patient.info/symptom-checker
Symptom checker & health information professional articles, forums etc.

266

US RESOURCES: (also informative for those outside the US)

The National Eye Institute
https://nei.nih.gov/
A US-based organisation with an A-Z directory providing eye health information in English and Spanish. The informative site includes information on low vision as well as research topics.
E-mail: 2020@nei.nih.gov
Tel: (301) 496-5248 - English and Spanish
Mail: National Eye Institute Information Office,
31 Center Drive MSC 2510, Bethesda, MD 20892-2510

Medical News Today - Knowledge Center
www.medicalnewstoday.com/knowledge-center
US-based. This is a useful online source of information on the latest advances in various medical conditions.

AMD Alliance International
www.amdalliance.org

American Macular Degeneration Foundation
Tel: 1-888-622-8527

Association for Macular Diseases
Tel: 212-605-3719 www.macula.org

Lighthouse Guild
Tel: 800-284-04422 www.lighthouse.org

Macular Degeneration Partnership
(There is an informative video on this site showing how a 'walk in the park' appears to a woman with AMD) Tel: 888-430-9898
www.ad.org

The Macula Foundation www.maculafoundation.org
Tel: 800-622-8524

Statement about the two charities supported by the sale of this book:

The RNIB '#Seetheneed' Project http://www.rnib.org.uk/see

Being told you are losing your sight is life changing, as you try to come to terms with the huge emotional, psychological and financial impact of sight loss. Staff in eye departments across the UK are under huge pressure. They must diagnose and treat increasing numbers of patients quickly, and simply do not have the time they would like to fully discuss the support that is available. At this distressing time, it is vital that all patients have access to timely emotional and practical support.

At this critical time, the role of sight loss advisers offers hospitals an innovative solution to fulfil an unmet need and ensure nobody faces sight loss alone. Sight loss advisers complement the work of other staff in the eye department and ensure that patients are provided with quality information, support and advice.

The RNIB '#Seetheneed' report sets out why sight loss advisers provide a cost effective solution for the NHS to improve the quality of services and outcomes for individual patients. The presence of this support service is integral to the delivery of high quality eye care. That's why RNIB is urgently calling for hospital managers to ensure that every eye department across the UK has access to a qualified sight loss adviser.

RNIB, working in conjunction with City University, London, also offers an accredited training course which provides prospective sight loss advisers with an excellent working knowledge of the services available for people with sight loss, and an understanding of various eye diseases.

The London Eye Hospital Trust

The LEH Trust has a mission to reduce treatable blindness worldwide through the direct provision of treatment and surgery and to fund education and research projects to complement this aim. In particular, the LEH trust would like to make a significant impact in the worldwide treatment of Trachoma, one of the leading causes of childhood blindness which is entirely preventable and treatable and can potentially be eradicated.

A Closing Note

For those readers who like to look at the end of a book first, I will say that this book has a happy ending, but might I suggest that you read Chapter 22: 'Seeing Less' to find out what led up to my writing this book before you consider putting it to one side? I would also prefer you to purchase this book rather than just flick through the pages quickly and put it back on the shelf in the bookshop, simply because I want the eye charities mentioned on the previous page to benefit from the proceeds of its sale. I hope you will find the information in these pages useful and also enjoy sharing my story...

Liz Lenton